The Theology of the Gospel of Mark

This book presents the reader with a comprehensive view of the theology underlying the first narrative account of the life of Jesus. In chapter one Dr Telford introduces the background of the text and its general message, attempting briefly to place the Gospel (and therefore its theology) in its historical setting. In the second chapter, he describes and analyses the Gospel's theology, again from an historical perspective and with particular regard to its original context. In the third chapter, Telford goes on to examine the Gospel in relation to other relevant writings of the New Testament. Briefly reviewing this larger corpus and highlighting parallels and contrasts, where appropriate, he seeks to locate the Gospel's theology in its wider canonical context. The fourth and final chapter ranges even further afield, commenting on the Gospel's history of interpretation and on its significance in the contemporary context.

w. r. telford is lecturer in Christian Origins and the New Testament in the Department of Religious Studies at the University of Newcastle in the United Kingdom. He has written two books: *The Barren Temple and the Withered Tree: a Redaction-Critical Analysis of the Cursing of the Fig-tree Pericope in Mark's Gospel and its Relation to the Cleansing of the Temple Tradition* (1980), and *Mark* (1995). Editor of *The Interpretation of Mark* (1985, 2nd edn 1995), he has also contributed to a variety of edited works and journals, including *Theology*, the *Scottish Journal of Theology*, the *Epworth Review*, the *Journal of Biblical Literature* and the *Journal of Theological Studies*.

NEW TESTAMENT THEOLOGY

General Editor: James D. G. Dunn,
Lightfoot Professor of Divinity, University of Durham

This series sets out to provide a programmatic survey of the individual writings of the New Testament. It aims to remedy the deficiency of available published material which concentrates on the New Testament writers' theological concerns. New Testament specialists here write at greater length than is usually possible in the introduction to commentaries or as part of other New Testament theologies, and explore the theological themes and issues of their chosen books without being tied to a commentary format, or to a thematic structure provided from elsewhere. When complete, the series will cover all the New Testament writings, and will thus provide an attractive, and timely, range of texts around which courses can be developed.

Titles published in the series

THE THEOLOGY OF
THE
GOSPEL OF MARK

W. R. TELFORD

CAMBRIDGE
UNIVERSITY PRESS

PUBLISHED BY THE PRESS SYNDICATE OF THE UNIVERSITY OF CAMBRIDGE
The Pitt Building, Trumpington Street, Cambridge CB2 1RP

CAMBRIDGE UNIVERSITY PRESS
The Edinburgh Building, Cambridge, CB2 2RU, UK http://www.cup.cam.ac.uk
40 West 20th Street, New York, NY 10011–4211, USA http://www.cup.org
10 Stamford Road, Oakleigh, Melbourne 3166, Australia

First published 1999

Printed in the United Kingdom at the University Press, Cambridge

Typeset in Baskerville 11/12.5 pt [CE]

A catalogue record for this book is available from the British Library

Library of Congress Cataloguing in Publication data
Telford, William.
The theology of the Gospel of Mark / W. R. Telford.
p. cm. (New Testament theology)
Includes bibliographical references and index.
ISBN 0 521 43366 5 (hardback) – ISBN 0 521 43977 9 (paperback)
1. Bible. N.T. Mark – Theology. 1. Title. 11. Series.
BS585.2.T45 1999
226.3′06–dc21 98–35098 CIP

ISBN 0 521 43366 5 hardback
ISBN 0 521 43977 9 paperback

For Andrena

Contents

Editor's preface

Although the New Testament is usually taught within Departments or Schools or Faculties of Theology/Divinity/Religion, theological study of the individual New Testament writings is often minimal or at best patchy. The reasons for this are not hard to discern.

For one thing, the traditional style of studying a New Testament document is by means of straight exegesis, often verse by verse. Theological concerns jostle with interesting historical, textual, grammatical and literary issues, often at the cost of the theological. Such exegesis is usually very time-consuming, so that only one or two key writings can be treated in any depth within a crowded three-year syllabus.

For another, there is a marked lack of suitable textbooks round which courses could be developed. Commentaries are likely to lose theological comment within a mass of other detail in the same way as exegetical lectures. The section on the theology of a document in the Introduction to a commentary is often very brief and may do little more than pick out elements within the writing under a sequence of headings drawn from systematic theology. Excursuses usually deal with only one or two selected topics. Likewise larger works on New Testament Theology usually treat Paul's letters as a whole and, having devoted the great bulk of their space to Jesus, Paul and John, can spare only a few pages for others.

In consequence, there is little incentive on the part of teacher or student to engage with a particular New Testament document, and students have to be content with a general overview, at best complemented by in-depth study of (parts of) two or three New Testament writings. A serious corrollary to this is the degree to which students are thereby incapacitated in the task of integrating their New Testament study with the rest of their Theology or Religion courses, since often they are capable only of drawing on the general overview or on a sequence of particular verses treated atomistically. The growing importance of a literary-critical approach to individual documents simply highlights the present deficiencies even more. Having been given little experience in handling individual New Testament writings as such at a theological level, most students are very ill-prepared to develop a properly integrated literary and theological response to particular texts. Ordinands too need more help than they currently receive from textbooks, so that their preaching from particular passages may be better informed theologically.

There is need therefore for a series to bridge the gap between too brief an introduction and too full a commentary where theological discussion is lost among too many other concerns. It is our aim to provide such a series. That is, a series where New Testament specialists are able to write at a greater length on the theology of individual writings than is usually possible in the introductions to commentaries or as part of New Testament Theologies, and to explore the theological themes and issues of these writings without being tied to a commentary format or to a thematic structure provided from elsewhere. The volumes seek both to describe each document's theology, and to engage theologically with it, noting also its canonical context and any specific influence it may have had on the history of Christian faith and life. They are directed at those who already have one or two years of full-time New Testament and theological study behind them.

University of Durham   JAMES D. G. DUNN

Preface

My interest in the Gospel of Mark began when in 1972 I
embarked on doctoral work at Cambridge (England) under the
expert supervision of Dr Ernst Bammel, whose recent death has
brought great sadness to all those who knew him and benefited
from his immense erudition and scholarship. My fascination
with the Gospel has further developed during my time of
teaching and research in the Department of Religious Studies
at the University of Newcastle. My thanks, in the first instance,
therefore, go to those students of mine whose diligence and
enthusiasm has always made the business of teaching such a
pleasant and stimulating one for me. This book was written
over a period of two years, and for the most part in a number
of concentrated sessions spent in Cambridge and in Hawarden. I should also like to thank, therefore, the Staff of the
Cambridge University Library (that venerable institution
within whose redoubtable walls I have spent so many produc-
tive hours!), the Bursar and Staff of Westcott House, Cambridge, and the Trustees, Warden, and Staff of St Deiniol's
Library, Hawarden (this unique institution which offers such a
welcome and such a service to all those engaged in the pursuit
of what Gladstone himself described as 'divine learning'). All
of these have given me in my limited periods of research the
facilities and the incentive to finish the book. Particular thanks
go to the Trustees of St Deiniol's for awarding me a Murray
McGregor Fellowship, and to Dr Peter Jagger, and his worthy
successor as Warden, Revd Peter Francis, for their friendship
and encouragement. For making it possible for me to have a
period of study leave, my appreciation goes to my colleagues at

xiii

Newcastle, the Dean of the Faculty of Arts and the University Research Committee, and for general encouragement as well as helpful advice, thanks are due to my colleagues in Studiorum Novi Testamenti Societas (SNTS) and at the British New Testament Conference. A particular word of thanks should be given to Professor Jimmy Dunn, the Editor of this series, for his infinite patience. This quality was also exhibited in no small measure by my loving wife, Andrena, whose enduring forbearance and cheerfulness have been a constant source of strength.

Abbreviations

BETL	Bibliotheca Ephemeridum Theologicarum Lovaniensium
BJRL	*Bulletin of the John Rylands Library*
BTB	*Biblical Theology Bulletin*
BZNW	Beihefte zur Zeitschrift für die neutestamentliche Wissenschaft und die Kunde der älteren Kirche
CBQ	*Catholic Biblical Quarterly*
DBI	*The Dictionary of Biblical Interpretation*, eds. R. J. Collins, J. L. Houlden (London: SCM Press; Philadelphia, PA: Trinity Press International, 1990)
ETL	*Ephemerides Theologicae Lovanienses*
EvTh	*Evangelische Theologie*
ExpT	*Expository Times*
IDB	*The Interpreter's Dictionary of the Bible*, ed. G. A. Buttrick (New York and Nashville, TN: Abingdon Press, 1962)
IDB(S)	*The Interpreter's Dictionary of the Bible, Supplementary Volume*, ed. K. Crim (Nashville, TN: Abingdon Press, 1976)
Int	*Interpretation*
JAAR	*Journal of the American Academy of Religion*
JBL	*Journal of Biblical Literature*
JR	*Journal of Religion*
JTSouthAfr	*Journal of Theology for South Africa*
JSNT	*Journal for the Study of the New Testament*
JSNTSS	Journal for the Study of the New Testament Supplement Series
JTS	*Journal of Theological Studies*

NovT	*Novum Testamentum*
NTA	*New Testament Abstracts*
NTS	*New Testament Studies*
PerspRelSt	*Perspectives in Religious Studies*
SBL	Society of Biblical Literature
SBLDS	Society of Biblical Literature Dissertation Series
SJT	Scottish Journal of Theology
SNTSMS	Society of New Testament Studies Monograph Series
TZ	*Theologische Zeitschrift*
WUNT	Wissenschaftliche Untersuchungen zum Neuen Testament
ZNW	*Zeitschrift für die neutestamentliche Wissenschaft*
ZThK	*Zeitschrift für Theologie und Kirche*

CHAPTER I

The historical setting of the Gospel of Mark

INTRODUCTION

The words 'The Theology of the Gospel of Mark', in the title of this book are deceptively simple. The three major expressions of which the title is composed, however, are far from straight-forward. They beg a number of important questions. Firstly, what do we mean by the word 'Theology' in connection with the Gospel of Mark? In focusing upon Mark as 'theology' rather than as 'history' or as 'literature', what aspects of the Gospel have we in mind? Secondly, what is intended by the use of the term 'Gospel' as applied to this first century text? What does the word mean, and how appropriate a description is it from a historical, literary or theological point of view? Thirdly, who is meant or what indeed is conveyed by the traditional attribution 'Mark'? Was the Gospel written by the John Mark of the New Testament, as tradition claims, or is this a fiction? Where the theology of the Gospel is concerned, does it matter?

An act of literary communication involves, in essence, an author, a text and a reader, and the process of interpreting that text must take into account all three. What then do we mean in overall terms by 'The Theology of the Gospel of Mark'? Do we mean the theology of the *author* – in other words, the religious ideas, the philosophical perspective, the theological convictions, in short, the ideology which motivated the evangelist to write, which was a product of his own age, culture and tradition, and which influenced the treatment of his sources? Do we mean the theology of the *text* itself, considered as a whole – in other words, the religious message which it conveys, irrespective of its historical context, of the sources it draws upon or of the intention of its original author? Is 'The Theology of the Gospel of Mark' a theology constructed by the *reader* (or the 'interpretative community') from the text – in other words, a product of 'engagement' between the reader and the text, a religious dialogue or 'revelation' engendered by the interaction of the text with the reader's experience past or present?

Given the Gospel's use of sources, we might even ask, furthermore, whether the Gospel of Mark has a unified theology at all! One relatively conservative critic issues the following warning:

> If Mark has preserved material which does not fully correspond to the view which he himself holds then are we at liberty to speak of a theology of the Gospel of Mark? Must we not rather speak of Mark's theology? If a valid distinction can be drawn between these two then it may be that we should not look for a coherent and consistent theology in the Gospel but be prepared to find unevenness since he laid his theology over an existing theology, or theologies, in the tradition he received.[1]

If, on the other hand, there is a consistent theology in the Gospel – and a considerable body of recent Markan scholarship, one notes, is now highlighting the literary and theological features which integrate the Markan text[2] – the question remains as to how we might gain access to 'The Theology of the Gospel of Mark'? If the theology resides in the mind of the evangelist, then is it to be recovered, as many insist, by using the historical-critical tools of source, form and redaction criti-

---

[1] E. Best, 'Mark's Preservation of the Tradition' in W. R. Telford (ed.), *The Interpretation of Mark* (Edinburgh: T. & T. Clark, 1995), pp. 163–4.

[2] E.g. T. J. Geddert, *Watchwords. Mark 13 in Markan Eschatology* (JSNTSS 26; Sheffield: JSOT Press, 1989); J. D. Kingsbury, *The Christology of Mark's Gospel* (Philadelphia, PA: Fortress Press, 1983); J. D. Kingsbury, *Conflict in Mark. Jesus, Authorities, Disciples* (Philadelphia, PA: Fortress Press, 1989); B. L. Mack, *A Myth of Innocence. Mark and Christian Origins* (Philadelphia, PA: Fortress Press, 1988); C. D. Marshall, *Faith as a Theme in Mark's Narrative* (SNTSMS, 64; Cambridge: Cambridge University Press, 1989); D. Rhoads and D. Michie, *Mark as Story. An Introduction to the Narrative of a Gospel* (Philadelphia, PA: Fortress Press, 1982); J. Sergeant, *Lion let Loose. The Structure and Meaning of St Mark's Gospel* (Exeter: Paternoster, 1988); M. R. Thompson, *The Role of Disbelief in Mark. A New Approach to the Second Gospel* (New York and Mahwah, NJ: Paulist Press, 1989); M. A. Tolbert, *Sowing the Gospel: Mark's World in Literary-Historical Perspective* (Minneapolis, MN: Fortress Press, 1989).

cism, that is, by separating tradition and redaction and so determining Mark's contribution to the developing Jesus tradition?[3] If the theology is rooted in the text as a whole, then is it best approached, as others argue, by holistic methods such as narrative criticism (and its sister discipline narrative theology)?[4] If the theology, on the other hand, is a construct arising out of the reader's engagement with the text, then should not other literary approaches such as reader-response criticism be employed to illuminate this process?[5]

So much for some of the questions raised by our title. It is time now to offer some answers, or at least to indicate what I myself understand by 'The Theology of the Gospel of Mark', what aspects of the subject I plan to cover in this book, and what approach I shall be taking to it. The term 'theology' comes from two Greek words, *theos* meaning 'God' and *logos* meaning 'word', or, by extension, 'rational discourse'. In its narrow sense, 'theology' means 'rational discourse about God'. In its broader sense, it refers to a complex of related subjects in Christian doctrine, subsuming such topics as Christology (from *Christos* meaning 'Christ' or 'Messiah'; and hence doctrine or understanding concerning the person or nature of Christ), soteriology (from *sōtēria* meaning 'salvation'; and hence doctrine or understanding concerning the work of Christ), pneumatology (from *pneuma* meaning 'spirit'; and hence doctrine or understanding concerning the Holy Spirit), cosmology (from *kosmos* meaning 'world' or 'universe'; and hence doctrine or

[3] For these methods, see C. E. Carlston, 'Form Criticism, NT' in *IDB(S)*, pp. 345–8; R. T. Fortna, 'Redaction Criticism, NT' in *IDB(S)*, pp. 733–5; K. Grobel, 'Form Criticism' in *IDB*, pp. 320–1; J. Muddiman, 'Form Criticism' in *DBI*, pp. 240–3; E. P. Sanders and M. Davies, *Studying the Synoptic Gospels* (London: SCM Press; Philadelphia, PA: Trinity Press International, 1989), pp. 51–223; S. S. Smalley, 'Redaction Criticism' in I. H. Marshall (ed.), *New Testament Interpretation* (Exeter: Paternoster, 1977), pp. 181–95; W. R. Telford, *Mark* (New Testament Guides; Sheffield: Sheffield Academic Press, 1995), pp. 37–85; S. H. Travis, 'Form Criticism' in Marshall (ed.), *Interpretation*, pp. 153–64; C. M. Tuckett, *Reading the New Testament* (London: SPCK, 1987), pp. 78–135; C. M. Tuckett, 'Redaction Criticism' in *DBI*, pp. 580–2; C. M. Tuckett, 'Source Criticism (NT)', in *DBI*, pp. 646–8; D. Wenham, 'Source Criticism' in Marshall (ed.), *Interpretation*, pp. 139–52.

[4] See D. F. Ford, 'Narrative Theology' in *DBI*, pp. 489–91; R. C. Tannehill, 'Narrative Criticism' in *DBI*, pp. 488–9; Telford, *Mark*, pp. 90–2.

[5] See M. Davies, 'Reader-Response Criticism' in *DBI*, pp. 578–80; Telford, *Mark*, pp. 92–3.

understanding concerning the world), eschatology (from *eschatos* meaning 'last' or 'final'; and hence doctrine or understanding concerning the end of the world or final matters), anthropology (from *anthrōpos* meaning 'man'; and hence doctrine or understanding concerning the nature of man), ecclesiology (from *ekklēsia* meaning 'assembly' or 'church'; and hence doctrine or understanding concerning the church or believing community) and ethics (from *ethos* meaning 'custom' or 'usage'; and hence doctrine or understanding concerning the moral behaviour governing the relationship between the Christian believer, the believing community and the world).

Although these categories belong to the vocabulary of Christian doctrine in its later and more developed state, and are hence familiar to those steeped in systematic theology, they are nevertheless convenient to some extent for the analysis of first-century Christian texts like the Gospel of Mark provided they are used with caution. The Gospel of Mark reflects Christian tradition at an early stage of development and does not present us with anything approaching a systematic theology. The 'Theology' of the Gospel of Mark (as I intend to use the term) refers in a broad sense to the religious understanding, ideas and beliefs entertained by this ancient writer concerning the nature of God, the person and work of Jesus, the role of the Spirit, the nature of man and the world, the end of that world and so on. A major emphasis in this book therefore will be on theology as 'religious ideology', that is, on what was believed by the evangelist, as reflected in his narrative, and, in particular, to what extent these beliefs were a product of, a development from or even a challenge to the religious culture and tradition to which he was indebted.

Our second term 'Gospel' also requires some comment. The word (Old English, *godspel*) is a literal translation of the Greek term *euangelion*, which in ordinary usage meant 'good news', such as that announced when a battle was won or a Roman ruler was enthroned.[6] The expression is a favourite one of the evangelist, and is used by him to describe Jesus' teaching

---

[6] R. P. Martin, *Mark – Evangelist and Theologian* (Exeter: Paternoster, 1979), p. 22.

(1.14–15; 8.35; 10.29; 13.10; 14.9) without, however, specifying its precise content. The text actually begins with the word (1.1 'The beginning of the *gospel* of Jesus Christ') but it is not clear whether it is used in Mark with its usual connotation of 'good news' or as a technical term for the religious or doctrinal content of the message preached by (or perhaps about) Jesus (see Rom. 1.1–4).[7] It has been suggested, although this is less likely, that in 1.1 it may even refer to the literary genre in which that oral proclamation is contained. What is clear, however, is that the term 'Gospel' was being used in a generic sense by Christians in the second century, the earliest datable example of its functioning as a literary type occurring in the writings of Justin Martyr.[8] In a similar way perhaps to the process by which the term 'apocalypse', which occurs in Revelation 1.1, came to be transferred to other texts bearing the characteristic features of the Revelation of John, the term 'Gospel' was derived from the use of the term *euangelion* in the text of Mark and subsequently employed as a generic description for texts in which that 'good news' was to be found.

Its appropriateness as a description of the text, at least from a theological point of view, is apparent. If the 'Gospel' genre was a unique one in the ancient world, and Mark, as has been suggested, was the originator of it, the term adequately describes its special features, namely, that it is 'kerygmatic in nature and evangelical in design.'[9] On the other hand, from a literary point of view, it is inappropriate, derivative and even misleading as a generic description of the text. No genre can be said to be without roots in antecedent literary types and treating Mark as unique draws attention away from a number of potential models in the ancient world by which Mark could have been influenced in the overall conception of his work. Much recent research has been conducted on this subject, and discussion can be found elsewhere[10] but it is worth here

---

[7] R. A. Guelich, ' "The Beginning of the Gospel". Mark 1:1–15', *Biblical Research*, 27 (1982), pp. 5–15; K. Kertelge, 'The Epiphany of Jesus in the Gospel (Mark)' in Telford (ed.), *Interpretation*, pp. 106–7; Martin, *Mark*, pp. 24–8.

[8] *Apology*, 66 (*c.* 150 CE) and Martin, *Mark*, p. 19.

[9] Martin, *Mark*, p. 21.

[10] D. E. Aune, *The New Testament and its Literary Environment* (Philadelphia, PA: Westmin-

commenting on the implications of the question of genre for theology. Establishing the genre of a literary work provides us with our first clue as to its origin, meaning and purpose, and without such indications, the theology cannot be fully appreciated. Two conflicting models for the emergence of the Gospel are currently espoused. The first has been described as the model of 'aggregate growth'. Based on the results of form criticism, this sees the Gospel text as an 'evolutionary'[11] document, the end result of a somewhat impersonal, collective, immanent process by which the diverse oral traditions of the early Christian community came eventually to be written down. This approach often anchors the text in a cultic rather than literary tradition and as a result tends to diminish not only the literary but also the theological creativity of the one(s) responsible for its final form. Based on the results of redaction criticism and the newer literary methods, the second model sees the Gospel text as a 'revolutionary' document, the result of authorial creativity adopting or adapting existing genres (Graeco-Roman biography, Hellenistic romance, Greek tragedy, or, within the Jewish field, apocalyptic or wisdom literature have been some of the parallels cited). By anchoring the text to a self-conscious literary tradition and enterprise, this approach tends by contrast to elevate the literary and theological creativity of the author.

But who was the 'Mark' who was ultimately responsible for 'The Theology of the Gospel of Mark'? This third question will be addressed in my next section but here let me anticipate the discussion by stating that I, in common with many Markan scholars nowadays, regard the available evidence as insufficient

ster Press, 1987); R. A. Guelich, 'The Gospel Genre' in P. Stuhlmacher (ed.), *Das Evangelium und die Evangelien. Vorträge vom Tübinger Symposium 1982* (Tübingen: Mohr–Siebeck, 1983), pp. 173–208; W. H. Mare, 'Genre Criticism and the Gospels' in J. H. Skilton (ed.), *The Gospels Today. A Guide to some Recent Developments* (Philadelphia, PA: Skilton House, 1990), pp. 82–101; Sanders and Davies, *Gospels*, pp. 25–47; M. J. Suggs, 'Gospel, genre' in *IDB(S)*, pp. 370–2; C. H. Talbert, *What is a Gospel? The Genre of the Canonical Gospels* (London: SPCK; Philadelphia, PA: Fortress Press, 1978); W. R. Telford, 'The Interpretation of Mark: a History of Developments and Issues' in Telford (ed.), *Interpretation*, pp. 15–17; Telford, *Mark*, pp. 94–100.
[11] L. W. Hurtado, 'The Gospel of Mark: Evolutionary or Revolutionary Document?', *JSNT*, 40 (1990), pp. 15–32.

to establish the actual *identity* of its author, and hence to support its traditional attribution to the John Mark of the New Testament.[12] That is not to say that we cannot compile some kind of *profile* of the author – indeed in seeking to illuminate his theology I shall be attempting in this respect to do so – but the internal evidence of the text hardly permits the drawing of an identikit picture which would link the author with any named members of the early church. Few hard facts indeed are known about such figures, legend, historical naivety or the romantic imagination often supplying what we think we know about them. For convenience, however, and following convention, I shall continue to refer to the text's anonymous author as 'Mark' but with a disclaimer, as in the modern novel or film, that the character 'Mark' in this book is a literary fiction, and is not intended to signify an identification with any actual person in the New Testament. In light of this, I might further comment on why I have chosen to refer to the author throughout as 'he'. This is not merely a matter of consistency and convenience. The gender of the author, I recognize, is to some extent an open question. While it remains a possibility that the author of this work was female, the balance of probability nevertheless argues in favour of a male author given the preponderance of literary activity by male writers in the ancient world and the early church. In the final chapter we shall in fact be considering the way women are presented in the Gospel, a treatment which will have implications for the gender of the author.

Having raised some issues and offered some definitions, let me now summarize the overall plan of the book and highlight some of the distinctive features of the approach that I shall be taking to 'The Theology of the Gospel of Mark'. In this first chapter, I shall say something about the background of the text and its general message, attempting briefly to place the Gospel (and therefore its theology) in its historical setting. In a second

---

[12] The most recent comprehensive treatment of the traditions surrounding Mark is that by C. C. Black, *Mark. Images of an Apostolic Interpreter* (Studies on Personalities of the New Testament; Columbia, SC: University of South Carolina Press, 1994). Black concludes that 'we lack enough hard, pertinent evidence to confirm the historicity of the connection between the apostle Peter and the Second Evangelist or his Gospel' (p. 205).

major chapter, I shall describe and analyse the Gospel's theology, again from a historical perspective and with particular regard to its original context. Special emphasis will be given to three important and interrelated aspects of Mark's theology, namely his Christology, soteriology and eschatology. In chapter 3 we shall examine the Gospel in relation to other relevant writings of the New Testament. Briefly reviewing this larger corpus and highlighting parallels and contrasts, where appropriate, I shall seek to locate the Gospel's theology in its wider canonical context. The fourth and final chapter will range even further afield, commenting on the Gospel's history of interpretation and on its significance in the contemporary context.

Three emphases in particular will characterize the approach that will be taken. The first, as this outline demonstrates, is the importance of *context* in understanding the theology of the Gospel of Mark. For some literary approaches, texts may be interpreted purely with regard to their own internal relations or 'narrative world' and without reference to speculative extrinsic factors.[13] I shall assume, however, that without an appreciation of the ancient context in which the Gospel was conceived (the historical setting out of which it emerged, the literary and cultural environment in which it was written, the theological situation to which it was addressed), the theology of Mark cannot be adequately understood. It is for this reason, therefore, that I have also taken particular care to preface my discussion of individual features of Mark's thought or treatment of the tradition (whether it be the parables, the miracles or the Kingdom of God), with general background explaining how these were understood in the various traditions to which he was heir (for example, the Old Testament, apocalyptic Judaism, the wider Hellenistic world, or the immediate pre-Markan tradition). In focusing upon the ancient context, however, I shall also be mindful of the contemporary context within which this study of Mark's theology is also conducted, whether it be the university, where the Gospel functions as a resource for historical reconstruction, sociological investigation or literary analysis, or

---

[13] For example, Kingsbury, *Christology*.

the church where it functions as scripture (both religiously and ethically), or society in general where it functions, for good or ill, as an influence, cultural, ethical, political or otherwise.

My second emphasis will be on the importance of *method*. The principal method employed will be the historical-critical one (especially redaction criticism) but I shall also draw upon the insights of the newer literary approaches where appropriate. Where a holistic perspective on the text is relevant I shall adopt it. Account will be taken of the role of the reader in the construction of the theology of Mark, whether the ancient reader to whom the text was intended to speak, or the modern reader who comes to it with very different eyes. I shall also be conscious in particular of my own reading of the text, a critical academic one which attempts to construct, using categories that in part would have been alien to the evangelist, a much more systematic or self-conscious account of his theology than he himself would perhaps have recognized!

A third emphasis will be on the importance of *Mark as a theologian*. For me, as already indicated, 'The Theology of the Gospel of Mark' is largely the theology of its author, the evangelist, although he himself has taken over traditions with their own theological stamp. It is also the theology of the text for whose final form he was responsible. Where Mark's theology differs from or is in tension with that of his sources I shall endeavour to illuminate its distinctiveness. Where no tension appears to exist, I shall assume that he took over the tradition because he agreed with the theology it reflected. My focus, therefore, will be on the contribution of the evangelist to the theology of the developing Jesus movement and in this I would join forces with those who see in Mark a theologian of some considerable creativity.[14]

AUTHORSHIP, DATE AND PROVENANCE

In speaking of Mark as a theologian, we immediately run up against a traditional view of the Gospel which attributes it, as

---

[14] See Telford, 'History of Developments' in Telford (ed.), *Interpretation*, pp. 24–5.

already mentioned, to the John Mark of the New Testament and regards it as a simple and largely unvarnished historical account of the reminiscences of the apostle Peter. This account, moreover, is frequently viewed as crude from a literary point of view and unsophisticated from a theological one. Since this again raises the question of authorship in relation to theology, let me deal with it briefly. A fuller discussion can be found elsewhere[15] but let me here summarize some of the main points of the argument.

The traditional view of authorship can be traced to the early second century and is based on the testimony of Papias, bishop of Hierapolis, who, according to Eusebius (*Ecclesiastical History* III.39.14–16), attributed it to an unknown contemporary, 'the Elder'. In favour of its authenticity is the strength and virtual unanimity of the church tradition, at least between the second and the fifth century; the 'understated' nature of the testimony, namely its ascription to a non-apostle; the widely held view that this Gospel was also used as a source by the authors of at least two of the three later canonical Gospels (Matthew and Luke), a state of affairs which may also attest to the strength of the tradition lying behind it; the prominence given to Peter in the Gospel (the so-called 'Petrine passages' are 1.16–39; 2.1–14; 3.13–19; 4.35–5.43; 6.7–13, 30–56; 8.15–9.48; 10.32–52; 11.1–33; 13.3–4, 32–7; 14.17–50, 53–4, 66–72) and even, it has been claimed, the appearance of John Mark himself as the enigmatic (but anonymous) young man in Gethsemane who flees away naked leaving his garment behind (14.51–2)!

Against this position, however, there are weighty objections. That early church tradition was virtually unanimous in supporting the claim is not surprising since the later church fathers were almost certainly dependent upon Papias, and hence offer no independent attestation. Papias' evidence itself is unreliable and often ambiguous. The identification of 'Mark' with the John Mark of the New Testament is not actually made by Papias himself (although he may have intended this figure) and is not explicitly made indeed until Jerome. If the 'John Mark' of

---

[15] See Telford, *Mark*, pp. 15–20.

the New Testament is meant, then we have to reckon with the fact that the New Testament traditions about him (if indeed they are all referring to the one person)[16] connect him with Paul, and not with Peter (see Acts 12.12, 25; 13.5, 13; 15.37, 39; Col. 4.10; 2 Tim. 4.11; Phlm. 24).[17] The one exception is 1 Peter 5.13 where a connection between 'Mark' and the apostle Peter is posited ('my son Mark'). Since this epistle is widely regarded as pseudonymous, the most that can be said is that it too witnesses to a late first-century or early second-century tradition that associated the apostle with a 'Mark' (even perhaps *the* John Mark), although no connection is made, of course, between this 'Mark' and the writer of the Gospel. We might even speculate that this was the source of the Papias tradition. Ascribing the Gospel to Peter's 'son Mark', even although he was not an apostle, may have given the Gospel all the legitimacy it needed in the eyes of those who had by this time come to value it. As for Matthew and Luke's use of Mark, this cannot be used in support of the Papias tradition since neither of these writers identify it as a source, and, far from capitalizing on its alleged Petrine authority, feel free to alter it as they wish.

Where the internal evidence is concerned, the clues given as to the Gospel's real author provide little correlation with the New Testament traditions about John Mark. The author of our text shows unfamiliarity with the geography of Palestine (e.g. 5.1; 6.45; 7.31; 8.22; 10.1; 11.1), Jewish customs (7.2–4; 10.2; 14.1; 14.64) and even the Jewish leadership groups (e.g. 3.6; 6.17; 8.15; 12.13).[18] The Gospel was written in Greek with Gentiles in mind (compare e.g. the Aramaic translations in 3.17; 5.41; 7.11; 7.34; 14.36; 15.22, 34) and offers harsh criticism of Jews and Judaism, a subject I shall take up later. Peter is not significantly more prominent in Mark than he is in the other Gospels (for which Petrine authority is not claimed), and an unflattering

---

[16] According to Black, three different figures emerge when one examines the New Testament evidence, the Lukan 'Mark' (aligned with a more parochial Jewish Christianity), the Pauline 'Mark' (Paul's servant and co-worker) and the Petrine Mark (Peter's faithful 'son'). 'Indeed, it seems that there is not one but at least two, and perhaps three, figures of Mark explicit in the Christian canon' (p. 66).

[17] See P. Parker, 'The Authorship of the Second Gospel', *PerspRelSt*, 5 (1978), pp. 4–9.

[18] For discussion, see the standard commentaries where these passages are concerned.

picture is frequently painted of him (e.g. 8.33; 9.5–6; 14.30–1, 66ff.). It is pure romantic fiction, moreover, to suppose that in 14.51–2 we have the hallmarks of eye-witness testimony and that there John Mark is signing his name to his work. While the vivid details within the Gospel indicate the author's closeness to the oral tradition, the nature and variety of the material to be found in Mark, as form critics have pointed out, testifies to the fact that the Gospel is a product of a long process of 'community tradition' and not of direct eye-witness testimony.[19] In sum, it is only the external evidence of the Papias tradition which supports the traditional view of authorship and this evidence is problematic. The internal evidence of the text, which is ultimately decisive, tilts strongly against it. Indeed without Papias' testimony the Gospel itself would hardly have suggested it.[20] When we consider, however, that it was the religious value of the Gospel which led the early church to assert its link with Peter and not *vice versa*, then the matter of its actual authorship is not ultimately decisive for the question of its theology. What does matter is that this anonymous writer, whoever he was, created, to our knowledge, the first extensive and coherent narrative account of the teaching and activity of Jesus, an early literary representation which was at the same time a *religious* interpretation of traditions about the founder of Christianity which were circulating in the first-century Mediterranean world.

But how early was it written and where in the Mediterranean world was it composed? A general consensus would now accept a date not much earlier than 65 CE and not much later than 75, that is, some time before or after the fall of Jerusalem which occurred in 70.[21] A substantially earlier date is usually dismissed

---

[19] See D. E. Nineham, 'Eye-Witness Testimony and the Gospel Tradition', *JTS*, 9 (1958), pp. 13–25, 243–52; 11 (1960), pp. 253–64.

[20] K. Niederwimmer, 'Johannes Markus und die Frage nach dem Verfasser des zweiten Evangeliums', *ZNW*, 58 (1967), pp. 172–88.

[21] For some recent discussion, see, for example, F. F. Bruce, 'The Date and Character of Mark' in E. Bammel and C. F. D. Moule (eds.), *Jesus and the Politics of His Day* (Cambridge: Cambridge University Press, 1984), pp. 69–89; E. E. Ellis, 'The Date and Provenance of Mark's Gospel' in F. van Segbroeck *et al.* (eds.), *The Four Gospels 1992* (Leuven: Leuven University Press/Peeters, 1992), pp. 801–15; M. Hengel, 'The Gospel of Mark. Time of Origin and Situation' in M. Hengel (ed.), *Studies in the Gospel*

since it takes insufficient account of the development of the tradition before Mark as well as the internal evidence (especially of chapter 13) which suggests that events in the sixties formed the backdrop for the final form of the text. Where opinions differ would be in the fixing of a more precise date within this general period. Some would argue for the mid-sixties, that is, in the aftermath of the Neronian persecution,[22] and this would explain the evangelist's interest in the subject of suffering, persecution and martyrdom (e.g. 1.14; 4.17; 6.17–29; 8.31–9.1; 9.11–13, 30–2; 10.29–30, 32–4, 38–9, 45; 13.9, 11–13; 14.41). Others would opt for the second half of the sixties during the period of unrest and apocalyptic fervour occasioned by both the Romano-Jewish War and the civil war throughout the Empire (e.g. 13.6–8, 17–23, 24–31).[23] Others still, taking the prediction of the destruction of the Temple as a *vaticinium ex eventu* (13.1–2), or prophecy after the event, would hold that it was written shortly after the fall of Jerusalem when eschatological expectation had perhaps begun to be tempered by the delay in Jesus' second return or *parousia* (e.g. 13.10, 32–7).[24] This would be my own view. Where the Gospel's theology is concerned, the more precise datings are not hugely significant, except insofar as the earlier of these three datings might lead us perhaps to accord more significance to the theme of 'suffering discipleship' in Mark's theology, and the latter datings to the importance of eschatology.

Where provenance is concerned, four hypotheses dominate the field, namely Rome, Galilee, Antioch and small-town, rural

of Mark (Philadelphia, PA: Fortress Press, 1985), pp. 1–30; D. Senior, ' "With Swords and Clubs" … the Setting of Mark's Community and His Critique of Abusive Power', *BTB*, 17 (1987), pp. 10–20.

22 See Tacitus, *Annals*, 15.44 and C. K. Barrett, *The New Testament Background. Selected Documents* (London: SPCK, 1987), pp. 15–16 as well as V. Taylor, *The Gospel According to St Mark* (London: Macmillan; New York: St Martin's Press, 1966), pp. 31–2 ; W. L. Lane, *The Gospel According to Mark. The English Text with Introduction, Exposition and Notes* (The New International Commentary on the New Testament, 2; Grand Rapids, MI: Eerdmans, 1974), pp. 17–21.

23 W. Marxsen, *Introduction to the New Testament. An Approach to its Problems* (Oxford: Blackwell, 1968), p. 143.

24 S. G. F. Brandon, 'The Date of the Markan Gospel', *NTS*, 7 (1960–1), pp. 126–41; J. Marcus, 'The Jewish War and the *Sitz im Leben* of Mark', *JBL*, 111 (1992), pp. 441–62.

Syria. The first of these, Rome, is the traditional place of origin for Mark's Gospel. It is supported by external evidence (chiefly the Anti-Marcionite Prologue, Irenaeus and Clement of Alexandria) but this again may simply be a deduction from 1 Peter 5.13 where Mark, Peter and Rome (or 'Babylon') are connected. Certain internal clues have been adduced in its favour such as the frequent Latinisms (e.g. 5.9 *legion*; 6.27 *speculator* or military executioner; 12.42 *quadrans*, a Roman coin), the indications of Gentile addressees or the evidence which links the Gospel with the Neronian persecution in 64, or the anti-Jewish sentiments prevailing shortly after 70 in consequence of the Romano-Jewish War. None of these is obviously decisive. The fact that Mark came to be used by Matthew and Luke within a relatively short time after its composition suggests to some that it emanated from an important church-centre like Rome but this consideration has to be balanced with the evidence of its relative neglect in subsequent church history.

In favour of the alternative, Galilee, is the author's clear dependence on Palestinian traditions, his special interest in Galilee (e.g. 1.14, 16, 28, 39; 3.7; 7.31; 14.28; 16.7) and his use of Galilean and Judaean place-names throughout without explanation. Such a location would also be consistent with the evidence linking the Gospel with the events of the war and the eschatological excitement it precipitated in Palestine. A major city like Antioch in Syria, however, would be equally fitting, with its mixture of Roman and Jewish culture, its links with the primitive Jesus movement (see Acts 11.19–30), and even, if one were to accept the traditional view of the Gospel's authorship, with Peter (see Gal. 2.11), with Mark's uncle Barnabas (see Acts 11.22–6) and also with Cyrene (see Acts 1.20) from where the (unexplained) Simon of Mark's text is said to have come (Mk 15.21)! On the other hand, if the Gospel's cultural and linguistic links are with eastern Mediterranean village life, as is claimed, and given that it portrays Jesus' ministry and that of his disciples as an itinerant and rural one, a major urban centre like Antioch may not be appropriate (Mark displays, it is said, an aversion to the city). Rural and small-town southern Syria has therefore been suggested as a more suitable place of

origin.[25] While Rome is the most popular of all these alterna-
tives, the question of provenance is clearly still an open one.

THE MARKAN COMMUNITY

In the introduction I emphasized the importance of the historical context for the interpretation of the theology of Mark. The
above discussion illustrates, however, some of the difficulties
which confront us when we try to reconstruct the historical
setting by working back from the textual evidence. These
difficulties are also apparent when we seek to answer the
question of Mark's addressees. So far we have encountered
evidence to support the view that Greek-speaking Gentiles were
in view, but can we be more specific? Three overlapping terms
are frequently employed in this debate, 'readership', 'audience'
and 'community', and certain distinct issues lurk behind them.
Was the Gospel of Mark addressed to a 'readership'? Obviously
it was (e.g. 13.14 'let the reader understand') but a 'readership' is
not the same thing as a 'community'. A 'readership' may be
general, diverse in interests or background, and widely diffused.
A 'community', on the other hand, implies a particular social
configuration, with its own special organization, needs, activities, beliefs and traditions. Were Mark's addressees a widely
disseminated 'readership', or members of a localized, self-
conscious 'community', a group, sect or cult with its own
religious identity? Some scholars, taking a literary-historical
approach[26] and having a concern to place Mark in its first-
century literary context by investigating, for example, its genre,
would obviously prefer to speak in terms of 'readership' rather
than 'community', while those influenced by form criticism
tend to reverse the emphasis, as already mentioned.

In speaking further of Mark's 'audience' should we interpret
the word in its literal sense? Was the text intended to be read
silently by the individual, read aloud by a group in a public

---

[25] H. C. Kee, *Community of the New Age. Studies in Mark's Gospel* (Philadelphia, PA:
Westminster Press, 1977), pp. 100–5.
[26] See, for example, Tolbert, *Sowing.*

setting,[27] or even performed on a stage? A growing body of recent opinion would argue that we ought to think in terms of 'auditors' rather than 'readers'.[28] Because of its compositional techniques, structure and style, the Gospel should be considered as 'oral traditional literature', an oral/aural narrative which was designed for performance before and in interaction with a live audience, and the evangelist perhaps as an itinerant story-teller or oral performer. Some indeed would assert (for example, Boomershine or Dewey) that methodologies based on silent reading of texts have a potential for distorting the original intention of the text and that the dynamics of orality should be taken more seriously in its interpretation.

Such questions are avoided by those who take a strictly literary approach like narrative criticism. Here the boundaries of the text and its own narrative world are not transgressed and discussion of the 'implied author' speaking through the 'narrator' to the 'implied reader' leaves the 'real author' and the 'historical reader' out of account and a matter merely for speculation. What are the signs that behind the Gospel of Mark, however, lay not simply a 'readership', real or implied, but a 'community'? An historical-critical approach based on form criticism would point to a number of features in the Markan text which would suggest an affirmative answer; for

---

[27] E. Best, 'The Gospel of Mark: Who was the Reader?', *Irish Biblical Studies*, 11 (1989), pp. 124–32. In commenting on Mk 13.14 ('let the reader understand'), Best claims that the 'reader' in question would be an active participant in communal worship (when the Gospel was read aloud) and that the phrase, a gloss, was a private note to this public reader to call attention to the solecism 'standing where he [sic] should not'.

[28] M. A. Beavis, *Mark's Audience. The Literary and Social History of Mark 4.11–12* (JSNTSS, 33; Sheffield: JSOT Press, 1989); T. E. Boomershine, 'Peter's Denial as Polemic or Confession: the Implications of Media Criticism for Biblical Hermeneutics', *Semeia*, 39 (1987), pp. 47–68; P. J. J. Botha, 'The Historical Setting of Mark's Gospel: Problems and Possibilities', *JSNT*, 51 (1993), pp. 27–55; C. Bryan, *A Preface to Mark. Notes on the Gospel in Its Literary and Cultural Settings* (Oxford: Oxford University Press, 1993); J. Dewey, 'Oral Methods of Structuring Narrative in Mark', *Int*, 43 (1989), pp. 32–44; J. Dewey, 'Mark as Interwoven Tapestry. Forecasts and Echoes for a Listening Audience', *CBQ*, 53 (1991), pp. 221–36; J. Dewey, 'Mark as Aural Narrative: Structures as Clues to Understanding', *Sewanee Theological Review [Sewanee, TN]*, 36 (1992), pp. 45–56. I recently heard the distinguished actor Alec McCowen give his one-man rendition of the Gospel of Mark in Newcastle Cathedral (Sunday, 17 March 1996) and anyone who has listened to this forceful recital (given in the King James Authorised Version) will appreciate how suitable this Gospel is for oral performance.

example, the nature of the material used (its parenetic, catechetical and polemical characteristics), the content of the issues addressed (e.g. political questions concerning leadership and discipleship; legal and cultic issues concerning the sabbath, purity, fasting, table fellowship; social issues concerning marriage and divorce, poverty and riches; doctrinal issues concerning the authority and status of Jesus, the Kingdom of God, the coming age, resurrection etc.), the mood engendered or atmosphere created (the apocalyptic overtones and the eschatological urgency, the references to suffering and the hints of persecution, real or anticipated). All these suggest a 'community' (rather than simply a 'readership'), which faces a common threat, is in tension with its Jewish heritage, is oppressed, possibly persecuted,[29] is in need of moral guidance, sees Jesus as a paradigm for its faith and expects a speedy resolution of its problems.

Features such as these are not sufficient, of course, to provide a definitive clue to the identity of the Markan community. This, like the Gospel's provenance, still remains an open question.[30] Such factors could apply to urban Gentile Christians in Rome suffering persecution (see V. Taylor, S. G. F. Brandon), Jewish Christians in Galilee awaiting the parousia (W. Marxsen) or to a rural and ethnically inclusive community in southern Syria with an apocalyptic orientation (H. C. Kee).[31] They remind us, however, that Mark's theology had its roots in a community experience and that it cannot easily be detached from the social, political and cultural exigencies which affected it.

---

[29] See B. M. F. van Iersel, 'The Gospel According to St Mark – Written for a Persecuted Community?', *Nederlands Theologisch Tijdschrift*, 34 (1980), pp. 15–36.

[30] See J. R. Donahue, 'The Quest for the Community of Mark's Gospel' in van Segbroeck *et al.* (eds.), *Four Gospels*, pp. 817–38.

[31] For some recent work which builds on the sociological insights of Kee, see J. S. Suh, *Discipleship and Community. Mark's Gospel in Sociological Perspective* (Nexus Monograph Series 1; Claremont, CA: Center for Asian-American Ministries, School of Theology at Claremont, 1991). See also R. L. Rohrbaugh, 'The Social Location of the Marcan Audience', *BTB*, 23 (1993), pp. 114–27 as well as *Int*, 47 (1993), pp. 380–95; H. Waetjen, *A Re-ordering of Power. A Sociopolitical Reading of Mark's Gospel* (Minneapolis, MN: Fortress Press, 1989).

THE TRADITION BEFORE MARK

If behind Mark there lay a 'community' or 'communities', there also lay, it should be emphasized, a 'tradition' or 'traditions'. Whatever literary or theological creativity was demonstrated by the Markan author, he did not invent the basic material in his Gospel. That material had a pre-history. Sayings and stories about Jesus had been circulating for a generation in various Jewish- or Gentile-Christian communities before they came to literary expression and theological (re)interpretation at the hands of our anonymous writer. These mainly oral traditions took the form, for the most part, of discrete, independent, self-contained units, except possibly for the more extensive passion narrative. The particular 'forms' taken by this oral material were not accidental but a product of the function (*Sitz im Leben*) of the material in its community setting (for example, preaching, teaching, instruction to catechumens, worship, exhortation, discipline, apologetic, polemic). Having played a significant role in these various cultic activities, they carried as a result their own theological stamp or colouring. This by now familiar view of the origin of the Gospel material owes much to classical form criticism[32] and it is one which, despite a number of modifications, is still influential in academic circles. It is the basic model with which I myself shall work, although it will be qualified by the results of redaction criticism and tempered by the insights of the newer literary criticism.

But how can we be sure that Mark did not invent the basic material in his Gospel but used sources? This subject I have treated at greater length elsewhere[33] but in general a number of factors would indicate this, namely, considerable disjunction in the narrative especially when we read it in the original language, obvious insertions (e.g. 7.3–4), puzzling parentheses (e.g. 11.13c), some lack of logical coherence, especially in passages where what appears to be offered is an amalgam of originally separate sayings (e.g. 4.1–34; 8.34–9.1; 9.33–50, especially

---

[32] See R. Bultmann, *The History of the Synoptic Tradition* (Oxford: Blackwell, 1968).
[33] See Telford, 'History of Developments' in Telford (ed.), *Interpretation*, pp. 17–24; Telford, *Mark*, pp. 46–56.

49–50; 11.22–5; 13.3–37), overlaps with Q (e.g. Mk 8.35 and Mt. 10.39 = Lk. 17.33) or with John (e.g. Mk 11.15–18 and Jn 2.13–22), frequent repetition including doublets (e.g. the two feeding accounts of 6.30–44 and 8.1–10) or triplets (e.g. the three passion predictions of 8.31, 9.31, 10.33–4), suggestive patterning (e.g. the repetition of the sea miracle, three healing miracles and one feeding miracle pattern which some scholars have observed in 4.35–5.43/6.30–44 and 6.45–53/7.24–8.26),[34] and numerous inconsistencies and discrepancies (compare 9.1 with 13.32). Some of these features could, of course, be put down to the conscious (and even awkward) literary activity of the evangelist himself (certain instances of repetition, for example, may reflect authorial emphasis rather than the incorporation of sources) but the overall impression is that the evangelist has drawn on extraneous and at times conflicting material.

If Mark did use source material, then we might further ask whether this material came to him in extensive written form, in a number of smaller collections (either oral or written) or in single oral units? Prior to the advent and influence of form criticism, an older view maintained that the Gospel was either an abridgement of an earlier more extensive written source, a primitive Gospel, or, conversely, that it was an expansion of an earlier less extensive written source, a proto-Mark or *Urmarkus*. This theory is no longer popular, the diversity of the Gospel's contents suggesting that Mark is the compilation of a multiplicity of sources rather than an edited version of a single one. Did the evangelist take over, then, a larger number of less extensive written sources? Given the degree of homogeneity in the Markan style and hence the difficulty in establishing the parameters of such alleged sources, this hypothesis too has become less compelling, with the eclipse of classical source criticism by form criticism favouring Markan dependence on an oral rather than a literary tradition. Consequently, recent Markan scholarship has tended to talk in vaguer and more general terms of the 'sources', 'traditions', 'collections' or even

[34] See P. J. Achtemeier, 'Towards the Isolation of pre-Markan Miracle Catenae', *JBL*, 89 (1970), pp. 245–91.

'cycles' underlying sections of the Gospel without claiming that it can isolate these in any more precise way.

Discussion has centred in particular around the question of pre-Markan collections or traditions underlying the prologue (1.1–15; Jesus and John the Baptist), 'the [so-called] day in Capernaum' (1.21–39), the controversy passages (2.1–3.6; 7.1–23; 11–12), the parable discourse (4.1–34), the miracle pericopae (1.21–2.12; 4.35–5.43; 6.31–52; 7.24–8.10), the sayings complexes (3.22–30; 8.34–9.1; 9.33–50; 10; 11.22–5), the apocalyptic discourse (13) and the passion narrative (14–15). For some, Mark's debt to such collections is extensive (e.g. R. Pesch), for others moderate (e.g. J. Gnilka), for others limited (e.g. H.-W. Kuhn, D. Lührmann).[35] My own estimation of the consensus[36] is that there is general agreement in favour of Mark's use of a collection of controversies (in 2.1–3.6 but not in 7.1–23 or 11–12), parables (in 4), sayings (in 10) and a passion narrative. Opinions are more divided in the case of the miracles (especially 4.35ff.) and the apocalypse (13) and in general a negative judgment would be delivered against a coherent underlying source in 1.1–15 and 1.29–39. In sum, there are many who would echo the judgment of W. G. Kümmel that (with the qualified exception of the passion narrative) 'we cannot go beyond declaring that Mk is probably based on no extensive written sources, but that more likely the evangelist has woven together small collections of individual traditions and detailed bits of tradition into a more or less coherent presentation'.[37]

But of what did these 'detailed bits of tradition' consist? Here

---

[35] J. Gnilka, *Das Evangelium nach Markus* (Evangelisch-Katholischer Kommentar zum Neuen Testament, II 1/2; Zurich, Einsiedeln and Cologne: Benziger, 1978; Neukirchen-Vluyn: Neukirchener Verlag, 1979); H.-W. Kuhn, *Ältere Sammlungen im Markusevangelium* (Studien zum Alten und Neuen Testaments, 8; Göttingen: Vandenhoeck & Ruprecht, 1971); D. Lührmann, *Das Markusevangelium* (Handbuch zum Neuen Testament, 3; Tübingen: Mohr–Siebeck, 1987); R. Pesch, *Das Markusevangelium* (Herders Theologischer Kommentar zum Neuen Testament, II, 1/2; Freiburg, Basle and Vienna: Herder, 1976; 1977).

[36] W. R. Telford, 'The Pre-Markan Tradition in Recent Research (1980–1990)' in van Segbroeck *et al.* (eds.), *Four Gospels*, pp. 693–723.

[37] W. G. Kümmel, *Introduction to the New Testament* (London: SCM Press, 1975), p. 85.

classical form criticism (particularly as represented by Bultmann) has offered us a substantial and, despite developments in
the discipline and criticisms of it,[38] still influential categoriza-
tion. In Mark, from the (so-called) 'sayings tradition', we can
discern *apophthegms*: sayings introduced with a brief narrative
framework (e.g. 2.18–19a; 3.31–5; 12.14–17); *gnomic* or *wisdom
sayings*: proverbs or aphorisms which embody conventional
secular wisdom or general religious truth (e.g. 2.21–2; 4.21–2;
8.35–7; 10.31), *prophetic* and *apocalyptic sayings*: predictions, ad-
monitions, warnings of impending crisis, summonses to repentance, promises of future reward, etc. (e.g. 8.38; 9.1; 12.38–40;
13 *passim*), *legal sayings*: sayings expressing Jesus' attitude to the
Jewish Law, and *community rules*: sayings setting forth the regulations of the community in respect of its internal organization
and discipline as well as its mission (e.g. 2.27; 7.15; 9.42;
10.11–12; 10.42–4; 11.25; 12.29–30), *Christological sayings* or 'I-
sayings': sayings which express the purpose of Jesus' coming, his
special relationship with God, his passion and resurrection (e.g.
2.17b; 2.19b, 20; 2.28; 10.45) and *parables* (e.g. 4.1–34; 13.28–9,
34–7). From the (so-called) 'narrative tradition', we have *miracle
stories*, with their emphasis on divine power (e.g. 1.29–31; 7.31–7;
8.22–6; 9.14–27), *historical stories* and *legends*, with their personal
(biographical) or cultic orientation and their folkloric conventions (e.g. 11.1–10; 14.12–16) and *myths*, where the 'otherworldly'
breaks in on the human scene (1.9–11; 1.12–13; 9.2–8). Reflected in all these forms was the theology of the community or
communities which created and transmitted them, and it was
these forms, together with the longer passion narrative (an
account itself coloured by a religious view of Jesus) which Mark
took over and shaped into his own distinctive theological
presentation of Jesus.

THE MESSAGE OF MARK

In making this last statement, I am parting company to an
appreciable degree from the form critic's evaluation of the

---

[38] See Telford, *Mark*, pp. 66–9.

evangelist's literary and theological achievement. In common
with a now strongly established view, I would hold that the
evangelist was not a mere compiler, collector or editor of
traditions but one who was to a large degree responsible for the
final form of the Gospel. This revised estimate is principally a
product both of the redaction-critical approach which has
dominated Gospel study since the 1960s and the newer literary
approaches which have been applied to Mark increasingly since
the late 1970s.

Redaction criticism (and its sister discipline composition
criticism) has uncovered the extent to which the evangelist
selected, arranged, linked, altered, modified, reshaped, expanded and in some cases even created the material of which
his Gospel is composed. Where the traditions needed to be
woven together into a connected presentation, for example, it
was he who provided the seams which link the individual
sayings or stories together or the summary passages linking
sections of the narrative (e.g. 1.21–2; 1.39; 2.13; 3.7–12; 4.1;
6.6b; 6.30–4, 53–6). Where individual traditions lacked indications of time or place, it was he who frequently supplied them
with a chronological, topographical or geographical setting
(e.g. 1.9; 2.1, 13; 3.13; 4.1; 6.1; 7.24, 31). Where such traditions
required comment or explanation, he introduced parenthetical
statements (e.g. 2.15b; 3.21b, 30; 5.41b; 7.3–4, 19c; 13.14b;
15.16b, 34). Redaction criticism has also highlighted the fact
that in his extensive editorial work, the evangelist was motivated more by literary and theological concerns than by purely
historical ones.

The newer literary approaches, with their holistic emphasis,
have in turn asserted that a narrow 'source-editing' model for
the compositional process (the investigation of summary passages, seams, insertions etc.) provides us with an inadequate
basis for gaining a complete understanding of the evangelist's
literary or theological enterprise. Increasing attention has been
paid to recurrent themes, motifs or interests within the Gospel
and a growing recognition accorded to those features (both
literary and theological) which give the Markan text its unity
and progression. This coherence can be seen, it is maintained,

in the Gospel's style,[39] its literary techniques and rhetorical devices (for example, in its consistent demonstration of linear and concentric, or 'sandwich' patterning)[40] and its narrative development (plot, characters and settings).[41] Many would now find themselves in agreement with R. C. Tannehill's judgment that 'Mk is a single unified story because of its progressive narrative lines.'[42] In short, the textually disintegrative factors (the disjunctions, discrepancies, ambiguities, inconsistencies, etc.) which have led form critics to investigate the pre-history of the text and its external or socio-historical context, are now being counterbalanced in scholarly discussion by an increasing emphasis on the textually integrative ones, that is, those which direct us to the unity of the text and its internal relations.

All this has important implications for the question of Mark as 'theologian' and for the extent of his literary and theological creativity. The matter is still being fiercely debated.[43] A number of scholars, following Bultmann, would be unwilling to concede

[39] See, for example, F. Neirynck, *Duality in Mark. Contributions to the Study of the Markan Redaction* (BETL, 31; Leuven: Leuven University Press/Peeters, 1988). 'There is a sort of homogeneity in Mark, from the wording of sentences to the composition of the gospel. After the study of these data one has a strong impression of the unity of the gospel of Mark. It can be formulated as a methodological principle that the categories we distinguished hold together and that no pericope in Mark can be treated in isolation' (p. 37).

[40] E.g. *Triadism* (the grouping of units in sequences of three) or *montage* (the juxtaposition of units to suggest meaning by association). One common form of concentric patterning is *chiasmus* where materials are placed in a sandwich pattern (e.g. *A–B–B'–A'*) in such a way that inner and outer elements correspond to each other and the central unit, where it occurs, is highlighted (e.g. *A–B–C–B'–A'*). Others are *inclusio*, a framing device where, for emphasis, an opening or leading idea or phrase is repeated at the conclusion of a unit (or series of units), and *intercalation*, which involves the dovetailing or interlacing of one unit with another in an *A–B–A* pattern. See J. Dewey, *Markan Public Debate. Literary Technique, Concentric Structure, and Theology in Mark 2:1–3:6* (SBLDS, 48; Chico, CA: Scholars Press, 1980); J. Dewey, 'The Literary Structure of the Controversy Stories in Mark 2:1–3:6' in Telford (ed.), *Interpretation*, pp. 141–51; Telford, *Mark*, 102–4; B. M. F. van Iersel, *Reading Mark* (Edinburgh: T. & T. Clark, 1989).

[41] 'At the levels of narrator, plot, characterisation, theology and literary style one can discover a unity and integrity in the gospel that makes it both appropriate and necessary to study the work as a genuine narrative, as a single, coherent, intelligible story' (Marshall, *Faith*, p. 26). See also Rhoads and Michie, *Mark*; D. Rhoads, 'Narrative Criticism and the Gospel of Mark', *JAAR*, 50 (1982), pp. 411–34.

[42] R. C. Tannehill, 'The Gospel of Mark as Narrative Christology', *Semeia*, 16 (1979), p. 77.

[43] See Telford, 'History of Developments' in Telford (ed.), *Interpretation*, pp. 24–5.

that Mark was master of his material and would prefer to see the tradition exerting a stronger influence on the theology of the Gospel than the conservative redactor who gave it written expression. The issue has not been resolved but, as I said in the introduction, I would join forces with those who see in Mark a theologian of some considerable creativity.

The extent of his literary and theological engagement with his material can be seen in a number of ways. It can be observed, for example, in his consistent use of an 'omniscient, intrusive, third-person narrator'[44] (behind whom, in my view, stands ultimately not only the implied author but also the real one). Present in every scene, this narrator is not bound by time and space. He is able to know and thence to inform the implied reader what his characters think and feel, so establishing them in the reader's mind as 'reliable' or 'unreliable' characters. Evincing a definite and consistent 'point of view', he guides the reader throughout the text and suborns him or her into accepting his own ideological stance. This will be important when we examine the evangelist's Christology.

Described by one early form critic (M. Dibelius) as 'the book of secret epiphanies', the Gospel of Mark is replete with elements which tease the mind and invite the reader to theological contemplation (e.g. 8.14–21). One device used by the narrator is irony, a narrative strategy directed to the reader and occurring, according to a recent literary study, 'when the elements of the story-line provoke the reader to see beneath the surface of the text to deeper significances'.[45] By withholding information from characters in the world of the narrative but disclosing it to the reader, irony gains the confidence of the reader and enlists him or her in the process of interpretation. This is particularly so in the case of 'the [so-called] messianic secret', which we shall shortly be examining, but irony is a pervasive feature of the Markan Gospel, as the work of

---

[44] See N. R. Petersen, ' "Point of View" in Mark's Narrative', *Semeia*, 12 (1978), pp. 97–121.

[45] J. Camery-Hoggatt, *Irony in Mark's Gospel* (SNTSMS, 72; Cambridge: Cambridge University Press, 1992), p. 1.

Camery-Hoggatt and others have shown.[46] When the Jewish authorities are mocking Jesus as a false prophet inside the trial chamber, for example, his prophetic powers are being simultaneously vindicated for the reader by Peter's denial in the courtyard outside (14.30 and 14.65, 66–72).

This last example illustrates one of the literary devices used by the Markan redactor, and already commented on, namely that of intercalation, the dovetailing or interlacing of one pericope with another in an *A–B–A* pattern (14.53, 54, 55–65, 66–72). In each case, the evangelist begins to tell a story, interrupts it by inserting another, and then returns to the original in order to complete it (3.21, *22–30*, 31–5; 4.1–9, *10–12*, 13–20; 5.21–4, *25–34*, 35–43; 6.7–13, *14–29*, 30; 11.12–14, *15–19*, 20–5; 14.1–2, *3–9*, 10–11; 14.17–21, *22–6*, 27–31; 15.40–1, *42–6*, 15.47–16.8). These intercalations not only function in a literary way (to create suspense or tension in the narrative) but they also invite the reader to draw a theological lesson from the linked passages by treating them in a mutually interpretative way. Jesus' action in cursing the fig-tree (11.12–14, 22–5), for example, is intended to be viewed in connection with his action in the Temple (11.15–19), both traditions taken in conjunction with each other hinting at a deeper religious symbolism.[47] This observation is reinforced in a recent study which concludes that the Markan sandwiches 'emphasize the major motifs of the Gospel, especially the meaning of faith, discipleship, bearing witness, and the dangers of apostasy... the middle story nearly always provides the key to the theological purpose of the sandwich'.[48]

If the Markan redactor can be shown to make a subtle use of interlinked traditions in this way, juxtaposing internal elements

---

[46] See R. M. Fowler, *Let the Reader Understand. Reader-Response Criticism and the Gospel of Mark* (Minneapolis, MN: Fortress Press, 1991), *passim* ; R. M. Fowler, 'The Rhetoric of Direction and Indirection in the Gospel of Mark' in Telford (ed.), *Interpretation*, pp. 221–4; Rhoads and Michie, *Mark*, pp. 59–67; G. Van Oyen, 'Intercalation and Irony in the Gospel of Mark' in van Segbroeck *et al.* (eds.), *Four Gospels*, pp. 949–74.

[47] See W. R. Telford, *The Barren Temple and the Withered Tree. A Redaction-Critical Analysis of the Cursing of the Fig-tree Pericope in Mark's Gospel and its Relation to the Cleansing of the Temple Tradition* (JSNTSS, 1; Sheffield: JSOT Press, 1980), esp. pp. 48–9.

[48] J. R. Edwards, 'Markan Sandwiches. The Significance of Interpolations in Markan Narratives', *NovT*, 31 (1989), pp. 193–216.

of the text for theological effect, he also demonstrates a similar subtlety in the sphere of intertextuality. A coherent thread running through the Gospel is its references to the Old Testament, a rich tapestry of quotations and allusions being presented to the reader with an implicit invitation to interpret the story of Jesus theologically in the light of these. Clearly the evangelist owed much to the tradition in this regard since the Old Testament was a formative influence on the developing Jesus tradition prior to Mark, whether serving to promote a 'messianic' Christology in general, or contributing to the formulation of the passion narrative in particular. Mark's hand was also at work, however, in this process, the Jewish scriptures being used by him to develop or counteract the Christology implicit in the tradition or traditions before him.[49]

As a final example, I might point to the theological resonances sounded by Mark's topographical and geographical settings. The first part of the Gospel is set in Galilee and its surrounding area, the second part in Jerusalem, with Jesus' journey from Galilee to Jerusalem forming the bridge or centrepiece. Within this overall framework, the Markan characters are encountered in a variety of places: in the *wilderness* (e.g. 1.4, 12, 35; 6.31; 8.4); at the *sea* (1.16; 2.13; 3.7; 4.1; 5.21; 7.31); in the *house* (2.1, 15; 3.20; 7.17, 24; 9.33; 10.10); in the *synagogue* (1.21; 3.1); getting in/out of a *boat* (3.9; 4.1, 36; 5.2, 21; 6.32, 45, 54; 8.10, 14); in the *hills/*on a *mountain* (3.13; 6.46; 9.2; 13.3); on the *way/road* (8.27; 9.33, 34; 10.17, 32, 46, 52); in the *temple* (11.11, 15, 27) or in the *tomb* (5.2; 16.5). Some of these locations have been taken over from the tradition, others are attributable to the evangelist himself, but whatever their precise origin, it is clear that most of them possess rich religious overtones which would not have escaped the ancient reader, whether Jew (e.g. 'the wilderness', 'the mountain', 'the synagogue', 'the temple') or Gentile Christian (e.g. 'the house', the early Christian meeting-

---

[49] For the relation between Mark's Christology and the Old Testament, see Kee, *Community*, esp. pp. 116–44; J. Marcus, *The Way of the Lord. Christological Exegesis of the Old Testament in the Gospel of Mark* (Louisville, KY: Westminster John Knox Press, 1992); R. Schneck, *Isaiah in the Gospel of Mark, I–VIII* (BIBAL DISSERTATION SERIES 1; VALLEJO, CA: BIBAL, 1994).

place, or 'the way', a metaphor for discipleship and the early Christian movement's self-designation, according to Acts 9.2; 19.9, 23; 22.4; 24.14). The narrative opposition between Galilee and Jerusalem (Galilee is where Jesus is welcomed, Jerusalem where he is rejected) or between the land and the sea (especially Jesus' frequent lake crossings) can also be read with regard to their theological and even mythological associations as well as to their historical ones.[50]

Where does this leave us then with respect to the question of Mark's theological creativity? We have certainly come a long way from the notion that 'the author of Mk was a clumsy writer unworthy of mention in any history of literature'[51] or that he was theologically unsophisticated. On the other hand, given his dependence on tradition, it is possible to exaggerate his literary ability and theological profundity, as well as to overemphasize the gulf separating his story world and the real world, his text and its historical context, as the following judgement does:

The gospel of Mark is a story world artistically constructed by an immensely creative and powerful storyteller. It is an integrated narrative in which all of its content is coherently related to itself and constitutes an independent, self-contained, and systematic universe with its own inherent structures of time and space ... consequently it can be comprehended only in terms of itself and not by any historical investigation of its content in relation to the quest for the historical Jesus.[52]

Mark's story world is less coherent than literary critics claim, as we noted when considering some of the evidence of disjunctions, discrepancies and inconsistencies in the text. His story world often interpenetrates with the world of his own community, his real life concerns impinging on the narrative world he has created.[53] It is possible that he was conservative at some

[50] See, for example, D. Blatherwick, 'The Markan Silhouette', *NTS*, 17 (1970–1), pp. 184–92; E. S. Malbon, *Narrative Space and Mythic Meaning in Mark* (New Voices in Biblical Studies; San Francisco: Harper & Row, 1986); E. S. Malbon, 'Galilee and Jerusalem: History and Literature in Marcan Interpretation' in Telford (ed.), *Interpretation*, pp. 253–68; van Iersel, *Mark*.

[51] E. Trocmé, *The Formation of the Gospel According to Mark* (London: SPCK, 1975), p. 72.

[52] Waetjen, *Re-ordering*, p. 1.

[53] See H. Räisänen, *The 'Messianic Secret' in Mark* (Studies of the New Testament and its World; Edinburgh: T. & T. Clark, 1990), p. 21.

points in dealing with his tradition, and creative, even radical, at others. Consequently, I shall attempt to give due weight to both the textually integrative and the textually disintegrative factors, the former justifying the synchronic approach (that is, one directed to the Gospel's final form, interrelationships and effects), the latter the diachronic one (that is, one attuned to the pre-history of its component parts).

What then was the message of Mark and can we determine his leading ideas, a task Bultmann considered misguided?[54] My answer to these questions will emerge as we proceed, but here let me summarize what scholars would now identify as the major themes, motifs or concerns which motivated the evangelist in the creation of his Gospel.

(a) the *secrecy* motif and the writer's interest in the true but hidden *identity of Jesus.*

(b) an interest in the *passion* of Jesus (his suffering, death and resurrection) and its significance for Christology.

(c) an interest in the nature and coming of the *Kingdom of God* and in the question of Jesus' return as *Son of Man.*

(d) an interest in *Galilee.*

(e) his use of the term 'gospel' (*euangelion*).

(f) an interest in *Gentiles* and the Gentile mission.

(g) an interest in *persecution, suffering* and *martyrdom* and the true nature of *discipleship.*

(h) his harsh treatment of the *Jewish leadership groups,* Jesus' *family* and especially his original *disciples.*

Any valid theory of the Gospel's overall theological purpose must take into account all of these distinctive features and assess them accordingly, and this I shall attempt to do. The question of the Gospel's provenance as well as the nature of the Markan community was still, as we saw, an open one. This is also the case for the Gospel's overall purpose. The three most popular theories suggest that Mark's purpose was parenetic (E. Best), kerygmatic (E. Schweizer) or Christological (N. Perrin). According to Best, 'Mark's purpose was pastoral. He wrote primarily

---

[54] Bultmann, *History,* p. 349.

to build up his readers in faith.'[55] With a suffering church in mind, he intended his theology of the cross to equip them to face persecution as well as resist the temptation of their culture. In the opinion of Schweizer, the evangelist's desire to communicate the kerygma or message of the cross was uppermost, the Gospel being about 'the amazing, incomprehensible condescension and love of God which in Jesus seeks the world. But the world is so blinded that it cannot recognize him although he does everything to help it find him'.[56] For Perrin, 'a major aspect of the Marcan purpose is Christological; he is concerned with correcting a false Christology prevalent in his church and to teach both a true Christology and its consequences for Christian discipleship'.[57] Since it is the third of these three views which comes closest to my own estimate of the Markan purpose, I shall therefore begin this study of the theology of the Gospel of Mark with his treatment of the person of Jesus.

= polemical

---

[55] E. Best, *Mark. The Gospel as Story* (Studies of the New Testament and its World; Edinburgh: T. & T. Clark, 1983), p. 51.

[56] E. Schweizer, 'Mark's Theological Achievement' in Telford (ed.), *Interpretation*, p. 80.

[57] N. Perrin, 'The Christology of Mark: a Study in Methodology' in Telford (ed.), *Interpretation*, p. 129.

CHAPTER 2

The theology of Mark

THE PERSON OF JESUS

'Who then is this?': the nature and significance of Markan Christology

In reading the Gospel of Mark from beginning to end, one is immediately struck by the number of narrative images by which its central figure is characterized.[1] He appears as an authoritative teacher (1.21–2), a charismatic prophet (8.27–8) and a popular healer and exorcist (1.32–4). He is described as the 'Nazarene' (10.47) and addressed as 'Teacher' (4.38), 'Rabbi' (9.5), or 'Lord' (7.28). He is acclaimed as the 'Holy One of God' (1.24), greeted as the 'Son of David' (10.47) and confessed as 'Christ' (8.29) or 'Son of God' (15.39). He speaks of himself, however, as the 'Son of Man' and defines his role as that of a servant (10.45). Given this multifaceted representation, how then do we determine Mark's Christology, his understanding of the person of Jesus?

The traditional route has been by way of an analysis of these titles or epithets as well as of the attributes predicated of him. Markan Christology, however, is not simply the sum-total of these, laid side by side, as it were. The picture is more complex than that, and for at least two reasons. In the first place, the evangelist is not simply presenting his own view of Jesus but also taking over, as we have seen, from the early Christian movement before him, both Jewish and Gentile, a variety of traditions which understood Jesus in different ways. Each of these

[1] See E. K. Broadhead, *Prophet, Son, Messiah. Narrative Form and Function in Mark 14–16* (JSNTSS, 97; Sheffield: JSOT Press, 1994).

traditions bears its own Christological stamp. Some appear to
hit historical bedrock (Jesus as teacher, prophet or healer),[2] or
go back to the primitive Jewish-Christian tradition (Jesus as
Messiah, apocalyptic Son of Man, royal Son of David or
suffering Servant).[3] Others may reflect perhaps an estimate of
Jesus more widely current within Hellenistic Jewish or Gentile
Christianity (Jesus as Lord, Son of God, 'divine man'[4]). The
traditions incorporated, therefore, come from different strata of
the developing tradition about him and some, as a result, are
not only dissimilar but contradictory. In the second place, the
evangelist may have taken over traditional material with a
certain Christological slant for a variety of reasons. He may
have done so because he approved of the estimate of Jesus
presented by it. He may have done so, conversely, because he
disapproved of it and wished to qualify, extend or even contradict what it conveyed about the significance of Jesus. A third
possibility is that he was neutral about it and incorporated a
particular tradition for other than its Christological content or
function.

[2] See W. R. Telford, 'Major Trends and Interpretive Issues in the Study of Jesus' in
B. Chilton and C. A. Evans (eds.), *Studying the Historical Jesus* (Leiden, New York and
Cologne: E. J. Brill, 1994), esp. p. 55.

[3] The term *Nazarēnos* used of Jesus (1.24; 10.47; 14.67; 16.6) preserves this primitive
character, and was probably taken over undeveloped by Mark from the tradition. For
a recent discussion, however, of its wider narrative role, see E. K. Broadhead, 'Jesus
the Nazarene: Narrative Strategy and Christological Imagery in the Gospel of Mark',
JSNT, 52 (1993), pp. 3–18.

[4] Although the 'divine man' or *theios anēr* has been under attack as a unified type or
clearly definable concept in the ancient world, it does retain its usefulness in
describing what is an essentially Hellenistic (rather than Jewish) conception of divinity
in which the figure portrayed is a being hovering between the human and the divine,
and who shares a relationship with God which is essentially ontological or metaphysical rather than ethical. For a selection of the discussion, see H. D. Betz, 'Jesus as
Divine Man' in F. T. Trotter (ed.), *Jesus and the Historian. Written in Honor of E. C. Colwell*
(Philadelphia, PA: Westminster Press, 1968), pp. 114–33; L. Bieler, *ΘΕΙΟΣ ΑΝΗΡ.
Das Bild des 'göttlichen Menschen' in Spätantike und Frühchristentum* (Darmstadt: Wis-
senschaftliche Buchgesellschaft, 1935/1936); B. Blackburn, *Theos Anēr and the Markan
Miracle Traditions. A Critique of the Theios Anēr Concept as an Interpretative Background of the
Miracle Traditions used by Mark* (WUNT, 2/60; Tübingen: Mohr–Siebeck, 1991);
C. Holladay, *'Theios Anēr' in Hellenistic-Judaism: A Critique of this Category in New Testament
Christology* (SBLDS, 40; Missoula, MT: Scholars Press, 1977); J. D. Kingsbury, 'The
"Divine Man" as the Key to Mark's Christology – the End of an Era?', *Int*, 35 (1981),
pp. 243–57; D. L. Tiede, *The Charismatic Figure as Miracle-Worker* (SBLDS, 1; Missoula,
MT: Scholars Press, 1972).

As a result, careful discrimination needs to be exercised in any analysis of titles used or attributes predicated of Jesus in Mark. Some of the titles were important for him, others less so. Some appear frequently, others less so. Some reflect his own view of Jesus' significance, others that of the pre-Markan tradition. Some may present, in his view, an inadequate or even false image of Jesus. Some are shared by some other early Christian writers (e.g. Paul), or by the later evangelists. Some Christological traditions present in other earlier or later writers are absent (for example, belief in Jesus' pre-existence as a divine being, or the tradition of his virgin birth).

Given this complexity, it is not surprising that scholars have questioned whether there is a Markan Christology at all, the evangelist having merely synthesized the various images, it is argued, rather than imposing his own Christological viewpoint upon them.[5] More recently, and in line with the newer literary approaches, there has been a tendency to interpret the Christology of the narrative in its own terms without recourse to hypothetical reconstructions of pre-Markan tradition.[6] However, redaction criticism,[7] informed by literary insights, can take us some way towards an answer to the question posed at the beginning of this chapter, but we need to proceed cautiously.

In general, we should note the nature and frequency of the titles and attributes, observing their pattern and arrangement. In particular, we should ask ourselves at what points in the narrative the major titles appear (at the beginning of the Gospel or the end? in a significant or climactic scene – a confession scene? a worship passage? a controversy episode?) and on whose lips (an opponent? a disciple? Jesus himself? a super-natural being – a demon, or angel? a neutral observer?). Which titles or attributes appear more often in obviously redactional

[5] See, for example, E. Trocmé, 'Is there a Markan Christology?' in B. Lindars and S. S. Smalley (eds.), *Christ and Spirit in the New Testament. In Honour of Charles Francis Digby Moule* (Cambridge: Cambridge University Press, 1973), pp. 3–13.
[6] See, for example, J. D. Kingsbury, *The Christology of Mark's Gospel* (Philadelphia, PA: Fortress Press, 1983).
[7] See R. H. Stein, 'The Proper Methodology for Ascertaining a Markan Redaction History', *NovT*, 13 (1971), pp. 181–98.

passages (e.g. seams or summary passages) and which are added to manifestly pre-Markan material? Does the evangelist preserve or alter the meaning of a title taken over from the tradition, and if the latter, how so? Does he use one title, for example, to interpret or qualify another? Does he juxtapose several titles? These are the some of the methods employed by Matthew and Luke in redacting Mark. Comparison, indeed, with Matthew and Luke is instructive for, as first century readers of Mark, they are sensitive to his treatment of the tradition and in particular to his Christological presentation.

With these questions and considerations in mind, let us now briefly discuss the major titles to be found in the Markan text, saying something about their frequency, meaning, background and significance.[8] The title 'Teacher' (*didaskalos*) appears as a noun some twelve times in the Gospel (4.38; 5.35; 9.17, 38; 10.17, 20, 35; 12.14, 19, 32; 13.1; 14.14), its corresponding verb (*didaskein*) fifteen times, that is 'more often than in any other New Testament book'.[9] 'And he began to teach' is a recurrent Markan expression (e.g. 4.1; 6.2, 34; 8.31; see also 10.1). In depicting Jesus as acting in this characteristic way, it would be fair to say that the tradition of 'Jesus the Teacher' was important for Mark in a way that it was not, for example, for Paul. The evangelist seems to approve of the title since it appears on one

[8] For a fuller discussion of the following titles, see the standard treatments to be found in O. Cullmann, *The Christology of the New Testament* (The New Testament Library; Philadelphia, PA: Westminster Press, 1959); J. D. G. Dunn, *Unity and Diversity in the New Testament. An Inquiry into the Character of Earliest Christianity* (London: SCM Press, 1977), pp. 33–59; R. H. Fuller, *The Mission and Achievement of Jesus* (Studies in Biblical Theology 12; London: SCM Press, 1954), pp. 79–117; R. H. Fuller, *The Foundations of New Testament Christology* (London: Lutterworth Press; New York: Scribner, 1965); F. Hahn, *The Titles of Jesus in Christology. Their History in Early Christianity* (London: Lutterworth Press; New York: World Publishing Company, 1969); H. C. Kee, *Community of the New Age. Studies in Mark's Gospel* (Philadelphia, PA: Westminster Press, 1977), pp. 116–44; W. G. Kümmel, *The Theology of the New Testament According to its Major Witnesses Jesus – Paul – John* (Nashville, TN and New York: Abingdon Press, 1973); C. F. D. Moule, *The Origin of Christology* (Cambridge: Cambridge University Press, 1977); V. Taylor, *The Gospel According to St Mark* (London: Macmillan; New York: St Martin's Press, 1966), pp. 117–22; G. Vermes, *Jesus the Jew. A Historian's Reading of the Gospels* (London: SCM Press, 1983).

[9] C. F. Evans, *The Beginning of the Gospel. Four Lectures on St Mark's Gospel* (London: SPCK, 1968), p. 47, *gratia* R. P. Martin, *Mark – Evangelist and Theologian* (Exeter: Paternoster, 1979), p. 111. Cf. also 1.21–2, 27; 2.13; 4.1–2; 6.2, 34; 8.31; 9.31; 10.1; 11.17, 18; 12.14, 35, 38; 14.49.

occasion as Jesus' self-designation (14.14 'The Teacher says . . .').
On the other hand, it is also his opponents' term of address in
chapter 12. In the majority of cases it appears on the lips of his
disciples, although Matthew, it should be noted, alters the title
to the more reverential 'Lord' in 4.38 (Mt. 8.25). In four cases,
the Jewish equivalent, 'Rabbi' or 'Rabbouni' is used, once on
the lips of a blind Jew, Bartimaeus, before he is cured (10.51),
once on the lips of Judas in the act of betrayal (14.45) and twice
on the lips of his disciples in contexts where they fail to
recognize the true significance of Jesus or his actions (9.5; 11.21).

It has also been frequently observed that although Jesus is
presented as a teacher in this Gospel, Mark does not communicate as much as the other evangelists do of the actual content of
Jesus' teaching.[10] A strong emphasis is given to the passion
narrative, with material reflecting Jesus' conflict with the Jewish
authorities over the Law (2.1–3.6; 7.1–23; 11.27–12.44) providing an explanation for the events leading up to it. The
evangelist can be seen employing elements of the sayings
tradition, therefore, for his own purposes and in particular to
illustrate and develop some of his main themes, namely the
secret of the Kingdom of God (4.1–34), the nature and cost of
discipleship (8.34–9.1; 9.33–10.31) and the coming of the Son of
Man (13). It is uncertain whether he knew the 'sayings source'
Q underlying the Gospels of Matthew and Luke, although that
source demonstrates the importance of 'Jesus the Teacher' for a
very early Jewish-Christian community. While there is some
anachronism in his portrayal of Jesus as a teacher of the
Christian 'word' (2.2; 4.14ff., 33) or 'gospel' (1.1, 15; 8.35; 10.29;
13.10; 14.9), there is no doubting the historicity of the tradition
itself. I would conclude therefore that the evangelist has taken
over a tradition which was important for him but, at the same
time, may intend to intimate to his readers that seeing or

---

[10] See M. E. Boring, 'The Paucity of Sayings in Mark. A Hypothesis' in P. J. Achtemeier
(ed.), *Society of Biblical Literature 1977 Seminar Papers* (Missoula, MT: Scholars Press,
1977), pp. 371–7; M. Smith, 'Forms, Motives and Omissions in Mark's Account of the
Teaching of Jesus' in J. Reumann (ed.), *Understanding the Sacred Text. Essays in Honor of
Morton S. Enslin on the Hebrew Bible and Christian Origins* (Valley Forge, PA: Judson Press,
1972), pp. 153–64.

addressing Jesus merely as 'Rabbi' or 'Teacher' represents a less than adequate understanding of his Christological significance. A similar conclusion can be reached with regard to the title 'Prophet' (6.3–4,14–16; 8.27–8; [13.22]). In 6.4, in the context of his rejection at Nazareth, the title is given as a self-designation of Jesus. The setting of this passage, a biographical apophthegm according to Bultmann, was probably composed by Mark but the punch line saying ('A prophet is not without honour . . .') is in essence pre-Markan.[11] In two other passages (6.14–16; 8.27–8), possibly a doublet, we are told that the popular Jewish estimate of Jesus was that he was a prophet. The evangelist elsewhere makes little of this title (compare, however, 11.32 and 13.22) although it is clear that it not only belonged to his tradition but is a key element in characterizing the historical Jesus' social type.[12] In the second of these passages, the important confession scene at Caesarea Philippi, the evangelist can be seen significantly qualifying the image of Jesus as prophet. Here Jesus himself poses the Christological question ('Who do men say that I am?'). The reader is then told that while 'prophet' was the estimate of the Jewish populace, the verdict of Peter, a major disciple and prominent leader of the early Jewish-Christian community, was 'You are the Christ' (8.29).

This brings us to what many regard as the key declaration in Mark, the Christological affirmation not only of the Jewish-Christian tradition before him but of the evangelist himself. Jesus is the Christ, the Messiah, the 'Anointed One' (*Christos*). Before we jump to this conclusion, however, we should remind ourselves of the meaning and background of this term for Jews.[13] While there was no uniform Messianic expectation in Jewish circles of the period, two prominent strands of the Messianic hope do stand out. In the first place, the term

---

[11] R. Bultmann, *The History of the Synoptic Tradition* (Oxford: Blackwell, 1968), pp. 31–2, 75, 102. A version of the saying appears without its narrative framework in the Oxyrhynchus Papyrus I.5. Cf. also Jn 4.44.

[12] See D. Hill, *New Testament Prophecy* (Marshall's Theological Library; London: Marshall, Morgan & Scott, 1979), pp. 48–69 for the marshalling of the evidence. 'It is true that from the historian's point of view the working concept which guided Jesus in the task of his ministry was that of "prophet" ' (p. 68).

[13] See E. Rivkin, 'Messiah, Jewish' in *IDB(S)*, pp. 588–91.

'Messiah' was used of an earthly, political figure, a warrior-king who by his military exploits and passion for justice would lead his people into victory over their Gentile overlords, establish God's Kingdom and restore the land of Israel to his chosen people, the Jews. According to popular belief he would be descended from King David, and, in some sources, is even accorded the title 'Son of David'.[14] A second (though less common, less coherent and therefore more disputed) strand of the Messianic hope was the belief entertained in apocalyptic Judaism in an exalted, transcendent, heavenly figure (styled variously as 'one like a son of man', 'that Son of Man' or 'the Man') who would appear at the end-time to judge the world, punish the wicked and vindicate the righteous.[15]

Three key questions may therefore now be addressed. How important is the term 'Christ' in actuality for Mark, what particular understandings lay behind his use of the term, and was he inviting his readers to see in Peter's confession of Jesus as the 'Christ' a Christology that they should themselves embrace? We should begin by noting that the term 'Christ' is not in itself very prominent in the Gospel. There are only seven instances of its use (1.1; 8.29; 9.41; 12.35–7; 13.21, 22; 14.61; 15.32) and one of these (9.41) may be spurious. It is never applied by the Markan Jesus to himself. Where it is used, it is frequently qualified by other titles used in conjunction with it, principally 'Son of God' (or its equivalent) or 'Son of Man' (e.g. 8.29–31; 14.61–2).

The title 'Son of David' appears in three passages in the Gospel, twice directly (10.47–8; 12.35–7) and in a third by implication (11.10). On the first of these occasions it makes an unannounced appearance, again on the lips of the blind Jew, Bartimaeus, who, the reader is told, is subsequently cured of his (Christological?) blindness and follows Jesus 'on the way' (of discipleship?). In the second related passage, the Jewish populace, in a Messianic context, ostensibly greet Jesus as such (11.10). In the third passage (12.35–7), however, the Markan

---

[14] *Psalms of Solomon* 17.23–51 (C. K. Barrett, *The New Testament Background. Selected Documents* (London: SPCK, 1987), pp. 337–9). See also Vermes, *Jesus*, pp. 130–4.

[15] These expressions occur in Daniel, 1 Enoch and 4 Ezra, texts which we shall consider in more detail later in this chapter.

Jesus, in a characteristic piece of rabbinical exegesis, disputes the view that the 'Christ' can be the 'Son of David'. According to scripture (Ps. 110.1), David himself calls him 'Lord', so how can he be regarded as David's son? Opinions differ with regard to the interpretation of this passage but the essential point being conveyed by the evangelist to the reader, in my view, is that the designation 'Christ' is not to be understood in its Jewish, nationalistic, political and triumphalist 'Son of David' sense, but in the sense in which it later came to be understood by Hellenistic Christianity, that is, as a divine being who is to be identified with the community's exalted 'Lord'.[16] What I would detect in Mark therefore is a move away from a 'Son of David' Christology, one embodied, I suspect, in the characters of the Markan text (Peter, the disciples, blind Bartimaeus and the Jewish crowd who are later to crucify him). At the narrative level, this Christology may be implied in Peter's rejection of a non-triumphalist Messiahship (8.31–2) – one notes the Markan Jesus' stern reaction to this (8.33 'Get behind me, Satan') – as well as in the desire of his disciples to occupy a privileged position at Jesus' right and left hand 'in his glory' (10.35–45). At the historical level, although here one can only speculate, Mark may be in tension with a Jewish-Christian estimate of Jesus which laid considerable emphasis on Jesus as the 'Son of David'.[17] Paul seems to know of the tradition but, with his

---

[16] The title 'Lord' (*Kyrios*) has a wide semantic range, from an expression of respect when applied to a human being (a teacher or healer, for example) to a term of reverence when applied to God. Within Hellenistic Christianity the title is found applied to Jesus in his exalted status as 'Lord' of the church, the declaration 'Jesus is Lord' being the principal credal confession of Paul and his churches (Rom. 10.9; 1 Cor. 12.3; 2 Cor. 4.5). It is found on the lips of Jesus' disciples in the Gospels but is normally understood to apply to Jesus in the former sense, that is, as a term of respect rather than of post-Easter religious devotion (however Jn 20.28). In Mark, the title occurs sixteen times, eight times in relation to God. In five instances, it appears to refer to Jesus himself, occurring three times on his lips (2.28, 5.19, 11.3), once on the lips of a Gentile woman (7.28) and once where the evangelist is referring indirectly to Jesus (1.3; cf. 12.35–7). Some of these instances are disputed by scholars, or not interpreted as conveying an exalted or confessional estimate of Jesus. I myself am not so sure, preferring to see in these (mostly redactional) passages the believing confession of the evangelist or his post-Easter community breaking through. See W. R. Telford, *The Barren Temple and the Withered Tree* (JSNTSS, 1; Sheffield: JSOT Press, 1980), pp. 254–5.

[17] See J. B. Tyson, 'The Blindness of the Disciples in Mark', *JBL*, 80 (1961), pp. 261–8.

Gentile orientation, plays it down (Rom. 1.3), while Matthew, with his loyalty to the Jewish-Christian tradition, can be seen to play it up.[18]

If the evangelist has rejected a Jewish-Christian 'Son of David' Christology, then it might also be suggested that he gave a qualified acceptance to a 'Son of Man' Christology, perhaps because of its esoteric and transcendental overtones. The term is a frequent one in the Gospel (2.10, 28; [3.28]; 8.31, 38; 9.9, 12, 31; 10.33, 45; 13.26; 14.21, 41, 62) where it appears exclusively on the lips of Jesus as a self-designation. Scholars are uncertain as well as divided about its ultimate meaning, background and significance. We shall be examining the title in greater detail when we come to discuss Mark's soteriology but at this point we should note that one prominent element in the Markan use of the expression is its association with the theme of suffering. While the Markan Jesus, as 'Son of Man', will come at the end-time 'with great power and glory' (13.26), his divine destiny, it is emphasized, is to suffer and die (8.31). Here it is tempting to believe that the evangelist has taken over yet another strand of the Jewish-Christian tradition, one that identified Jesus with this apocalyptic Son of Man. In adopting these 'Son of Man' sayings, he has preserved the connotation of a triumphant, eschatological figure (identified with Jesus), but has qualified the Messianic overtones by stressing the *divine necessity* of the Son of Man's *redemptive suffering and death*.

It is the title 'Son of God', however, which most scholars agree is the most important title for Jesus in Markan estimation. It occurs eight times in the Gospel (1.1, 11; 3.11; 5.7; 9.7; 13.32; 14.61; 15.39), in each case in key contexts or episodes. It is used to identify Jesus by the evangelist himself in 1.1 (although a number of major textual witnesses, it should be said, omit it). It appears on the lips of God himself in affirmation of Jesus both at his baptism (1.11) and at his transfiguration (9.7). It is Jesus' self-designation in 13.32. In an 'inside view', the reader is also informed that this is the verdict of the supernatural world on

[18] See 1.1ff.; 1.20; 9.27; 12.23; 15.22; 20.30, 31; 21.5; 21.14–17 and Markan par.

Jesus following exorcisms (3.11; cf. 1.24[19]) as well as that of a Roman centurion at his crucifixion (15.39). All these may be said to provide 'reliable commentary' for the reader on the true nature of Jesus as the evangelist perceives him. But what did the title mean for Mark and his readers? Is it used by him to identify Jesus in Jewish terms as the Messianic king[20] or God's 'suffering righteous servant',[21] or is it employed in a more Hellenistic sense to denote Jesus as an epiphany of God, a miracle-worker, a 'divine man' (*theios anēr*) or supernatural being?[22] A number of scholars hold that the terms 'Son of God' and 'Christ' are synonymous, and this has contributed to the view that not only his sources but Mark himself harboured an essentially Messianic understanding of Jesus. This view, however, is to be challenged. While the Messiah may be *described* as having a filial relationship to God in an ethical or even adoptionist sense (e.g. 2 Sam. 7.14; Ps. 2.7), there is little evidence that 'Son of God' was a *title* for the Messiah in first-century Judaism, or that both terms were interchangeable.[23] On the contrary, Mark presents Jesus as having attributes which

---

[19] Here the title 'Holy One of God' is used, a rare term appearing elsewhere in the Gospels (apart from its Synoptic parallel in Lk 4.34) only in Jn 6.69.

[20] So Kee, *Community* or Kingsbury, *Christology*.

[21] See Fuller, *Mission*, pp. 86–95; L. S. Hay, 'The Son-of-God Christology in Mark', *The Journal of Bible and Religion*, 32 (1964), pp. 106–14; M. Hooker, *Jesus and the Servant. The Influence of the Servant Concept of Deutero-Isaiah in the New Testament* (London: SPCK, 1959); D. Lührmann, *Das Markusevangelium* (Handbuch zum Neuen Testament, 3; Tübingen: Mohr–Siebeck, 1987), pp. 38–40; T. W. Manson, *The Servant-Messiah. A Study of the Public Ministry of Jesus* (Cambridge: Cambridge University Press, 1953); C. Maurer, 'Knecht Gottes und Sohn Gottes im Passionsbericht des Markusevangeliums', *ZThK*, 50 (1953), pp. 1–38.

[22] See R. Bultmann, *Theology of the New Testament* (London: SCM Press, 1952/1955), Vol. I, pp. 128–33; J. Schreiber, 'Die Christologie des Markusevangeliums. Beobachtungen zur Theologie und Komposition des zweiten Evangeliums', *ZThK*, 58 (1961), pp. 154–83; S. Schulz, 'Markus und das Alte Testament', *ZThK*, 58 (1961), pp. 184–97.

[23] See J. Jeremias, *The Parables of Jesus* (London: SCM Press, 1972), p. 73; Vermes, *Jesus*, p. 199; see also p. 9. In light of 4Q246, the 'Son of God' text found at Qumran, some scholars have urged less caution with respect to such an identification; see e.g. J. C. O'Neill, 'What is Joseph and Aseneth About?', *Henoch*, 16 (1994), p. 195. For a sample of the discussion, see J. A. Fitzmyer, '4Q246: The "Son of God" Document from Qumran', *Biblica*, 74 (1993), pp. 153–74 and J. J. Collins, 'A Pre-Christian "Son of God" among the Dead Sea Scrolls', *Biblical Review*, 9 (1993), pp. 34–8, 57. See also J. J. Collins, *The Scepter and the Star. The Messiahs of the Dead Sea Scrolls and other Ancient Literature* (Garden City, NY: Doubleday, 1995), ch. 7.

conform much more to those of a 'divine man' (*theios anēr*) in the Hellenistic world than that of the Davidic Messiah.[24]

He is endowed with power (*dynamis*) and authority (*exousia*), both key terms for the evangelist (e.g. 1.22, 27; 2.10; 5.30; 6.2, 14; 11.28, 29, 33; 13.26).[25] This power extends in particular over nature, giving him the ability to calm storms, for example, or walk on water (4.35–41; 6.45–52). He works miracles (1.21–34; 3.10–12; 4.35–5.43; 6.2, 14; 6.35–56; 7.24–8.26, 9.14–27; 11.12–14) and possesses supernatural knowledge (e.g. 2.8; 5.32; 11.2–6; 13.1–2; 14.13–16). He is metamorphosed before his disciples in divine splendour (9.2–9). In this last passage, the transfiguration scene, we find the climax to the confession at Caesarea Philippi and the answer indeed to the question whether Mark's readers were being invited to see in Peter's confession of Jesus as the 'Christ' a Christology that they should themselves embrace. Here on a high mountain (the place of revelation) Jesus is declared to be God's 'Son' (9.7) and not merely the 'prophet' of Jewish estimation (8.28) or the 'Christ' of Jewish-Christian confession (8.29). Here again let me quote Bultmann:

> One must recognize that the title, which originally denoted the messianic king, now takes on a new meaning which is self-evident to Gentile hearers. Now it comes to mean *the divinity of Christ, his divine nature*, by virtue of which he is differentiated from the human sphere; it makes the claim that Christ is of divine origin and is filled with divine 'power'.[26]

This is not to say, of course, that Mark is operating with a later Nicene or Chalcedonian understanding of Jesus' divinity.[27]

---

[24] 'The synoptic gospels ... picture Jesus as the Son of God who reveals his divine power and authority through his miracles ... This is the vein in which the Gospel of Mark tells its story' (Bultmann, *Theology*, Vol. I, pp. 130–1).

[25] J. R. Edwards, 'The Authority of Jesus in the Gospel of Mark', *Journal of the Evangelical Theological Society*, 37 (1994), pp. 217–33.

[26] Bultmann, *Theology*, pp. 128–9.

[27] See M. E. Boring, 'The Christology of Mark: Hermeneutical Issues for Systematic Theology', *Semeia*, 30 (1984), pp. 125–53; J. D. G. Dunn, *Christology in the Making. A New Testament Inquiry into the Origins of the Doctrine of Incarnation* (London: SCM Press, 1989), esp. pp. 60–4; J.-J. Marin, *The Christology of Mark. Does Mark's Christology Support the Chalcedonian Formula 'Truly Man and Truly God?'* (European University Studies, Series 23: Theology 417; Berne, Frankfurt, New York and Paris: Lang, 1991).

Notions of the Son of God's pre-existence, mediatorial role in
creation, descent from heaven, incarnation or sinlessness are as
yet undeveloped.[28] What he does represent, however, is an
advance on earlier Christology. He wished his readers to see
more primitive (and, in my opinion, more historical) understandings of Jesus' person and mission (teacher, prophet, healer)
'superseded' by more exalted ones ('Lord', 'Christ', 'Son of
Man', 'Son of God'). The evangelist demonstrates some reluctance, however, over the images of Jesus as royal Son of David
or apocalyptic Son of Man, rejecting, I believe, the first, and
qualifying the second. For Mark, the traditional estimates of
Jesus' significance are inadequate unless they reckon both with
his status as the supernatural but concealed 'Son of God' and
with the divine necessity of his redemptive suffering and death.
In short, to see Jesus in terms of a Jewish Messianic triumphalism is a false Christology. To see how Mark combats such a
view, we must next turn to the literary means by which his 'Son
of God' Christology is brought home to his readers, in other
words, to the secrecy motif which is a characteristic feature of
his Gospel.

'And he charged them to tell no one': the secrecy motif in the Second Gospel

Anyone who reads the Gospel of Mark is immediately struck by
the air of mystery which surrounds the Markan Jesus' person
and activity. There are three aspects of the evangelist's presentation of Jesus in particular where a habitual secretiveness is
predicated of him. In the first place, there are the puzzling
commands to silence. Jesus is shown, for example, silencing
supernatural beings, the demons, after exorcisms, because they
are said to recognize who he is (1.25, 34; 3.11–12). He is depicted
as silencing human beings, those he has cured, after healings,
and commanding them (or witnesses) not to tell anyone about
their restoration (1.44; 5.43; 7.36; 8.26). He is portrayed as
silencing his own disciples, the inner circle, after revelation,

---

[28] See, however, J. Schreiber, *Die Markuspassion. Eine Redaktionsgeschichtliche Untersuchung*
(BZNW, 68; Berlin and New York: Walter de Gruyter, 1993), pp. 210–59 for evidence
of 'pre-existence' in connection with the Markan Jesus.

strictly ordering them not to spread it about that he was the Messiah (8.30), or commanding them to tell no one about the vision that they had seen until after the resurrection (9.9).

The last of these commands to silence touches upon a second aspect of the evangelist's presentation of Jesus, that is, the secret instruction given to his disciples. The Markan Jesus appears repeatedly in private sessions with his disciples in which they are invited to understand the true nature, meaning and significance of his teaching, person and work (e.g. 4.11–12, 33–4; 7.17–23; 8.31–3; 9.2–8, 28–9; 9.30–2; 10.10–12, 32–4; 13.3–37). Just as frequently, however, they are shown either failing to understand him (as in the first part of the Gospel; 4.41; 6.52; 8.14–21) or positively misunderstanding him (as, to an increasing degree, in the second part of the Gospel; 8.32–3; 9.5–6, 9–13, 32, 34, 38; 10.13–14, 32, 35–45). This failure to comprehend Jesus' true significance, according to Mark, also extends to Jesus' original family and friends, as well as to the Jewish authorities (3.20–35; 6.1–6).

A third aspect of the secretiveness attributed to Jesus concerns his teaching itself. Strangely, the evangelist informs his readers that the purpose of Jesus' parables was not to enlighten his Jewish audience, but to mystify them, not to reveal the truth to them but to conceal it from them: 'To you has been given the secret of the kingdom of God, but for those outside everything is in parables; so that they may indeed see but not perceive, and may indeed hear but not understand; lest they should turn again, and be forgiven' (4.11–12).

These three aspects of the Markan Jesus' conduct are also complemented by other behavioural features. He is presented frequently withdrawing himself from public view, and sometimes even attempting deliberately to conceal himself from the crowds (e.g. 1.35–7, 45; 3.7; 4.35; 6.31, 45–7; 7.24; 9.30). This reticence of his extends also to the Jewish authorities. To these opponents he pointedly refuses to present his 'Christological credentials', on one occasion to the Pharisees by denying them a sign (8.11–13), on another to the chief priests, the scribes and the elders by failing to disclose the source of his authority (11.27–33).

These observations were first brought to the attention of scholars by W. Wrede in his epoch-making book, *Das Messiasge-heimnis in den Evangelien* [*The Messianic Secret in the Gospels*] (1901).[29] When most, if not all, of these features are taken together, he argued, they comprise a secrecy motif which runs consistently throughout the Gospel. Their overall effect, he claimed, is to present Jesus as the bearer of a concealed Messianic dignity or status, as the Messiah *incognito*. The question which then arises is this: 'How is the evangelist's curious presentation to be explained?'

Two main types of explanation have been advanced.[30] Firstly, there have been historical explanations. In line with this approach, the motive of concealment has been seen as a facet of the historical Jesus' own behaviour and teaching, a character-istic of his, in other words, which is correctly reported by Mark.[31] Secondly, there have been literary or theological ex-planations. The basic thrust of this approach is to view the secrecy motif as a literary or theological device (or perhaps better, a literary device with a theological import) whereby various traditions about the historical Jesus have been presented to the reader within the overall perspective of the Christology (and soteriology) adopted within the Markan community some time *after* Jesus' death and the rise of the Easter-belief in his resurrection or, to put it another way, through the lens of the early church's dogma or the evangelist's ideology.[32]

Each of these explanations seeks, therefore, to find a solution

[29] English translation, J. C. Greig, *The Messianic Secret* (The Library of Theological Translations; Cambridge and London: James Clarke & Co., 1971).

[30] For a more comprehensive overview, see J. L. Blevins, *The Messianic Secret in Markan Research 1901–1976* (Washington, DC: University Press of America, 1981); C. M. Tuckett, 'Introduction: The Problem of the Messianic Secret' in C. M. Tuckett (ed.), *The Messianic Secret* (London: SPCK; Philadelphia, PA: Fortress Press, 1983), pp. 1–28; C. M. Tuckett, 'Messianic Secret' in *DBI*, pp. 445–6; H. Räisänen, *The 'Messianic Secret' in Mark* (Studies of the New Testament and its World; Edinburgh: T. & T. Clark, 1990); D. E. Aune, 'The Problem of the Messianic Secret', *NovT*, 11 (1969), pp. 1–31.

[31] Among the adherents of this view, to varying degrees, may be counted A. Schweitzer, W. Sanday, A. S. Peake, F. C. Burkitt, T. W. Manson, W. Barclay, W. D. Davies, V. Taylor, E. Sjöberg, R. P. Martin, J. G. D. Dunn and D. E. Aune.

[32] Among the adherents of this view, to varying degrees, may be counted W. Wrede, R. H. Lightfoot, D. E. Nineham, T. A. Burkill, N. Perrin, R. H. Fuller, T. J. Weeden, J. Schreiber and J. B. Tyson.

at the various levels of the tradition. Historical explanations trace the secrecy motif back to the primary level of the tradition, that is, to Jesus himself, attributing the motive of concealment directly to him. Literary or theological explanations trace the motive of concealment back to the secondary or tertiary levels of the tradition, attributing it, in smaller measure, to the tradition of the early church in the post-resurrection period or, in greater measure, to the evangelist himself, as a product of his redaction. In either case, it is a theological device serving to further the claims of a particular post-resurrection Christology.

Where historical explanations are concerned, one popular and prevailing view has it that Jesus was reluctant to make a Messianic claim in public in order to avoid precipitating a political and, with it, a violent revolution.[33] A modification of this theme, which has Jesus eschewing such prudential motives, claims, in the words of D. E. Aune, that 'Jesus did not openly claim to be the Messiah during his ministry because his own conception of the Messianic office was quite different from that of his contemporaries. Jesus spiritualized the Jewish messianic expectations, which were primarily politically oriented. Through the use of the relatively neutral title "Son of Man", Jesus reinterpreted the messianic role and filled it with new meaning.'[34] The true Messianic role, in other words, was one that demanded suffering and death in a spirit of self-sacrificing love. A further variation on these historical explanations, one which has the advantage of rooting Jesus' alleged motivations in the religio-cultural ideas prevalent in his day, is that he was acting in keeping with a current Jewish apocalyptic conception that if the Messiah appeared on earth *before* the *eschaton*, then he must necessarily appear as one hidden until the coming of the new age.[35]

The problem with explanations such as these is that they are conjectures supplying motivations for the Markan Jesus which are simply not given by the evangelist. While plausible in themselves, such suggestions do not account for all of the evidence offered by the text and indeed often run counter to it.

---

[33] See Aune, 'Messianic', p. 9.   [34] *Ibid.*
[35] E. Sjöberg, cited *ibid.*, pp. 10–13.

If the Jesus of history was actually opposed to a political conception of Messiahship, then why is he not shown openly denouncing such conceptions? Why is his teaching on Messiahship not more pronounced? In the words of D. E. Nineham, had Jesus 'feared that the character of his Messiahship might be misunderstood, could he not have forestalled such misunderstandings by patient and unambiguous teaching on the subject?'[36] No such clear teaching is given by Mark, perhaps because in the tradition no such specific teaching emanating from Jesus had been handed down.

On the other hand, the Gospel itself attests the existence of certain traditions which did in fact represent Jesus as appearing openly to accept and even actively encourage popular Messianic claims for himself. Three such examples are the Triumphal Entry into Jerusalem (11.1–10), the Cleansing of the Temple (11.15–19) and the Trial before the High Priest (14.53–65). In the first of these, Jesus' disciples are represented as according him a Messianic ovation. If Jesus had actually given his disciples teaching on the true nature of his Messiahship, why are they presented by Mark as repeatedly misunderstanding him (e.g. 10.35–45)? If the disciples, moreover, had actually been told of his imminent death and resurrection in advance (8.31; 9.31; 10.33–4), why were they taken by surprise, despite these repeated warnings? Viewed historically, their conduct is incomprehensible, if not reprehensible.

Likewise, viewed historically, the injunctions to secrecy are quite implausible. How could secrecy be plausibly enjoined if demons are shown as shouting out who Jesus is? How could the cures performed be reasonably expected to have been kept a secret (particularly the raising of Jairus' daughter! 5.43)? Indeed, the evangelist informs us that the injunction to secrecy was often broken despite stern warnings against disclosure (1.45; 7.36)? Why too are there apparent discrepancies in Jesus' behaviour? In some cases of exorcism or healing, no injunction to secrecy is given (e.g. 2.1–12; 3.1–6; 5.6–8). On one occasion the opposite is the case and disclosure is commanded (5.19–20).

[36] D. E. Nineham, *The Gospel of St Mark* (Pelican Commentary; London and New York: A. & C. Black, 1968), p. 32.

How is this selective policy to be explained historically?[37]
Where Messianic self-disclosure is concerned, it is noteworthy
that no secrecy appears to surround the Markan Jesus' open
and public use of the term 'Son of Man' in 2.10 and 2.28 (see
also 8.38) nor in his confession before the High Priest in
14.61–62.

Those who argue for the historicity of the Markan presentation must also reckon with the Johannine presentation which
contradicts it. In the Fourth Gospel, reticence has been thrown
to the wind and the Johannine Jesus is quite content to expatiate
on his status as God's divine emissary in long Christological
discourses, both public and private (e.g. Jn 5.17–47; 6.22–71;
7.14–52; 8.12–59). Either John's account is historical (where
Jesus' Messianic consciousness and self-disclosure is concerned),
in which case Mark's is not, or Mark's account is historical in
which case John's is not. Most scholars would prefer to hold
that neither is historical in this regard, each account reflecting
rather the theology of the respective writers and the religious
communities or traditions to which they belong.

The secrecy motif, then, despite its continuing problems, is
better understood at the literary or theological level than at the
historical one, and this is borne out by the fact that in the
majority of cases where it appears (and especially in the injunctions which are explicitly Christological), it is found in redactional passages (1.34; 3.11–12; 8.30; 9.9; 14.62).

Although W. Wrede was writing before the advent of redaction criticism, he criticized historical explanations for many of
the reasons given above. The Markan presentation, he argued,
if historical, is shot through with contradictions. For Wrede,
Mark (and to some extent the pre-Markan tradition) has
imposed a Messianic significance ('the secret') upon traditions
about the historical Jesus which were originally non-Messianic
in nature. '[T]he Gospel of Mark', he therefore judged,
'belongs to the history of dogma'.[38] On the basis of the
Markan evidence, Wrede claimed that no one had held that
Jesus was the Messiah (far less Jesus himself) until after the

---

[37] See also 10.48 where the command to silence issues from the crowd.
[38] Wrede, *Secret*, p. 131.

resurrection. After this event or moment of revelation (whatever it was or however interpreted), the early church was convinced that he was the Messiah and that he was coming shortly. Hence a process began in which traditions about Jesus in his lifetime which were not originally Messianic were invested with Messianic significance. This process culminated in Mark's Gospel.

To explain why Jesus had not claimed to be Messiah during his life and had not been recognized as such, the early church and Mark in particular offered the following response: Jesus did know himself to be the Messiah but had attempted to keep it a secret. The supernatural world, however, had recognized him. (Who could dispute this?!) Jesus had also revealed it to his disciples in secret, although his miracles were also indirect evidence. Jesus had warned them nevertheless that his true status (and mission) could only be divulged after his death and resurrection (hence 9.9).

Wrede's explanation for the Markan secrecy motif has not survived in the radical form in which he first presented it. From the very start, it drew critical fire, especially from historically oriented scholars in Britain. W. Sanday described Wrede's book as 'not only very wrong, but distinctly wrongheaded'.[39] T. W. Manson claimed 'the further we travel along the Wredestrasse, the clearer it becomes that it is the road to nowhere'.[40] V. Taylor regarded it as 'radical and polemical to a degree'.[41] R. H. Lightfoot was one of the few British scholars who gave it a sympathetic hearing, holding that 'we may believe not only that Wrede's very honest work was necessary, but that its results have been for the most part to the good ... It is unlikely that anyone, after a study of Wrede's volume, will be

[39] *The Life of Christ in Recent Research* (Oxford, 1907), p. 70, *gratia* R. H. Lightfoot, *History and Interpretation in the Gospels* (London: Hodder & Stoughton, 1934), p. 17.

[40] T. W. Manson, 'The life of Jesus: some tendencies in present-day research' in D. Daube and W. D. Davies (eds.), *The Background of the New Testament and its Eschatology. In Honour of Charles Harold Dodd* (Cambridge: Cambridge University Press, 1956), p. 216; *gratia* N. Perrin, 'The *Wredestrasse* becomes the *Hauptstrasse*: Reflections on the Reprinting of the Dodd Festschrift', *JR*, 46 (1966), p. 296.

[41] V. Taylor, 'Important and Influential Books (W. Wrede's, *Messianic Secret*)', *ExpT*, 65 (1953–4), p. 246.

inclined to regard St. Mark's gospel as a simple book; rather it is a book of simplicity and mystery combined.'[42]

Apart from attacking the unity of the secrecy motif and insisting, as many scholars still do,[43] that a number of the passages brought by Wrede under the umbrella of the 'Messianic secret' could be otherwise explained (for example, as conventional features of miracle stories), a number of valid objections were raised challenging Wrede's view that Jesus was not seen as Messiah in his lifetime. Four objections, in particular, were voiced.[44]

(1) The confession of Peter (8.27–9), the entry into Jerusalem (11.1–10), Jesus' confession before the High Priest (14.61–2) and his crucifixion as King of the Jews (15.1–33, esp. 15.26) run counter to the secret (as previously noted), show signs of being pre-Markan tradition and in themselves, it is claimed, are historically plausible.

(2) Jesus' crucifixion is unintelligible if it were not (in the primary tradition) that of a Messianic pretender.

(3) Jesus could never have been confessed as Messiah after the resurrection if he had not been recognized as such beforehand. Belief in his resurrection would not necessarily have created a corresponding belief in his Messiahship. It would merely have offered a vindication of such a claim.

(4) The early church would hardly have invented this article of faith given that it had to suffer opprobrium as a result of proclaiming a crucified Messiah.

For this reason some scholars continued (and still continue) to hold that the secrecy motif goes back to Jesus and that it was a facet of his Messianic self-consciousness. One such powerful advocate of this position, himself a critic of Wrede, was

---

[42] Lightfoot, *History*, p. 21.

[43] One popular approach is to distinguish between the injunctions which are explicitly Christological (*Das Messiasgeheimnis* or Messianic secret) and those which are related to the miracles (*Das Wundergeheimnis* or miracle secret). See U. Luz, 'The Secrecy Motif and the Marcan Christology' in Tuckett (ed.), *Secret*, pp. 75–96. For a contrary view which argues convincingly for the unity and coherence of Mark's secrecy motif, see F. Watson, 'The Social Function of Mark's Secrecy Motif', *JSNT*, 24 (1985), pp. 49–69.

[44] See, for example, V. Taylor, 'The Messianic Secret in Mark', *ExpT*, 49 (1947–8), pp. 146–51.

A. Schweitzer who held that Jesus had seen himself as Messiah, and was so regarded in the primitive tradition before Mark.[45]

While giving voice to what are valid objections, historical explanations have themselves, however, proved unconvincing, demonstrating a number of weaknesses, as discussed above. Not only do they make unwarranted assumptions about the nature of the Markan text (in particular that it offers a clear window into history) but they also fail to answer many of the points raised by Wrede. Markan scholarship has tended to move, therefore, in more recent times in a literary and theological direction, following Wrede's insights but modifying his somewhat over-simple reconstruction. A prominent view now is that Mark has not invested originally non-Messianic traditions about Jesus with a Messianic significance. Some of the traditions he took over, as has been already demonstrated, were already invested with such a significance. Mark is not introducing a particular Christology into his sources. Rather he is qualifying or correcting the Christology he found in them already![46]

One such influential theory has been proposed by T. J. Weeden.[47] Weeden has argued that Mark was seeking to combat a Hellenistic 'divine man' or *theios anēr* Christology which emphasized Jesus' power as a wonder-worker rather than the gospel ('the secret') of his redemptive suffering and death. Focusing upon the injunctions to secrecy surrounding the miracles, Weeden has suggested that Mark had inherited a miracle tradition in which Jesus was depicted as a wonder-working 'Son of God'. Such a view of Jesus, he claims, underlies the miracle stories the evangelist has taken over, accounts which essentially show him as a Hellenistic 'divine man' or *theios anēr*. This understanding of Jesus is one that the evangelist presents

---

[45] A. Schweitzer, *The Quest of the Historical Jesus. A Critical Study of its Progress from Reimarus to Wrede* (New York: Macmillan, 1959), pp. 328–48.

[46] 'It was not the *non*-messianic character of the units in the tradition which causes the evangelist trouble, but rather their messianic character', H. Conzelmann, 'Present and Future in the Synoptic Tradition', *Journal for Theology and the Church*, 5 (1968), pp. 42–3, *gratia* Martin, *Mark*, p. 94.

[47] T. J. Weeden, 'The Heresy that Necessitated Mark's Gospel' in W. R. Telford (ed.), *The Interpretation of Mark* (Edinburgh: T. & T. Clark, 1995), pp. 89–104.

the disciples, in his view, as sharing. Mark is concerned, however, to supplement or correct this Christological understanding by interpreting Jesus also as the Son of Man who must necessarily suffer. Inspired by a Pauline emphasis on the cross, he juxtaposes a *theologia gloriae* (as represented by this triumphalist 'divine man' Christology) with a *theologia crucis*. Where Mark's sources are concerned, this is achieved by the combination in the Gospel of a largely Hellenistic miracle tradition (in the first half) with a passion narrative preceded by passion predictions (in the second). From a literary and theological perspective, this Christological message is achieved overall by the secrecy motif. Through this device, the Markan reader is being informed that the true significance of Jesus cannot be appreciated only in his teaching and miracle-working activity. It can be apprehended only after his death and resurrection (9.9) in which the nature of his Messiahship can and will be seen in its true light.

This is an appealing explanation (particularly in its suggestion of a Pauline influence in Markan Christology) but, in my view, it is mistaken. It requires us, first of all, to evaluate Mark's use of the miracle tradition in a *negative* light, that is, as a tradition running counter to the evangelist's Christological tendencies or impulses and this is an interpretation which is to be resisted. Mark used the miracle tradition in a *positive* way, as I shall later argue, to enhance a 'Son of God' or epiphany Christology, and not to combat it. Secondly, the Christology for which the disciples are taken to be the textual representatives is a Hellenistic 'divine man' Christology. This would be a somewhat strange Christology for the evangelist to ascribe to Jesus' original Jewish followers, and an even stranger one for the evangelist to be resisting given the Hellenistic proclivities which we have reason to believe he himself entertained.

If we are to take a 'clash of Christologies' approach to the interpretation of Mark, as I myself in some measure am inclined to do, then there is stronger evidence within the Gospel to support the view that the disciples function as representatives of a triumphalist Jewish-Christian 'Son of David' or apocalyptic 'Son of Man' Christology. In this respect, the hypothesis of

J. B. Tyson is a much more plausible one.[48] Tyson has argued
that Mark sought to challenge a Jewish-Christian tradition
going back to the Jerusalem church which saw Jesus only as the
victorious royal Messiah, the Son of David, in favour of his real
status or significance (the 'secret' for Mark and Gentile Christianity) as the divine but unrecognized Son of God whose
suffering and death on the cross were redemptive. Such a
tradition might have seen Jesus as the future Messiah, the
triumphant Son of David who had cleansed the Temple and,
after his death and resurrection, would return shortly to restore
the kingdom. In that kingdom, by virtue of being his followers,
his disciples would occupy a privileged position (cf. Mt. 19.28 =
Lk. 22.29–30).

If Tyson is correct, how then might Mark be seen to challenge
such a Christology? In the first place, as I have noted elsewhere,
he appears to play down the triumphal entry tradition.[49] A
comparison with the more pronounced 'Son of David' elements
in the Matthean account clearly demonstrates this. The title
itself, as we have seen, only appears three times in the Gospel,
twice directly (10.47–8; 12.35–7) and in a third by implication
(11.10). In the first of these passages, it is on the lips of a blind
Jew who is henceforth cured of his blindness (10.46–52). In the
second, the evangelist has Jesus dispute the idea that the Christ
can be the Son of David (12.35–7). In the third, it is by
implication the terms in which Jesus is greeted by his own
disciples as well as the Jewish crowd (11.8–10). Mark might be
seen, therefore, to be placing this Christology and the attitudes
appropriate to it on the lips of the disciples and then showing
that they (along with the Jewish crowd of 11.10) are blind to
Jesus' true significance and need to be re-educated.

This re-education is particularly emphasized in the central
section of the Gospel (8.22–10.52), with its theme of true
discipleship and its use of the suffering Son of Man sayings. The
series of passages in this section are arranged in a formal
pattern (prediction–misunderstanding–corrective teaching) to

---

[48] J. B. Tyson, 'The Blindness of the Disciples in Mark' in Tuckett (ed.), *Secret*, pp.
35–43.
[49] See Telford, *Barren Temple*, p. 253 and n. 17.

which N. Perrin has drawn attention.[50] The Markan Jesus *predicts* that his mission as Son of Man is one that involves suffering, death and resurrection and, by implication, not one of military glory or political conquest (8.31; 9.31; 10.33–4). His disciples *misunderstand* and show that their conception is otherwise (8.32–3; 9.32–4; 10.35–7). He then *teaches* them the true nature of discipleship and of his mission, culminating in the saying about the Son of Man's giving of his life as a ransom for many (8.34–9.1; 9.35–50; 10.39–45).

To sum up, then, while *negatively* Mark may be seen as tilting against a Messianic 'Son of David' Christology, *positively* he may be seen as promoting a 'Son of God' Christology. The title 'Son of God' is capable of being interpreted in either a Jewish sense or a Hellenistic sense, my own view being that the evangelist understood it in the latter sense. 'Son of God' is not therefore a synonym for 'Messiah' in Mark, and hence there is in Mark strictly speaking not a 'Messianic' secret but a 'Son of God' secret, and when this is acknowledged, many of the conflicting elements in the Markan presentation begin to come together.

Essentially, the evangelist is inviting his readers to see Jesus as the Son of God. For, to repeat, let us see what he has done. Accepting the longer reading, the Gospel begins with the solemn affirmation 'The beginning of the gospel of Jesus Christ, *the Son of God*' (1.1; italics throughout mine). In a piece of 'reliable commentary', the narrator then places this Christology on the lips of God himself in two key scenes, the first at the beginning of the Gospel in the baptism scene (1.11; 'Thou art my beloved *Son*; with thee I am well pleased'), the second after the crucial 'confession' scene when the disciples are given a second opportunity to witness Jesus' true identity (9.7; 'This is my beloved *Son*; listen to him'). The narrator intimates that Jesus' true status as the divine Son of God was recognized by the supernatural world, the demons (3.11; 'And whenever the unclean spirits beheld him, they fell down before him and cried out, "You are the *Son of God*" '; 5.7). It was also recognized by

[50] See, for example, D. C. Duling and N. Perrin, *The New Testament. Proclamation and Parenesis. Myth and History* (New York: Harcourt Brace College, 1994), pp. 309–10.

one of the human characters in the story, significantly a Gentile, a Roman centurion, and at another climactic moment in the Markan drama, namely at the moment of his death (15.39; 'Truly this man was the *Son of God*'). This is also a revelatory moment for Christian theology, and the centurion may be seen perhaps as representing the confession of Gentile Christianity to Jesus.

On the other hand, this 'secret' into which the Christian reader has been initiated, is not divulged to the other human characters in the story. Most significantly, it is not ultimately recognized or confessed by Jesus' original followers. The evangelist, as we have seen, repeatedly points out to his readers that the Christology of Jesus' original Jewish disciples, the twelve, was in error. They failed to understand, indeed they misunderstood, the true significance of his person, message and mission, and their conduct in the story reflects this. At no point, even at the end of the Gospel, as we shall see, are they shown finally to come to this understanding or confession.

The conclusion that I have been increasingly drawn to, therefore, the more I have studied this Gospel, is that the author of Mark's Gospel writes as a representative of a Pauline-influenced Gentile Christianity which viewed Jesus (and, by means of the secrecy motif, invites the reader to view him) as the divine 'Son of God' who came to suffer and die on the cross. This Christology is in tension both with Jewish estimates of Jesus (teacher, prophet and healer) as well as Jewish-Christian ones. The latter emphasized (in keeping with Jewish monotheism) not his divinity (nor his cross?) but rather his triumphant status as the Jewish Messiah, either as the earthly Son of David or as one who, having been exalted to heaven, would return victoriously as God's eschatological agent, the apocalyptic Son of Man. Because of its political and nationalistic overtones, Mark has rejected the first but given a qualified acceptance to the second, perhaps, I suggest, because of its transcendent overtones.

Let me sum up. Thus far we have considered the person of Jesus in Mark, or the Markan Christology. We began here since Christology plays such a major role in the Gospel. We have seen

that Mark has taken over traditional material already stamped
with a particular estimate of Jesus' significance. Three traditions
in particular can be isolated, Jesus as teacher, Jesus as prophet
and Jesus as miracle-worker. These three traditions are likely
not only to be pre-Markan (since they are multiply attested,
occurring, for example, in Q) but also, according to many
scholars today, historical. Two further specifically Jewish-Christian traditions have been commented upon, namely Jesus as
royal Messiah or Son of David, and Jesus as apocalyptic Son of
Man. Mark, I have argued, was not only the transmitter but
also the interpreter of these traditions. The significance of his
Gospel (in literary and theological terms) is that it has welded a
number of these prevailing traditions about Jesus into a more or
less unified presentation. By both employing and correcting the
emphases of these separate traditions, by a discriminating use of
Christological titles, and, above all, by means of the secrecy
motif, Mark has presented these traditions in such a way as to
leave his readers in no doubt as to the significance that ought to
be attached to the historical figure of Jesus, namely, that he is
the supernatural 'Son of God'.

THE MESSAGE OF JESUS

'That hearing, they may hear and not understand': the nature and function of
the parables in Mark

We turn now to the message of Jesus in Mark, and in particular
to the traditions of Jesus as teacher and prophet. The tradition
of Jesus as miracle-worker will occupy our attention in a later
section. I shall be concerned to identify how Mark deals with
these traditions, especially in light of what I have said about his
'epiphany Christology' and the secrecy motif. One aspect of
this motif, as we saw, concerned Jesus' teaching, the purpose of
which, according to the evangelist (4.11–12), was not to enlighten his Jewish audience, but to mystify them, not to reveal
the truth to them but to conceal it from them. I shall focus on
the nature and function of the parables, therefore, and on the
'parables secret' and the so-called 'hardening' motif. How did

Mark understand the parables of Jesus which constituted the major form of his teaching, and how did he understand the Kingdom of God which constituted the central theme of his prophetic activity?

Let me set the context for the discussion by briefly summarizing what has been said about the parables of the Synoptic tradition in the recent history of scholarship. At its simplest, the parable is 'a brief narrative which forcefully illustrates a single idea'.[51] The definition of the parable has often been considered in conjunction with three other related literary forms, namely the simile, the metaphor and the allegory.[52] The simile is a form of speech in which one thing is said to be like another by virtue of one common property ('so be wise as serpents and innocent as doves' Mt. 10. 16). A metaphor is a stronger form of simile in which the comparison formula is dropped and one thing is said *to be* another by virtue of one common property ('Go and tell that fox ...' Lk. 13.32) The parable is an extended simile or metaphor. As such, it presents itself, in its most familiar form, as a story with a single point of comparison, a story from everyday life on which a judgment is invited. A parable is a form of communication, therefore, which is meant to strike for a verdict, to evoke a response. As used by the rabbis of Jesus' day, parables were often weapons of controversy, frequently improvised in the cut and thrust of debate. Designed essentially to clarify one main idea, or to emphasize one main point, the parable is therefore not to be confused with the allegory. An allegory is a story in which the various details have in themselves a veiled meaning, a classic exemplar of the genre being John Bunyan's *Pilgrim's Progress*. Designed essentially to be read and reflected upon, the allegory is often artificial as a result. It lacks the vividness and realism of the parable, whose individual details, drawn naturally from everyday life, serve, like feathers on an arrow, to bring the essential point home to the hearer.

Form-critical analysis of the parables in the Synoptic tradition

[51] L. Mowry, 'Parable' in *IDB*, p. 649.
[52] See C. H. Dodd, *The Parables of the Kingdom* (Fount Paperbacks; Glasgow: Collins, 1978), pp. 16–18.

has distinguished three main types.[53] In the first place, there is the parabolic or figurative saying (in German the *Bildwort* or 'image word') which conjures up in the mind of the hearer a brief but powerful image (for example, 'A city set on a hill cannot be hid' Mt. 5.14). Secondly, there is the simple parable or similitude (*Gleichnis* or 'comparison') which presents a more extended image, often with a comparison formula (for example, 'But to what shall I compare this generation? It is like children sitting in the market places and calling to their playmates, "We piped to you and you did not dance; we wailed, and you did not mourn"' Mt. 11.16–17 = Lk. 7.31–2). Thirdly, there is the narrative parable (*Parabel* or parable proper) which offers to the hearer a full story (for example, the Prodigal Son Lk. 15.11–32). Although a line cannot be drawn precisely between these three classes, C. H. Dodd offered the following as a rough guide: 'If we say that the first class has no more than one verb, the second more than one verb, in the present tense, and the third a series of verbs in an historic tense, we have a rough grammatical test.'[54]

The contention that parables need to be distinguished from allegories is one of the truisms of modern parable research. It owes itself to the work of A. Jülicher who issued a powerful challenge to the hitherto popular treatment of the parables as allegories.[55] While there is some overlap between the parable and the allegory and the one does not entirely rule out the other, even in the teaching of Jesus, the basic distinction between the two established by Jülicher is one which has been sustained by almost all subsequent parable research. The allegorical features in the parables as we now have them, he argued, are the product of the early church's subsequent theological reflection, of Christian hindsight, in other words, on events now seen as part of salvation history. Jülicher held that when this allegorical overlay was removed, the historical Jesus then stood out, not as a divine figure, but as a great moral teacher whose parables were designed to illustrate essential and

---

[53] *Ibid.*　　　[54] *Ibid.*, p. 18.
[55] A. Jülicher, *Die Gleichnisreden Jesu* (Darmstadt: Wissenschaftliche Buchgesellschaft, 1899).

timeless moral and spiritual truths about human life, society and relationships.

It was this latter view which was in turn challenged by C. H. Dodd in his *The Parables of the Kingdom*, first published in 1935. This epoch-making book offered a new perspective on the setting and message of the parables in the teaching of Jesus. Rather than a moral teacher, Dodd maintained, Jesus was an eschatological preacher, whose parables were designed to illustrate the eschatological nature of the Kingdom of God. This Kingdom Jesus had proclaimed not only as 'a transcendent order beyond space and time',[56] but also as one which had *already come* in his person and ministry. Thus was born the 'realized eschatology' with which the name of Dodd is associated.

A further contribution to the subject was made by J. Jeremias, the German scholar who has done more than any than other to reconstruct the form and setting of the parables in the ministry and teaching of Jesus.[57] Jeremias corrected Dodd's exaggerated emphasis on 'realized eschatology' by demonstrating that Jesus' view of the Kingdom in the parables, in its futuristic aspects, had much in common with current apocalyptic expectation (which saw the Kingdom of God as a supernatural event soon to come) and was not, therefore, as radical a departure from apocalyptic Judaism as Dodd had maintained. For Jeremias, Jesus too was an eschatological preacher but one whose parables expressed the conviction that the promised eschatological Kingdom of God (although future) was now *in process of realisation* ('inaugurated eschatology'), and hence called for a decision about his person and mission.

Further research on the parables has been characterized by the application to them of a more general literary criticism. Attention has been drawn to their literary aspects, to how they function as metaphor or as rhetoric. Some approaches have been occupied with the nature of language itself, as with 'the new hermeneutic'.[58] For E. Fuchs, the parables of Jesus were not only didactic or polemical in intent but 'language-events'

---

[56] Dodd, *Parables.* p. 45.   [57] Jeremias, *Parables.*

[58] Among those associated with this modern approach to the parables are E. Fuchs, E. Linnemann, E. Jüngel, A. Wilder, R. W. Funk, D. O. Via, Jr. and J. D. Crossan. For a

(*Sprachereignisse*), vividly conjuring up for his hearers the very reality with which they were concerned, namely the Kingdom of God.[59] For American scholarship on the parables, likewise, there has been an emphasis on the power of the parable as religious metaphor to mediate an experience of the transcendent.[60]

If, as Jeremias maintained, the parables belong to the bedrock of the tradition about Jesus,[61] then it is equally true to say that the process of recovering even what we can now discern as the eschatological orientation of his teaching has been a critically demanding one (and even today needs defence against those who are arguing for a non-eschatological Jesus). In investigating the parables, scholars have had to take account of their fate in the course of transmission and to consider the successive interpretative stages through which they have passed. To establish their setting and message in the teaching of Jesus (the first stage), it has been found necessary to determine their setting and message in the early church (the second stage) as well as their meaning and purpose for the evangelists (the third stage).

According to N. Perrin, '[T]he process of interpretation of the parables in the early Christian communities could well be described as the process of their domestication'.[62] The eschatological emphasis uppermost in the primary tradition was gradually toned down, modified or reinterpreted in light of the failure of imminent apocalyptic expectations, especially the delay of the parousia. This second stage development is apparent, for

helpful overview, see N. Perrin, *Jesus and the Language of the Kingdom. Symbol and Metaphor in New Testament Interpretation* (Philadelphia, PA: Fortress Press, 1976), pp. 89–193.

[59] 'Fuchs sees the parables as verbalizing Jesus' own understanding of existence in such a way that the parable mediates the possibility of sharing Jesus' understanding of existence, both to the immediate hearer and also to the subsequent interpreter' (Perrin, *Language*, p. 111).

[60] 'Modern research on the parables of Jesus, however, particularly the more recent work carried on in America [Wilder, Via, Funk, Crossan], has shown that the parables of Jesus were much more than illustrations explaining a difficult point, or than telling weapons in a controversy; they were bearers of the reality with which they were concerned ... It is the claim of this research that the parables of Jesus mediated to the hearer an experience of the Kingdom of God' (Perrin, *Language*, pp. 55–6).

[61] Jeremias, *Parables*, p. 11.   [62] Perrin, *Language*, p. 199.

example, in the so-called 'crisis' or 'parousia' parables, where a shift in emphasis from *warning* regarding the coming catastrophe to *correct conduct* in view of the delay can be observed (e.g. Mt. 24.43-4; Lk. 12.39-40).[63]

This process was particularly accentuated in the Hellenistic or Gentile-Christian phase of the spread of Christianity where apocalyptic thought and expectation were met with either incomprehension or suspicion. The parables were retold for the edification of the various Christian communities in which they were handed down and came naturally to reflect the current conditions and contemporary concerns of these communities in their different situations. As Jeremias pointed out, parables which can be traced back to the primary tradition often reflect Palestinian conditions or features whereas those which have been transmitted in a wider Hellenistic setting are frequently coloured by details (such as Hellenistic architecture, Roman judicial procedure, non-Palestinian agriculture) which are foreign to their original setting.[64] The parables likewise came to reflect subsequent events in Christian history and experience (for example, its missionary experience) and the attitudes adopted towards them (compare the differing attitudes to the Gentile mission reflected in the Matthean and Lukan versions of the parable of the Wedding Feast, Mt. 22.1-14 = Lk. 14.16-24).[65]

A third major stage in the development of the parables came with their incorporation into our written Gospels. By the time they came to be written down a process of allegorization had already been at work upon them.[66] Theological reflection, as we have noted, had already been conducted upon them by the early church in light of its own subsequent experience. They were treated as allegories reflecting major events in Christian salvation history.[67] At the same time, many were by this time found to be obscure and difficult to interpret, their original

---

[63] For a discussion of these and other such parables, see Dodd, *Parables*, pp. 115-30, esp. 124-8; Jeremias, *Parables*, pp. 48-63.

[64] Jeremias, *Parables*, pp. 26-7. [65] *Ibid.*, pp. 63-6.

[66] *Ibid.*, pp. 66-89.

[67] A classic and often repeated later example is Augustine's interpretation of the parable of the Good Samaritan. See Dodd, *Parables*, pp. 13-14.

context often lost, their original message unrecognized. They could be said to have resembled sermon illustrations for which there were no matching sermons. This was the situation which confronted the evangelists, particularly Mark. As a result, they too can be seen to have made their own distinctive contribution to the development and interpretation of the parables. Here form- and redaction-critical analysis has enabled scholars to determine the nature and extent of this contribution. Before considering Mark in particular, however, it is worth summarizing the scholarly consensus on the responsibility of the evangelists in general.

Although they themselves may have composed some of them (the parable of the tares in Mt. 13.24–30 has often been mooted as an example), it is now widely agreed that the parables were taken over for the most part from the tradition. Although collections of the parables were made from an early period, in some cases by the community, in other cases by the evangelists themselves, the evangelists nevertheless were responsible for the selection and arrangement of the parables in their respective gospels (e.g. Mk 4; Mt. 13 and 25; Lk. 9–18 *passim*). The act of collection and subsequent topical arrangement sometimes imposed a uniform but secondary interpretation on the separate parables and led to the tendency for some parables to become 'fused' (the clearest example is in Mt. 22.1–10, 11–14 where two originally independent parables have been linked together).[68]

In selecting and arranging parables in their respective Gospels, the evangelists frequently supplied their own (and often different) settings (contrast Lk. 19.11–27 *Jericho* with Mt. 25.14–30 *on the Mount of Olives*) and audiences (contrast Lk. 15.3–7 *the Pharisees and scribes* with Mt. 18.12–14 *the disciples*) for the parables of Jesus. In this latter example, the parable of the good shepherd and the lost sheep, the matter of audience is crucial for the meaning of the parable. In its Lukan context, the story illustrates God's love for those regarded by Jewish orthodoxy as outcasts (but who have a place nevertheless in God's Kingdom), while in Matthew, set within the context of Jesus'

---

[68] Jeremias, *Parables*, pp. 94–6.

instructions for the future church, it urges pastoral care for erring brothers within the community.[69] The Matthean example also illustrates how the parable was retold for the edification of the contemporary Jewish-Christian community from which his Gospel emerges.

For edificatory and hortatory purposes, the evangelists also often provided the parables with an application or series of different interpretations which are usually secondary and hence do not represent their original meaning (e.g. Mk 4.13–20; Lk. 18.14b; Mt. 20.16).[70] In these two latter examples, an isolated and independent saying attributed to Jesus elsewhere has been transferred to the parable as a suggested application (compare Lk. 18.14b with 14.11 and Mt. 20.16 with Mk 10.31, Mt. 19.30 and Lk. 13.30). On occasions, several (sometimes contradictory) applications are offered (e.g. Lk. 16.8b-13). Sometimes the same parable has different applications in different Gospels (contrast the differing interpretations of the Wedding Feast parable given in Mt. 22.14 and Lk. 14.12–14); sometimes an application lacking in one Gospel is supplied by another (compare Mt. 12.44c with the parallel Lk. 11.24–6). Many of these secondary interpretations take the form of moralizing generalizations applicable to the conditions of the later church living in and adapting to the world but not necessarily reflecting or preserving Jesus' original meaning (Lk. 16.9!).

Finally, the evangelists often presented the parables as allegories, as the tradition before them had done. It is clear, for example, that both Matthew and Luke had the later Gentile mission and even the Fall of Jerusalem in mind when relating the parable of the wedding feast (compare and contrast Lk. 14.16–24 esp. vv. 21–4 = Mt. 22.1–14 esp. vv. 6–7, 11–14).

If we now turn to Mark, we can see that he too has drawn on this rich vein of traditional material. Reproduced in his Gospel indeed are all three of the parable types isolated and classified by Dodd and Jeremias. Here we find the figurative or parabolic saying (*Bildwort*): 2.17a (the physician and the sick), 19a (the wedding guests and the bridegroom), 21 (the new patch on the

---

[69] *Ibid.*, pp. 38–40.   [70] *Ibid.*, pp. 103–14.

old garment), 22 (the new wine and the old wineskins); 3.23–7 (the divided kingdom and the divided house; the plundering of the strong man's house); 4.21 (the lamp and the lampstand), 24 (the measure given and received); 9.49–50 (the salt sayings); 10.25 (the camel and the eye of the needle); 13.28 (the blossoming of the fig tree). Simple parables or similitudes (*Gleichnisse*) are found: 4.26–9 (the growing seed), 30–2 (the mustard seed); 13.34–6 (the returning householder). Full blown narrative parables (*Parabeln*) are also represented: 4.1–8 (the sower); 12.1–9 (the vineyard).

The Markan parables have been selected from the tradition and arranged by the evangelist. A prominent grouping occurs in the discourse of chapter 4 (where all three classes incidentally are represented) but a series of linked parabolic sayings is also given in 2.17–22 and 3.23–7. One of the two prominent narrative parables is reserved for chapter 12 (12.1–9). Apart from the 'clustering' of the parables, one observes the conflation of originally separate parables into double parables linked by catchword connection (2.21–2; 3.24–5; 4.21–5).[71] One also notes that secondary expansion has occurred in a number of cases (e.g. 2.17b; 2.19b–20). The allegorization to which the parable tradition was subject is also clearly in evidence. The most famous example, of course, is the interpretation of the parable of the sower (4.13–20) upon which much ink has been expended. Here the explanation found on the lips of Jesus is manifestly artificial, with the various details of the parable, in particular the fate of the seed in respect of the different types of ground (the two are confused) being made to represent different responses to the 'word' or gospel preached by the church.[72]

Four other examples, however, may be commented upon. In the first place, the context in which the 'strong man' saying (3.27) is placed invites the reader to see Jesus as the stronger man who has bound Satan, in particular through the exorcisms by means of which he is revealed to the supernatural world as the Son of God (3.11–12). Secondly, the addition of the words 'As long as they have the bridegroom with them, they cannot

---

[71] On this last passage in particular, *ibid.*, pp. 91–2. [72] *Ibid.*, pp. 77–9.

fast. The days will come, when the bridegroom is taken away from them, and then they will fast in that day' (2.19b–20) to the parable of the wedding guests (2.18–19) acts clearly to identify the bridegroom with the Markan Jesus, an association not regarded as original. These additions point forward to a later church situation, to the practice of fasting in particular, and the hindsight they display in respect of Jesus' destiny reflects their secondary character.[73] Similarly, in the parable of the returning householder (13.34–6), the master of the house is a thinly disguised substitute for the Markan Jesus whose triumphant parousia as the Son of Man has just been predicted (13.24–7), and whose imminent betrayal, as the suffering Son of Man, by disciples who not only cannot keep watch ('lest he come suddenly and find you asleep'; 13.35–6 and 14.37–42) but also betray him ('at cockcrow'; cf. 13.35 and 14.30, 72), is about to be recounted.

A fourth example is the parable of the vineyard, which Jeremias described as 'pure allegory'. 'The vineyard is clearly Israel, the tenants are Israel's rulers and leaders, the owner of the vineyard is God, the messengers are the prophets, the son is Christ, the punishment of the husbandmen symbolizes the ruin of Israel, the "other people" (Mt. 21.43) are the Gentile church. The whole parable is evidently pure allegory'.[74] The parable clearly reflects the events of salvation history as seen by the early church. Of the identification of the 'son' with Jesus, Jeremias further adds:

But in the situation of Jesus, to which we are thus referred, the murder of the son formed an appropriate climax for the audience. They will have understood that Jesus saw himself as being the son, the last messenger, though it could not be taken for granted that the son had messianic significance, since no evidence is forthcoming for the application of the title 'Son of God' to the Messiah in pre-Christian Palestinian Judaism ... From which it follows that the christological point of the parable would have been hidden from the audience.[75]

---

[73] N. Perrin, *Rediscovering the Teaching of Jesus* (The New Testament Library; London: SCM Press; New York and Evanston, IL: Harper & Row, 1967), p. 79.

[74] Jeremias, *Parables*, p. 70. [75] *Ibid.*, pp. 72–3.

Also associated with the parable is Ps. 118.22–3 ('The very stone which the builders rejected has become the head of the corner'), a proof-text used by the early church (e.g. Acts 4.11; 1 Pet. 2.7) in which Jesus' rejection by the Jews but subsequent vindication by resurrection was prefigured, according to them.

Two further comments can be made. In the first place, the presence in the story of the 'beloved son' (12.6) would have recalled for the Markan reader the two previous passages in the Gospel in which the 'Son of God' secret had been disclosed, namely the baptism (1.11) and the transfiguration (9.7). Secondly, the fact that the secret of Jesus' identity is conveyed through the medium of a parable would have brought to mind another of the secrecy passages, namely the 'parables secret' of 4.11–12 ('To you has been given the secret of the kingdom of God, but for those outside everything is in parables so that they may indeed see but not perceive, and may indeed hear but not understand; lest they should turn again, and be forgiven'). Curiously, although the reader is not told that the Jewish authorities have recognized in the parable a claim on the part of the Markan Jesus to be the Son of God, some limited perception is nevertheless predicated of them ('for they perceived that they had told the parable against them' 12.12).

For Mark, then, the significance of the parables is not eschatological but *Christological*. The parables are not the means by which Jesus openly teaches, proclaims or points to the coming Kingdom of God. They are the means whereby he *secretly* intimates his true status and mission to those 'who have ears to hear' (4.9, 23). This comes out in the verses quoted above, the passage which can be seen as reflecting more than any other the Markan understanding of the parables, namely 4.10–12.

Here, as we have seen, the reader is told that the parables were vehicles not for instruction but for mystification. They were *meant*, therefore, to harden Jewish hearts. Attempts have been made to trace this motive back in some form to Jesus himself. Behind the word *parabole* in the Greek, it is argued, lies the Hebrew word *mashal* which, among other things in the Old Testament, can mean a 'riddle' or a 'dark saying', one which puzzles or makes one think.[76] In the tradition of apocalyptic Judaism, by which Jesus himself was also influenced, the 'parable' or 'similitude' was a common form for the revealing of secrets (especially of future events) whose interpretation was open only to the select few and granted to them by revelation.[77] The 'parables' in Jewish apocalyptic, however, are often allegories and Jesus' parables do not conform in type to them.[78] Even allowing for esoteric and enigmatic elements in the teaching of Jesus, such an obfuscatory motive, if regarded as historical, contradicts most of what modern scholarship has ascertained of the function of Jesus' parables within his own life situation.

Mk 4.11–12 must surely be seen, therefore, as 'originating in connection with the theological problem created by Jewish rejection of the Christian message and elaborated in different ways in Mark's source and in our three Synoptic gospels'.[79] In essence, C. E. Carlston is right although, given their links with the rest of the Gospel, I would prefer to regard these verses as Markan redaction rather than an alien insertion.[80] Three things ought to be kept in mind, however, when assessing these

[76] For a discussion of *māšāl* (parable) and the importance of the OT parables for understanding those of Jesus, see J. Drury, *The Parables in the Gospels* (London: SPCK, 1985) and more recently, 'Parable', *DBI*, pp. 509–11.

[77] See P. Patten, 'The Form and Function of Parable in Select Apocalyptic Literature and their Significance for Parables in the Gospel of Mark', *NTS*, 29 (1983), pp. 246–58; C. L. Mearns, 'Parables, Secrecy and Eschatology in Mark's Gospel', *SJT*, 44 (1991), pp. 423–42.

[78] '[I]t would seem to follow that the whole parabolic material was originally as free from allegorizing interpretations as were the special Lucan material and the Gospel of Thomas ... But it is only necessary to compare the undoubtedly pre-Christian animal allegories of Ethiopic Enoch, 85–90 ... with the vivid parables of Jesus, to realize how far removed he was from this kind of allegorizing' (Jeremias, *Parables*, pp. 88–90); see also Mowry, 'Parable' in *IDB*, p. 651.

[79] C. E. Carlston, 'Parable', *IDB(S)*, p. 641.

[80] Cf. W. Marxsen, 'Redaktionsgeschichtliche Erklärung der sogenannten Parabeltheorie des Markus', *ZThK*, 52 (1955), pp. 255–71; M. A. Beavis, *Mark's Audience. The Literary and Social History of Mark 4.11–12* (JSNTSS, 33; Sheffield: JSOT Press, 1989). J. Drury, too, is of the view that '[t]he presence of the 'hardening theory' (overt in verses 11 and 12, but evident in both parable and interpretation) with its corollary of dividing men into two camps, those who see and those who do not, is so major a theme of Marcan theology that it seems more economical to attribute the passage to him than to the twilit region of the early Church' (*Parables*, p. 371).

words in the Gospel. Firstly, as previously stated, when the parables came to be written down, many were already obscure, puzzling, enigmatic to Christian communities such as Mark's as well as to the evangelist. Secondly, the theology of the community as well as of the evangelist had advanced (particularly in respect of Christology and soteriology) and was based (perhaps as a result of the influence of Paul) not simply on Jesus' teaching but on claims regarding his status and mission which arose out of his death and alleged resurrection. Thirdly, these early communities had lived through and after a period in which Israel had decisively rejected not only these claims but also Jesus' original teaching. This meant that God's purpose had been thwarted. It meant too that Jesus' original teaching had either been false or ineffective. Paul himself can be seen grappling with this very problem of Israel's rejection of the gospel in chapters 9–11 of Romans.

It is out of these three factors (the enigmatic nature of the parables; Mark's own Christology; Jewish rejection of the gospel) that the Markan theory of the parables emerges. For Mark and his community, the very function of the parables has been reinterpreted. The parable is now seen, not as a vehicle for instruction or warning concerning the coming Kingdom of God, but as a vehicle for mystification. The parables reveal Jesus' message and status only to the initiated, in this case the Markan readership (whom I take to be largely Gentile-Christian). In fulfilment of the words of Isaiah (6.9–10), the parables were *meant* to harden Jewish hearts, *meant* to make them misunderstand, *meant* to conceal Jesus' message and status from them. Because that had been their historical *outcome*, this (according to theological reasoning) must have been their intended *effect*, for history is governed by God's purposes which cannot be thwarted. A predestinarian note is struck, therefore, in these verses, and the 'hardening' theory which is espoused (see also Jn 12.40; Acts 28.26ff.; Rom. 11.8; 2 Cor. 3.14; 4.3–4) may not only have functioned theologically for the community but also sociologically, bolstering the Markan community's sense of eliteness as well as its social cohesion in face of Jewish

hostility.[81] To them had been given the secret of the Kingdom of
God, but to outsiders everything was in parables. What, however,
did Mark mean by 'the secret of the Kingdom of God'? It is to this
question that we now turn, but before we do, let me sum up.

Thus far we have examined the parables of Jesus as they
come to us in the Gospel of Mark. After preliminary matters of
definition and classification, we examined their historical
setting in the life of Jesus where their meaning was eschatological and their function was to teach, indeed warn, his fellow
Jews about the imminent coming of the Kingdom of God. We
then moved on to their theological setting in the early church,
observing their fate in the course of transmission and in
particular the secondary interpretations and allegorization
which often served to distort or alter their original meaning. We
next discussed their literary setting in the Synoptic Gospels,
noting features of the editorial process conducted upon them
and commenting on their meaning and function for the evangelists. This introductory overview provided a context for Mark's
treatment of the parables in particular. We reviewed the nature
and function of the material in Mark, noting the different types
of parable incorporated by the evangelist before going on to
discuss the nature and significance of his redactional work upon
them. The conclusion was that the parables were seen by the
evangelist as cryptic utterances which were intended to conceal
Jesus' message from his hearers and reveal it only to the
initiated (in this case Mark's Christian readers). By virtue of
secondary additions and allegorical features attributable both
to pre-Markan tradition and to Mark (we cannot always differentiate between the two), parables were now seen as referring
not to the Kingdom of God as much as to the concealed nature
of the one who came proclaiming it, the divine Son of God.

'The time is fulfilled': the Kingdom of God in Mark

To investigate the meaning of the Kingdom of God for Mark,
we must as before place the discussion in a wider context by first

---

[81] F. Watson, 'The Social Function of Mark's Secrecy Motif', *JSNT*, 24 (1985), pp.
49–69.

reviewing how the term has generally been understood.[82] For the scholarly exegetes of the nineteenth century (A. Ritschl, F. Schleiermacher, etc.), 'Jesus', as I once elsewhere remarked, 'was a moral hero, an ethical giant cast in an essentially nineteenth century heroic mould, the proclaimer of the Kingdom of God as a lofty, universal, spiritual "idea" and, above all – a gentleman!'[83] The Kingdom of God was seen as 'the moral task to be carried out by the human race ... the organization of humanity through action inspired by love'.[84] Hence it was virtually identical with the church ('entering the Kingdom') or the spread of Christianity in the world (the steady growth of the Kingdom).

In support of this view, the Gospel of Mark was appealed to, particularly the so-called 'parables of growth' (Mk 4. 1–34). God's Kingdom was God's moral rule in the heart of the individual and a consequence of the individual's allowing God thus to reign in his heart and over his conscience would be the renovation of society and the growth of civilization. Nowhere has this view of the Kingdom been better expressed than in the splendidly emotive (and much repeated) words of the British scholar, T. W. Manson (1893–1958):

We may sum up the whole matter by saying that, as it appears in the life and teaching of Jesus, the sovereignty of God is essentially the working out, to a predetermined and inevitable end, of God's holy purpose. This purpose embraces in its scope both the natural world and the world of self-conscious beings. Its motive is love, its means service, and its end a state of things where the will of God is done on earth as in heaven. The sovereignty of God over nature is demonstrated not by the trampling march of supernatural power in some great cataclysm, but by his constant care over all his creatures, even the humblest. It is manifested in human life, not by legions of angels sweeping forward to crush the forces of evil, but by the realisation in those who accept its rule of a strange power to overcome evil with good. This power is recognised, by all who experience it, as the

---

[82] For a history of interpretation, see M. D. Hooker, 'Kingdom of God', *DBI*, pp. 374–77; B. Chilton, *The Kingdom of God in the Teaching of Jesus* (Issues in Religion and Theology, 5; London: SPCK; Philadelphia: Fortress, 1984), pp. 1–26; Perrin, *Language*; N. Perrin, *The Kingdom of God in the Teaching of Jesus* (The New Testament Library; London: SCM Press; Philadelphia, PA: Westminster Press, 1963).

[83] Telford, *Barren Temple*, p. 2.   [84] Perrin, *Kingdom*, p. 16.

strongest thing in the world, and as something which must finally prevail. In other words, the throne of the universe is founded upon a Father's love. This is probably the clue to 'the mystery of the Kingdom'.[85]

This essentially nineteenth-century view was challenged at the turn of the century, however, by 'the trampling march' of J. Weiss and A. Schweitzer. The 'Kingdom' concept should be interpreted not against the background of nineteenth-century idealistic Liberalism but against the background of first-century apocalyptic Judaism. In Jesus' mind there was an antithesis between God and Satan, and a metaphysical struggle between the two. The Kingdom of God would come about not by the material action of men but by the supernatural action of God. The Kingdom of God was not something gradually *evolving* by the action of men in history but the *eschatological irruption* of God (in apocalyptic fashion) into history, in the manner of a flood (e.g. Mt. 24.38–9 = Lk. 17.26–7).[86] The new age so brought about would be discontinuous with the old. Hence, J. Jeremias, for example, argued, the so-called 'parables of *growth*' are really 'parables of *contrast*'. In these parables (for example, the mustard seed, Mk 4.30–2), the emphasis is not on the biological process of growth (only uncertainly understood by the ancients) but on the sharp contrast between the smallness of the seed and the magnitude of the resultant (8–10 foot) shrub, illustrating the sharp discontinuity between the present age and the conditions that would prevail *extraordinarily* in the age to come.[87] To understand how this conception arose, let us summarize briefly how the concept of the Kingdom of God originated and developed, as we find it reflected in the literature of the Old Testament, apocalyptic Judaism and Rabbinic Judaism.[88]

While the expression 'Kingdom of God' itself hardly appears

---

[85] T. W. Manson, *The Teaching of Jesus. Studies of its Form and Content* (Cambridge: Cambridge University Press, 1931), p. 170.

[86] In commenting on the views of J. Weiss, Perrin writes: 'In the teaching of Jesus, however, the kingdom of God is conceived quite differently from this: it is the breaking out of an overpowering divine storm which erupts into history to destroy and to renew, and which a man can neither further nor influence' (*Kingdom*, p. 18).

[87] Jeremias, *Parables*, pp. 146–53.

[88] For a more comprehensive overview, see Perrin, *Language*; O. E. Evans, 'Kingdom of God', *IDB*, pp. 17–26; Manson, *Teaching*, esp. pp. 116ff.

in the Old Testament (although see 1 Chron. 28.5), the notion of God's 'kingship' (*malkûth*), 'kingly rule' or 'sovereignty' over the nation of Israel and subsequently over the nations of the world is a dominant emphasis (e.g. Exod. 15.18; 1 Chron. 29.11–12). Active in and from creation (e.g. Job 38–41), God's sovereignty extended universally and eternally over the present world order (e.g. Ps. 22.28; 103.19; 145.10–13; 146.10). For the prophets, Yahweh was alone supreme. Protector and defender of Israel, and a champion of righteousness and justice, he was actively at work in history, overseeing the affairs of the world (e.g. Jer. 27.5–11), using the authorities for his own purposes (e.g. Isa. 44.24–45.25), and calling the nations (as well as Israel) to account for their sins (e.g. Amos 1–2). History contradicted this belief, however, as the Jews were subjected to the domination and oppression of successive world empires. God, it appeared, was increasingly remote if not powerless. Belief in Yahweh's kingship came to be seen, therefore, not as a present experience or reality but as a future hope or expectation (e.g. Isa. 24.21–3; 33.22; Zeph. 3.14–18; Zech. 14.16). This belief is reflected in the later prophets who talked of the coming 'day of the Lord', a day in which God would intervene in judgment and in wrath, to punish the nations, to restore his people's fortunes, to demonstrate his own power and sovereignty (e.g. Isa. 2.12; 13.6, 9; Joel 1.15; 2.1; 3.14).

This view came to the fore in the intertestamental period and is encountered particularly in the literature of apocalyptic Judaism. Here the world was seen pre-eminently as the sphere of Satan's rule, not God's, and allied with him were the legions of demons and evil spirits who were responsible for the evil, corruption, sickness and death to which humankind was prone. Allied with Satan, too, were the Greek and Roman Empires to which the Jews became subject, and by whom they felt culturally, politically and religiously oppressed. God, it was believed, would shortly intervene to create a new world order and this new world order was termed, among other things, the 'Kingdom of God'. The term is used frequently in the literature of this period (200 BCE–100 CE) and almost invariably the thought is eschatological.

In some cases, as in the *Assumption of Moses* (a text probably written during the lifetime of Jesus), the emphasis is on God's intervention alone (with a subordinate role given to an angel), salvation is a collective experience and the emphasis is nationalistic:

> And then his kingdom shall appear throughout all his creation,
> And then Satan shall be no more,
> And sorrow shall depart with him.
> Then the hands of the angel shall be filled
> Who has been appointed chief,
> And he shall forthwith avenge them of their enemies
> For the Heavenly One will arise from his royal throne,
> And he will go forth from his holy habitation
> With indignation and wrath on account of his sons.
>
> . . .
>
> For the Most High will arise, the Eternal God alone,
> And he will appear to punish the Gentiles,
> And he will destroy all their idols.[89]

In other cases, as in the *Psalms of Solomon* (dated shortly after Pompey's capture of Jerusalem, *c.* 63 BCE), a prominent role is given to an earthly figure, a royal Messiah, the Son of David. Here again salvation is collective, the emphasis nationalistic, but the means of intervention is expressly political and military:

Behold, O Lord, and raise up unto them their king, the son of David,
At the time in the which thou seest, O God, that he may reign over
   Israel thy servant.
And gird him with strength, that he may shatter unrighteous rulers,
And that he may purge Jerusalem from nations that trample her down
   to destruction.

Wisely, righteously he shall thrust out sinners from the inheritance
He shall destroy the pride of the sinner as a potter's vessel.
With a rod of iron he shall break in pieces all their substance,
He shall destroy the godless nations with the word of his mouth;
At his rebuke nations shall flee before him.
And he shall reprove sinners for the thoughts of their heart.
And he shall gather together a holy people, whom he shall lead in
   righteousness,

---

[89] *Ass. Mos.* 10; see Barrett, *Background*, pp. 331–2.

And he shall judge the tribes of the people that has been sanctified by
  the Lord his God.
And he shall not suffer unrighteousness to lodge any more in their
  midst,
Nor shall there dwell with them any man that knoweth wickedness,
For he shall know them, that they are all sons of their God.
And he shall divide them according to their tribes upon the land,
And neither sojourner nor alien shall sojourn with them any more.[90]

In yet another passage, this time from Daniel (*c.* 167 BCE),
salvation is invested in a figure described, in contrast to the
beast-empires appearing in the seer's vision, as 'one like a son of
man'. Here salvation is again collective, but the emphasis is
universal and the means of intervention supernatural:

And four great beasts come up from the sea, diverse from one
another. The first was like a lion, and had eagle's wings ... And
behold another beast, a second, like to a bear ... After this I beheld,
and lo another, like a leopard, which had upon the back of it four
wings of a fowl; the beast had also four heads; and dominion was
given to it. After this I saw in the night visions, and behold a fourth
beast, terrible and powerful, and strong exceedingly; and it had great
iron teeth ... I beheld till thrones were placed, and one that was
ancient of days did sit: his raiment was white as snow, and the hair of
his head like pure wool; his throne was fiery flames, and the wheels
thereof burning fire ... the judgement was set, and the books were
opened ... I beheld even till the beast was slain, and his body
destroyed, and he was given to be burned with fire. And as for the rest
of the beasts their dominion was taken away: yet their lives were
prolonged for a season and a time. I saw in the night visions, and,
behold, there came with the clouds of heaven one like unto a son of
man, and he came even to the ancient of days, and they brought him
near before him. And there was given him dominion, and glory, and a
kingdom, that all the peoples, nations, and languages should serve
him: his dominion is an everlasting dominion, which shall not pass
away, and his kingdom that which shall not be destroyed.[91]

In 1 Enoch, specifically within the section known as the
Similitudes of Enoch (the dating is controversial but, according
to C. K. Barrett 'it is almost certainly earlier than the earliest

---

[90] *Ps. Sol.* 17.23ff.; see Barrett, *Background*, pp. 337–8.
[91] Dan. 7. 1–14; see Barrett, *Background*, pp. 340–1.

books of the New Testament'[92]), this 'one like a son of man' has become a supernatural, transcendent figure acting on God's behalf and commanding universal worship:

And in that place I saw the fountain of righteousness
Which was inexhaustible:
And around it were many fountains of wisdom:
And all the thirsty drank of them,
And were filled with wisdom,
And their dwellings were with the righteous and holy and elect.
And at that hour that Son of man was named
In the presence of the Lord of Spirits
And his name before the Head of Days.
Yea, before the sun and the signs were created,
Before the stars of the heaven were made,
His name was named before the Lord of Spirits.
He shall be a staff to the righteous whereon to stay themselves and not
   fall,
And he shall be the light of the Gentiles,
And the hope of those who are troubled of heart.
All who dwell on earth shall fall down and worship him
And will praise and bless and celebrate with song the Lord of Spirits.

. . .

And there was great joy amongst them,
And they blessed and glorified and extolled
Because the name of that Son of man had been revealed unto them.
And he sat on the throne of his glory,
And the sum of judgement was given unto the Son of man,
And he caused the sinners to pass away and be destroyed from off the
   face of the earth,
And those who have led the world astray.
With chains shall they be bound,
And in their assemblage-place of destruction shall they be impri-
   soned,
And all their works vanish from the face of the earth.

---

[92] Barrett, *Background* (1956), p. 252. Reflecting perhaps an increasingly less confident consensus among scholars, Barrett's judgment in his revised edition (1987, p. 341) was more cautious ('The date of the Similitudes is disputed, but may be contemporary with the New Testament'). C. Rowland suggests a date of 50 CE for the Similitudes, while acknowledging the difficulties involved in dating these and other apocalypses. See *The Open Heaven. A Study of Apocalyptic in Judaism and Early Christianity* (London: SPCK, 1982), p. 266.

And from henceforth there shall be nothing corruptible;
For that Son of man has appeared,
And has seated himself on the throne of his glory,
And all evil shall pass away before his face,
And the word of that Son of man shall go forth
And be strong before the Lord of Spirits

. . .

And he came to me and greeted me with his voice, and said unto me:
This is the Son of man who is born unto righteousness,
And righteousness abides over him,
And the righteousness of the Head of Days forsakes him not.
And he said unto me:
He proclaims unto thee peace in the name of the world to come

. . .

And so there shall be length of days with that Son of man,
And the righteous shall have peace and an upright way
In the name of the Lord of Spirits for ever and ever.[93]

In another variation on the Danielic tradition, 4 Ezra (or
2 Esdras, a text dated to the first century CE) presents an
eschatological figure, the (primal) 'Man' or pre-existent
Messiah who establishes God's dominion by slaying his enemies
with the breath of his lips:

And it came to pass after seven days that I dreamed a dream by night:
[and I beheld] and lo! there arose a violent wind from the sea and
stirred all its waves. And I beheld and lo! [The wind caused to come
up out of the heart of the seas as it were the form of a man. And I
beheld and lo!] this Man flew with the clouds of heaven. And
wherever he turned his countenance to look everything seen by him
trembled; and whithersoever the voice went out of his mouth, all that
heard his voice melted away as the wax melts when it feels the fire . . .
And after this I beheld, and lo! all who were gathered together against
him were seized with great fear; yet they dared to fight. And lo! when
he saw the assault of the multitude as they came he neither lifted his
hand, nor held spear nor any warlike weapon; but I saw only how he
sent out of his mouth as it were a fiery stream, and out of his lips a
flaming breath, and out of his tongue he shot forth a stream of sparks.
And these were all mingled together – the fiery stream, the flaming
breath, and the . . . storm, and fell upon the assault of the multitude
which was prepared to fight, and burned them all up, so that suddenly

---

[93] 1 Enoch 48; 69.26–9; 71.14–17; see Barrett, *Background*, pp. 341–3.

nothing more was to be seen of the innumerable multitude save only dust of ashes and smell of smoke.[94]

Despite differing expectations with regard to God's eschatological agents (angels/archangels, a Messiah or Messiahs, the Son of David, 'one like a son of man', 'that Son of man', the 'Man' etc.), what unites these passages is the fact that God's kingship is seen as a *future* hope rather than a present worldly reality, and the establishment of it either an earthly and political event, or a cosmic, supernatural and apocalyptic one.

One further dimension to the interpretation of the Kingdom of God is that supplied by the rabbis. While rabbinic thought held to this collective eschatological hope, it was also believed that God's kingship became a present reality or experience when the individual Jew took upon himself the yoke of the Torah and submitted himself to its prescriptions. Moral obedience to the Law, committing oneself to the scrupulous observance of the Torah, was described indeed as 'taking upon oneself the (yoke of the) kingdom (*malkûth*) of God'. This aspect of Jewish thought, the notion of the Kingdom achieving its reality, being 'present' or becoming effective through moral endeavour on the part of the individual has been said to provide an analogy not only for the 'moral' or 'interior' view of the Kingdom later to be developed in the nineteenth century but also for the thought of Jesus.[95]

Three aspects of the Kingdom of God in Jewish and Christian literature can therefore be identified, the Kingdom 'as an eternal fact, as a manifestation in the present life of men, and as a consummation still to come'.[96] It is the last of these conceptions, the eschatological one, however, which has come to dominate the discussion during this century. Where Jesus' teaching about the Kingdom is concerned, furthermore, it would appear that his view has more in common with that

---

[94] 4 Ezra 13.1–13; see Barrett, *Background*, p. 325.

[95] This was the view of T. W. Manson in particular (in *Teaching*) but critics have objected not only to his tendency to ignore the apocalyptic dimension in Jesus' teaching but also to his reliance on rabbinic material of a later date.

[96] Manson, *Teaching*, p. 136; see also Evans, 'Kingdom' in *IDB*, p. 17.

found in the literature of apocalyptic Judaism than it does with the rabbinical literature which post-dates it.

At this point, however, a swarm of difficulties awaits the exegete, for the complexity of our sources and the question of our methodology for interpreting them raises itself afresh. Jesus' teaching about the Kingdom is embedded in a plurality of traditions. It is found in Mark and in the tradition upon which he drew. It is found in Q. Kingdom sayings are found, in turn, in Matthew and in Luke where they have either been taken over from Mark, or from Q, or constitute special Matthean or Lukan material. Which, then, of the many Kingdom sayings in the Synoptic tradition (in Mark, there are 13, in Q 13, in special Matthean material 25, in special Lukan material 6), reflect Jesus' own conception and which that of the early church or evangelists?

When this Gospel material is examined critically, two broadly differing conceptions of the Kingdom of God emerge. In the first place, a number of these sayings clearly point to the Kingdom as an imminent future apocalyptic expectation in Jesus' message (e.g. Mk 1.14–15 par.; 9.1 par.; 14.25 par.; Mt. 6.10 par.; 8.11–12 par.; 10.7ff. (cf. v. 23) par.; 19.28 par.; Lk. 12.35–56 par.; 13.22–30 par.).[97] In a series of separate but related sayings, Jesus connects this proclamation with the coming of the Son of Man (e.g. Mk 13.24–7 par.; Mt. 10.23; Lk. 17.22–37 par.). On the other hand, there are other sayings in which the Kingdom seems to be regarded as a present reality or experience in the world (e.g. Mk 4.1–33 ('the parables of growth'); Mt. 11.2–6 = Lk. 7.18–23; Mt. 12.28 = Lk. 11.20; Mt. 13.16–17 = Lk. 10.23–4; Lk. 4.16–21; 10.18; 17.20–1).[98] The last passage is especially significant, given its 'realized' emphasis and its apparent repudiation of (apocalyptic) signs: 'Being asked by the Pharisees when the kingdom of God was coming, he answered them, "The kingdom of God is not coming with signs to be observed; nor will they say, 'Lo, here it is!' or 'There' for behold, the kingdom of God is in the midst of you"'

---

[97] The evidence is summarized in Perrin, *Kingdom*, pp. 83–4.
[98] The evidence is summarized in Perrin, *Kingdom*, pp. 74–8.

(Lk. 17.20–1). Was Jesus' conception of the Kingdom not only an eschatological one but also an apocalyptic one then?[99] Did Jesus, on the other hand, see the Kingdom as coming in other essentially non-apocalyptic ('spiritual', 'existential') terms? Clearly therefore problems confront us when we seek to differentiate Jesus' view from the various interpretations or reinterpretations of it by the early church and the evangelists, and especially when we consider the effect of the delay of the parousia and the failure of apocalyptic expectations upon these early Christians.

To account for these apparent discrepancies, three main theories have been advanced.[100] The first sees Jesus as an *eschatological prophet* who (like his contemporaries) expected and proclaimed the Kingdom as an *imminent*, eschatological event. Jesus' own view, moreover, as well as that of his immediate followers, was thoroughly apocalyptic in outlook. Those sayings of his embodying this apocalyptic outlook, the 'imminent' or 'future' sayings, are therefore authentic, while the 'present' or 'realized' ones which claim that the Kingdom of God has *already* come (in interior, moral, spiritual or existential terms) in Jesus' person and mission are the product of the early church's 'theological accommodation' to the failure of apocalyptic expectations (especially the parousia). Jesus' own eschatological orientation, in other words, has been gradually eclipsed in the tradition by the Christological interpretation attached

---

[99] B. D. Chilton comments on the difference between the two terms as follows: 'An "apocalyptic" writing typically conveys a "revelation" (*apocalypsis*) concerning the "end" (*eschaton*), sometimes by providing a calendar of occurrences leading up to and even including God's final acts. Apocalyptic is therefore eschatological, but eschatology need not be as detailed in respect of the final events as apocalyptic is' (*Kingdom*, p. 7).

[100] See, for example, E. S. Fiorenza, 'Eschatology of the NT', *IDB(S)*, pp. 276–7 who differentiates four. Some approaches have attempted to avoid the problem of these discrepancies, as N. Perrin does, for example, by claiming that ' "Kingdom of God" is not an *idea* or a *conception*, it is a *symbol*' (*Language*, p. 33) and hence open to a variety of apparently conflicting associations. By adopting what is essentially a modern and sophisticated literary approach, Perrin's 'interpretation is thus open to the accusation that he has read back twentieth-century attitudes into the words of Jesus' (Hooker, 'Kingdom' in *DBI*, p. 377); see also J. Riches and A. Millar, 'Conceptual Change in the Synoptic Tradition' in A. E. Harvey (ed.), *Alternative Approaches to New Testament Study* (London: SPCK, 1985), pp. 37–60.

subsequently to his words. This position has been called 'consistent' or 'thoroughgoing eschatology' and is associated with the names of J. Weiss and A. Schweitzer.

A second theory claims that the 'present' or 'realized' sayings are authentic while the 'future' or 'apocalyptic' sayings are secondary. Jesus himself made a radical departure from the apocalyptic outlook of his contemporaries in that he saw the Kingdom not in out-and-out apocalyptic terms but rather as 'a transcendent order beyond space and time' already present in his person and ministry. The sayings which talk of the Kingdom's future coming in apocalyptic terms (along with the parousia expectation itself) are therefore the product of a subsequent 're-Judaization' of Christianity, or even, as some have stated it, a contamination of an authentically Christian stream by Jewish apocalypticism. In this respect, the Fourth Gospel, and to an extent Paul, would preserve the essence of Jesus' own proclamation while the apocalyptic Christianity discernible in parts of the New Testament (e.g. Q, Mark (especially ch. 13), 1 & 2 Thessalonians and especially Revelation) would depart from it. This view has been called 'realized eschatology', as we have seen, and is associated with a mainly British school of scholarship represented by C. H. Dodd, T. W. Manson, C. F. D. Moule and J. A. T. Robinson.

A third mediating position holds that Jesus was an eschatological prophet who proclaimed that the Kingdom of God had been *inaugurated* in his person and ministry, but who looked for its dramatic consummation *in the future*. For this view, a number of *both* 'present' and 'future' sayings originate with Jesus and they must therefore be kept in tension with one another (the 'already' with the 'not yet'). This solution has been called for this reason 'inaugurated eschatology', 'proleptic eschatology' or an 'eschatology in process of realizing itself', and is associated with scholars such as W. G. Kümmel, R. H. Fuller and J. Jeremias.

While the third of these positions can be said to represent the current consensus (at least where European scholarship is concerned), and is probably the most cautious or balanced evaluation of the evidence, my own inclinations favour the first.

A certain 'hermeneutic of suspicion' can be directed to the second and to an extent the third. One notes in these positions, for example, a certain distrust of apocalyptic and a desire on the part of scholars to dissociate Jesus from a perspective considered simplistic, fanatical or irrelevant. The vagueness of expressions such as the Kingdom's coming 'in his own person and ministry' may disguise an exegete's own Christological assumptions, and the desire to harmonize Jesus' teaching, for the sake of theological continuity, with that of Paul and John, his or her apologetic ones. Apart from the fact that apocalyptic conceptions can be traced back to the very early tradition,[101] it seems more plausible to me that a 'realized' eschatological perspective with its emphasis on Christology rather than eschatology would have received a greater impetus from the delay of the parousia and the failure of apocalyptic expectations than that Jewish apocalypticism later 'contaminated' a Christian stream which in its origin and at its source was after all a Jewish sect!

This position we can see borne out by subsequent developments in the New Testament where, in Bultmann's famous dictum, 'The Proclaimer becomes the Proclaimed'. Where Jesus asked his disciples to pray for the Kingdom to come (Mt. 6.10 = Lk. 11.2), the primitive community in turn prayed for Jesus to come (1 Cor. 16.22; Rev. 22.20). Christ himself is the focus for Paul, and not the Kingdom to which he pointed. For John, the Kingdom of God is mentioned but twice (3.3, 5) and its equivalent 'eternal life' is seen as a *present* gift in union with Christ. For the rest of the New Testament, the references are relatively few. Jesus is central and not the Kingdom and that Kingdom, moreover, is seen as bound up with his person and mission, his death and resurrection.

How does Mark understand the Kingdom of God in the teaching of Jesus and where does he stand in the stream of such developments? Let me comment first of all on the nature of the

---

[101] This is acknowledged by a fourth position described by Fiorenza as 'apocalyptic eschatology'. Here apocalyptic is viewed as 'the mother of all Christian theology' (E. Käsemann) but at the same time attributed not to Jesus but to 'the post-Easter enthusiasm of the primitive church'. See Fiorenza, 'Eschatology' in *IDB(S)*, p. 276.

Kingdom sayings in the Gospel. The evangelist reproduces some thirteen of these sayings in all (1.15; 4.11; 4.26, 30; 9.1; 9.47; 10.14–15 (twice), 23–5 (twice); 12.34; 14.25; 15.43). In six of these instances, a future and even an apocalyptic element can be said to be uppermost. In 9.1, after a warning concerning the apocalyptic coming of the Son of Man (8.38), the Markan Jesus' audience is informed that 'there are some standing here who will not taste death before they see the Kingdom of God come with power'. As is well known, C. H. Dodd has attempted to claim this verse for 'realized eschatology' by translating the verse as follows: 'There are some of those standing here who will not taste death until they *have seen that* the Kingdom of God *has come* with power.' 'The perfect participle', Dodd argues, 'indicates an action already complete from the standpoint of the subject of the main verb ... The bystanders are not promised that they shall see the Kingdom of God *coming*, but that they shall come to see that the Kingdom of God *has already come*, at some point before they became aware of it.'[102] Although this interpretation 'has not established itself, nor ... been driven from the field',[103] it suffers from the weakness that the verb 'to see' (*horan*) 'is never used of intellectual perception'[104] and it requires us, among other things, to interpret the Kingdom 'come *with power*' in 'realized' terms as either the resurrection, Pentecost or the era of the Christian church.

In Mark 9.47 and in 10.23–5, the Markan Jesus talks of the Kingdom as something to be entered, and as something for which no sacrifice is too costly to be prepared for it. Here it is used in conjunction with the term 'life' (Mk 9.43, 45) or 'eternal life' (Mk 10.17, 30), meaning 'the life of the Age to Come' or the Messianic age.[105] This future orientation is clearly seen in the last of these verses where the Markan Jesus promises a reward to his followers ('in the age to come eternal life') for the sacrifices made 'in this time'. In Mark 14.25 the future emphasis is also clear. In expectation of the imminent consummation of the Kingdom, Jesus promises not to drink wine again until he

---

[102] Dodd, *Parables*, p. 43n.   [103] Perrin, *Kingdom*, p. 66.
[104] Fuller, *Mission*, p. 27.   [105] Dodd, *Parables*, p. 35.

shares a Messianic meal with his disciples.[106] The final passage (Mk 15.43) too reflects a future orientation in that it describes Joseph of Arimathea as someone living in expectation of the fulfilment of Israel's eschatological hopes.

At the same time as future, imminent and even apocalyptic notions can be discerned in some of these sayings, present or realized elements are also apparent. In Mark 10.14–15, the Markan Jesus rebukes his disciples for turning away the children 'for to such belongs the kingdom of God' and informs them 'whoever does not receive the kingdom of God like a child shall not enter into it'. What receiving the Kingdom 'like a child' precisely means is disputed ('with the attitude of a child', namely in humility or innocence, or 'as children receive things', namely 'as a gift', the child being a symbol for dependence or powerlessness? see also Mt. 11.25 = Lk. 10.21) but in this passage has been found the closest parallel with the rabbinical conception ('taking upon oneself the yoke of the kingdom') in that it predicates a correct attitude or moral stance as determinative for one's reception of the Kingdom. Jesus' words to the scribe in 12.34 in response to the ethical insight he demonstrates ('You are not far from the kingdom of God') may convey a similar notion.

The four remaining passages have given rise to considerable debate in terms of their future or realized thrust. In Mark 1.14–15, the evangelist has Jesus announce: 'The time is fulfilled, and the kingdom of God is at hand; repent, and believe in the gospel.' Here, as with Matthew 12.28 = Luke 11.20, Dodd translates: 'The Kingdom of God *has come*.'[107] Contesting the linguistic evidence, other commentators have preferred to understand the words as indicating the imminence rather than the actual presence of the Kingdom of God.[108] The parables of

---

[106] Here it is not 'the transcendent order beyond space and time' which is in view but the traditional 'messianic banquet' (cf. Isa. 25.6; Zeph. 1.7; 1 Enoch 62. 13–14); see W. G. Kümmel, *Promise and Fulfilment. The Eschatological Message of Jesus* (Studies in Biblical Theology, 23; London: SCM Press, 1957), pp. 31–2; Evans, 'Kingdom' in *IDB*, p. 21; Perrin, *Kingdom*, pp. 72–3.

[107] 'Both imply the "arrival" of the Kingdom' (Dodd, *Parables*, p. 37).

[108] The normal usage of *eggizō* in the NT is 'to draw near' and not 'to arrive'. While the word can mean 'to arrive' in the LXX, as the translation of *nāga'* (Hebrew) or *meṭā'* (Aramaic), this usage is exceptional and there too it normally means 'to arrive'. If

the Kingdom (Mk 4.26ff.; 4.30ff.) likewise have drawn differing interpretations, those following Jeremias seeing them as future-oriented in respect of their climax (the eschatological harvest), those following Dodd seeing them as oriented to the present in respect of the secrecy and hiddenness of the Kingdom they envisage, an emphasis also strongly represented in Mark 4.11.

How then, to return to our question, did Mark understand the Kingdom of God? One view is to take the 'realized' elements as reflecting Jesus' distinctive thought and the apocalyptic ones as secondary, perhaps even Markan. While acknowledging that Jesus spoke of the Kingdom as future, V. Taylor, for example, was of the opinion that 'Mark's view of the Kingdom was eschatological' and that 'the main emphasis lies upon the Kingdom as future and, indeed, imminent'. The evangelist, he asserts, 'does not record, and perhaps has not assimilated, the more distinctive elements in the teaching of Jesus, implicit in Markan sayings but more clearly evident in Q (Luke xi. 20, xvii. 20f., Matt. xxi. 31) and in such parables as the Leaven (Luke xiii. 20f.), Treasure Hid in a Field (Matt. xiii. 44), and the Pearl Merchant (Matt. xiii. 45f.)'. These more distinctive elements, Taylor holds, include the notion that the Kingdom is 'present in himself and in his ministry'. 'In a true sense, therefore, He taught a "realized eschatology", and is Himself αὐτοβασιλεία.'[109]

For my own part, I think this view is misguided. Apart from the historicizing tendencies to which Taylor was prone and the Christological presuppositions to which he adhered, the position advanced by him fails adequately to distinguish between Mark's sources and his redaction, although, given that redaction criticism was in its infancy when he was writing, this is understandable.[110] The evangelist has certainly not introduced

the evangelist had wished to express himself unambiguously, he could have used *ephthasen* as in Mt. 12.28 = Lk. 11.20. See Evans, 'Kingdom' in *IDB*, p. 20; Kümmel, *Promise*, pp. 24–5.

[109] Taylor, *Mark*, p. 114.
[110] For a redaction-critical analysis of the Markan Kingdom sayings, see A. M. Ambrozic, *The Hidden Kingdom. A Redaction-critical Study of the References to the Kingdom of God in Mark's Gospel* (Catholic Biblical Quarterly Monograph Series, 2; Washington, DC: Catholic Biblical Association of America, 1972).

a secondary apocalyptic element into the tradition he received. That apocalyptic element, particularly an imminent future Kingdom conception, was already embedded in the parables and sayings of Jesus he inherited, as we have seen.

In the tradition before him, the so-called parables of growth (Mk 4.8, 26, 30) were really parables of contrast, as Jeremias has demonstrated, reflecting the dramatic difference between this age and the conditions prevailing in the age to come, a discontinuity reflected also in the parabolic sayings of Mark 2.21 and 22. In the parable of Mark 13.28–9, the dramatic fertility of the fig tree at the onset of summer was taken, I believe, by Jesus, as an analogy for the future (imminent) approach of the end-time.[111] Jesus' proclamation of the coming Kingdom of God in Mark 1.15 may be said to be typical of the eschatological prophets of that period and has an affinity with the Q saying of Matthew 12.28 = Luke 11.20. The evangelist's claim that in the exorcisms of Jesus the kingdom of Satan is being usurped and (by implication) that of God being established has its counterpart in the same Q saying. In the triumphal entry of Mark 11.1–10, Mark is operating with a received tradition of Jesus as the royal Messiah, the Son of David, about to establish the Kingdom (Mk 11.10) as I have argued. The Son of Man saying of Mark 8.38 and the closely associated Kingdom saying of Mark 9.1, with their future-oriented apocalyptic outlook, like-wise have their counterparts elsewhere in the tradition and hence can be argued to have independent attestation (e.g. Mt. 10.32–3 = Lk. 12.8–9 and Mt. 10.23 as well perhaps as Mk. 13.30). While the apocalyptic discourse itself (13.1–37) was undoubtedly redacted by the evangelist, it was nevertheless composed from traditional material, some of which we may suppose went back to Jesus himself. The concept of the Messianic banquet, likewise, which was reflected as we saw in Mark 14.25, was used in apocalyptic, has its parallel in Matthew 8.11–12 = Luke 13.28–9 and was employed by Jesus.[112]

If the evangelist has not introduced a futurist eschatology

---

[111] For a fuller treatment of this passage in Markan redaction, see Telford, *Barren Temple*, pp. 213–18.

[112] Perrin, *Kingdom*, p. 183.

into his sources, neither can it be said that he accentuated that element. The opposite, I believe, was the case. Mark, in the service of his Christology and soteriology, may have accentuated what 'present' or 'realized' elements there were in the tradition while at the same time altering, modifying or toning down the thorough-going nature of the apocalyptic expectations he found there. Five examples can be given.

We note first of all, that to Jesus' imminent eschatological proclamation ('The time is fulfilled, and the kingdom is at hand'), Mark has added the words 'Repent and believe *in the gospel*' (1.14–15). Jesus is presented as preaching the 'gospel', but it was the early church which preached the 'gospel' or the 'word', and that 'word' or 'gospel' spoke in its content and 'mystery' (e.g. Col. 1.25–6; Eph. 3.8–10) of the significance of Jesus' death and resurrection (Acts 8.4; Rom. 1.1–4, 16; 1 Cor. 1. 17; Gal. 1.6–9; 6.6; Col. 4.3; 2 Tim. 1.11; 4.2; Jas 1.21; 1 Pet. 2.8; 1 Jn 2.7). Since this could not have been the original content of Jesus' message, the expression is anachronistic on his lips and this is confirmed by the fact that other references to the word 'gospel' (Mk 8.35; 10.29; 13.10; 14.9) appear to be redactional.[113] In using this theologically 'loaded' word (which I believe confirms the evangelist's links with Pauline Christianity), Mark has therefore tempered Jesus' original eschatological proclamation of the coming Kingdom with associations which for his readers would have been Christological as well as soteriological.

A second point to note is that the evangelist has carried the secrecy motif into Jesus' preaching on the Kingdom. The Kingdom of God is now a secret or 'mystery' (Mk 4.11–12) as is Jesus' true identity as the Son of God. The so-called parables of growth in chapter 4, the original import of which may have been strongly eschatological, have been given this secret or mysterious element largely by virtue of the material with which they have been juxtaposed (Mk 4.21–5, esp. 22) and by means of his redaction upon them (see especially Mk 4.11–12, 33–4).

A third observation concerns the context in which one of the most future-oriented of the Kingdom sayings (Mk 9.1) has been

[113] W. Marxsen, *Mark the Evangelist. Studies on the Redaction History of the Gospel* (Nashville, TN and New York: Abingdon Press; London: SPCK, 1969), pp. 117–50.

placed. This saying originally predicted the coming of the Kingdom in Jesus' own generation (Mk 13.30) and possibly also referred to the triumphant coming of the Son of Man. In its Markan context, however (note the precise 'And after six days' Mk 9.2), it invites the reader to see the prediction fulfilled in the transfiguration, or better 'epiphany', scene which immediately follows. There, as in Jesus' baptism (Mk 1.11), the secret of Jesus' true status is again disclosed:. 'This is my beloved Son; listen to him' (Mk 9.7).

The view that the apocalyptic element in the Gospel is pre-Markan and that the evangelist has modified it in view of the delay in the parousia is one, moreover, that can be sustained from an examination of the eschatological discourse itself.[114] According to a number of the Kingdom of God/Son of Man sayings, Jesus' apocalyptic expectation was immediate (e.g. Mt. 10.5–8, 23; Mk 9.1; 14.25). By placing Jesus' prediction concerning the end-time or *eschaton* in connection with the events surrounding the destruction of Jerusalem some forty years after the death of Jesus (when, I believe, the Gospel itself was written), Mark has already extended the apocalyptic expectation or scheme. It is agreed that 13.1–4 are redactional verses. In 13.10, the reader is further informed that the interim period before the coming of the Son of Man will take into account the Gentile mission (a universal mission not foreseen by the earlier tradition; see Mt. 10.5–8, 23). In 13.30, the apocalyptic dénouement will occur within a 'generation' yet 13.32 makes its timing even more indefinite, and 13.33ff., as we have seen, urges only watchfulness (a degree of watchfulness, incidentally, which appears somewhat out of proportion given the circumstances of the householder's absence!). According to Mark's sources, Jesus, in common with apocalyptic, predicted the signs which would herald the Kingdom of God or its agent, the Son of Man. Curiously, however, the evangelist has Jesus earlier *refuse* such signs (8.11–13), a feature which may also be compared with the

---

[114] See E. Schweizer, 'Eschatology in Mark's Gospel' in E. E. Ellis and M. Wilcox (eds.), *Neotestamentica et Semitica (Fs. M. Black)* (Edinburgh: T. & T. Clark, 1969), pp. 114–18.

anti-apocalyptic thrust of Luke 17.20–1. One conclusion which might be reached, therefore, is that Mark has inserted the eschatological discourse into his Gospel in order to modify or tone down the tradition's apocalyptic overtones (perhaps in view of the fervour occasioned by the Romano-Jewish war), or even to disassociate these events from the end-time itself, urging ethical 'watchfulness' as the only appropriate response to a delayed parousia expectation.

My final example concerns the 'abstinence vow' declared by Jesus in Mark 14.25.[115] It is to be noted that Mark has placed this logion in the context of what would have been for his community and the reader a celebration of Jesus' salvific death. In Jesus' own teaching the underlying image, as we have observed, was that of the 'Messianic banquet', his own meals with his disciples, it has often been suggested, acting as a joyful foretaste of the Messianic age. After his death, the primitive community continued to celebrate these shared meals in excited anticipation of his imminent return. Where an earlier more apocalyptic conception saw salvation for the community in terms of participation in the age to come, a more Hellenistic one saw Jesus' death as securing salvation for the individual. Hence in Pauline communities, for example, these shared meals came to be a solemn celebration of his death. Although the saying of 14.25 retains its eschatological emphasis, by placing it in this latter context (14.22–4), Mark may be said to have lessened the impact of its original apocalyptic meaning.

In conclusion, then, I would maintain that Mark himself provides evidence of having interpreted the parables and sayings of Jesus in a 'realized' eschatological way. The Gospel of Mark in its eschatology, therefore, represents an early stage in the transformation of the apocalyptic hope of both Jesus and primitive Jewish Christianity. Jesus 'the Proclaimer' of the coming eschatological Kingdom of God is in process of being seen as 'the Proclaimed' in whose person and ministry the Kingdom was (in another sense) *already* present. This is 'the

---

[115] J. Jeremias, *The Eucharistic Words of Jesus* (Oxford: Blackwell, 1955), pp. 165–72.

secret (or 'mystery') of the Kingdom of God' (Mk 4.11). Eschatology, in other words, is on the way to being eclipsed by Christology and soteriology.

In this section, we have examined the Markan understanding of Jesus' teaching concerning the Kingdom of God. To put this in perspective, we considered first of all how the Kingdom was understood in the nineteenth century and we saw how the prevalent view of the Kingdom as an interior, essentially spiritual reality was challenged by J. Weiss and A. Schweitzer in favour of an eschatological one. We then went on to look at the meaning of the expression in the Old Testament, in the literature of apocalyptic Judaism and in Rabbinic Judaism. I underlined the fact that the understanding of the Kingdom that was determinative for Jesus' own thinking was the eschatological, and indeed, apocalyptic one, and that this conception of the Kingdom is embedded in sayings of the threefold Synoptic tradition that can be traced back to the primary tradition. We also took note of the theory that Jesus had radically departed from an apocalyptic conception of the coming Kingdom, that he had taught a 'realized eschatology' and that he believed apocalyptic expectations were now being fulfilled in a different way in his own person and work.

While acknowledging that a 'realized' element is detectable in the tradition before Mark, I was of the opinion that a 'realized' eschatology should be seen for the most part as a secondary theological development, a highly original, indeed creative response to the failure of primitive apocalyptic expectations. In light of the delay in the parousia or expected end-time, the early church turned its attention less and less to the message of the coming Kingdom which Jesus had proclaimed and more and more to the person of the one who had proclaimed it. The Kingdom was now seen (particularly in Hellenistic Jewish and Gentile communities) as bound up with his person, death and resurrection. Salvation came increasingly to be seen therefore as a present experience realized in union with him and not, as in the Jewish-Christian tradition, as participation in the bliss of the age to come.

It was this movement from eschatology to Christology which I argued could be detected in Mark's treatment of the apocalyptic sayings and parables of Jesus. For him the Kingdom is a secret or mystery intimately connected with Jesus' identity as the concealed Son of God. Mark, it has been noted, has employed a secrecy motif in the service of this epiphany Christology. He has used this motif as a Christological device to interpret, qualify and extend earlier Palestinian traditions of Jesus as teacher, prophet and healer. We have noted in particular how he used it in respect of Jesus' teaching, namely in his 'parables' or 'Kingdom of God' secret (Mk 4.11–12), and reference has also been made to its use in respect of his wonder-working activity, namely the 'miracles' secret (Mk 1.25, 34, 44; 3.11–12; 5.43; 7.36; 8.26). In turning now to the mission of Jesus in Mark, we shall first of all take up the third of these traditions inherited by Mark, that of Jesus as healer and exorcist, and examine the Markan treatment of the miracles.

THE MISSION OF JESUS

'If you only have faith': the nature and function of the miracles in Mark

As before, in order to place the evangelist's treatment in context, let me begin by saying something about the nature of miracles and miracle-workers in the ancient world. The first point to note is the climate of credulousness that there was among the ancients in respect of miracles, prodigies, omens, portents, or what, in biblical terms, were termed 'signs and wonders'. Even as educated and sophisticated a man as the Jewish historian Josephus, while railing against the misguided trust which had been placed by his fellow Jews in eschatological prophets, was nevertheless at pains to point out the omens which God had himself supplied regarding the imminent destruction of Jerusalem: 'Thus it was that the wretched people were deluded at that time by charlatans and pretended messengers of the deity; while they neither heeded nor believed in the manifest portents that foretold the coming desolation, but, as if thunderstruck and bereft of eyes and mind, disregarded the plain warnings of God.'[116]

These portents, Josephus goes on to mention, were the appearance of both a star and a comet, a bright light round the altar and the sanctuary, a cow giving birth to a lamb in the temple, the miraculous opening of the eastern gate of the inner court, chariots in the air and armed battalions in the clouds, and woes against Jerusalem uttered by an eschatological prophet named Jesus, the son of Ananias! When Mark tells us that Jesus too had announced the signs which would herald the fall of Jerusalem (13.1–31), or that the curtain of the temple was torn in two when Jesus died (15.38), or Matthew, in addition, that there was an earthquake at that time which woke the dead (Mt. 27.51–3), then we are encountering a similar religious mentality, the desire for God's apocalyptic intervention and for nature to be responsive to the historic events of human experience.

The world of the evangelists was a world in which magic, thaumaturgy, divination, augury, astrology, and a variety of other superstitions commanded widespread belief. Miracle was no problem, in a sense, for the ancients since they had no developed concept of the laws of nature. Nature was not a closed system, operating in response to laws that could not be violated. Nature, history, human experience were the arena for the action of supernatural forces, gods, angels, divine men, spirits and demons.

Belief in spirits or demons was particularly strong in the New Testament period and thereafter, as both the Gospels and Acts (e.g. Mk 5.1–20; Lk. 11.24–6 = Mt. 12.43–5; Acts 19.11–20) and the Greek Magical Papyri attest.[117] Demons were of many kinds and, as J. M. Hull points out, they were often thought of as possessing bodies, of having physical needs or requiring a home.[118] Exorcism was a prominent feature of Hellenistic

---

[116] See Josephus, *Bellum Judaicum* VI.288 and *The Jewish War* (Loeb Classical Library; London: Heinemann, 1927; New York: G. P. Putnam, 1928), transl. H. St. J. Thackeray, pp. 459–61.

[117] See Barrett, *Background*, pp. 31–8.

[118] J. M. Hull, 'Demons in the NT', *IDB(S)*, p. 225.

magic. Originating in ancient Mesopotamia, it was rare in the
pre-Christian period but common in the first few Christian
centuries.[119]

This was a period too which saw a number of miracle-
workers, both human and divine, with a variety of claims being
made for them. The god, Asclepios, for example, was devoted
to healing. His temples were the hospitals of the ancient world
and a host of cures were attributed to him.[120] Jesus was not
unusual, then, in having a miracle tradition attached to him.
Indeed there are formal similarities between the stories reported of him and those told of other supernaturally endowed
men in the late Hellenistic period as well as of certain rabbis.[121]
Miracles and miracle-workers were, for the ancient world, to
put it crudely, two a penny. What makes the various accounts
distinctive is the range of theological significance attached to
the miracles, and the various religious estimates given to the
miracle-workers in respect of them.

In the Old Testament, for example, the key figures with
whom a miracle tradition is associated are Moses, Elijah and
Elisha (e.g. Exod. 4–14; 1 Kgs 17ff.; 2 Kgs 1ff.). It is of note,
however, that these three figures are not presented in OT
tradition as divine men, although there is evidence that they
were beginning to be thought of in such terms among Hellenistic Jews of Jesus' day. In the OT, the miracles that they
perform confirm their authority as chosen instruments of God,
and validate their role as God's messengers. The miracles, in
other words, point to the power of God whose agents they are,
rather than to their own supernatural status.[122]

A new element makes its appearance, according to H. C.
Kee, in the literature of apocalyptic Judaism, where miracle-
working occupies a central place.[123] Here miracles are inter-

[119] J. M. Hull, 'Exorcism in the NT', *IDB(S)*, pp. 312–4.
[120] S. V. McCasland, 'Miracle', *IDB*, p. 400; D. R. Cartlidge and D. L. Dungan,
Documents for the Study of the Gospels (Cleveland, OH, New York and London: Collins,
1980), pp. 151–3.
[121] H. C. Kee, 'Aretalogy', *IDB(S)*, p. 52.
[122] Of the miracle cycle in Exod. 4–14, H. C. Kee writes: 'It is not the divinity of Moses
that is manifested in these miracles, but the power and purpose of the God who is
using him as his chosen instrument' (Kee, *Community*, p. 25).
[123] 'But during the Hellenistic period in Jewish literature, a new motif begins to

preted eschatologically, that is, as signs of God's intervention to vindicate his people and establish his rule or kingdom (e.g. Dan. 6.27; 7; 9.15ff.). Two types of miracle would indicate when God's supernatural kingdom was about to appear. On the one hand, there would be signs in the heavens or cosmic disturbances.[124] On the other, there would be signs on earth, and one of these signs would be an increase in the number of healings, and especially exorcisms. To appreciate this connection, we must bear in mind the widespread belief in the ancient world that cases of epilepsy, manic depression, schizophrenia, hysteria etc. were the product of demon-possession. For the apocalyptist, demon-possession was evidence of Satan's domination or rule over the present age, and the exorcist was engaged, therefore, in warfare against Satan (Mk 3.22–7; Lk. 10.17–19).

In the texts of this period, a number of eschatological deliverers, therefore, are expected, and prominent among them is the eschatological prophet and miracle-worker.[125] Such figures did appear, many of them charlatans and deceivers, magicians who exploited these popular expectations and beliefs for gain or status.[126] Others, however, were sincere, believing that their paranormal (or magical) gifts and the effect they had on a credulous populace were genuine signs of the inbreaking of the Messianic age.[127]

manifest itself, a motif which had its beginnings in the later prophetic tradition and which was to exercise a potent effect on sectarian Judaism and on early Christianity as well. This motif consists of the affirmation that just as miracles in the past accompanied and made possible the great events by which God delivered his historic people, Israel, from their enemies, so he will act *in the very near future* on the analogy of the Exodus signs and wonders to free his new covenant people in the eschatological epoch which lies ahead. In short, *miracle-working becomes a central ingredient in Jewish eschatological literature*' (Kee, *Community*, p. 27).

[124] See, for example, Joel 2.30–1; *Sibylline Oracles* iii. 767–808 (Barrett, *Background*, pp. 333–4).

[125] Kee, *Community*, pp. 27–9.

[126] A sceptical account of these is given by Celsus; see Origen, *Against Celsus*, 7.9 and M. Smith, 'Aretalogies, Divine Men, the Gospels and Jesus', *JBL*, 90 (1971), p. 180.

[127] Josephus describes these figures thus: 'Besides these [the Sicarii or Jewish 'assassins'] there arose another body of villains, with purer hands but more impious intentions, who no less than the assassins ruined the peace of the city. Deceivers and impostors, under the pretence of divine inspiration fostering revolutionary changes, they persuaded the multitude to act like madmen, and led them out into the desert under the belief that God would there give them tokens of deliverance' (*B. J.* ii.258–9; Loeb, pp. 423–5). Among these was an Egyptian prophet who, intending to take

Exorcism was practised by the rabbis and miracle stories similar in form to the Gospel accounts appear in the rabbinical literature.[128] Honi the Circle-Drawer (or Onias the Righteous), a first century BCE figure, is reported, like Elijah, to have produced rain in response to prayer.[129] Hanina ben Dosa, a first-century Galilean contemporary of Jesus, is reputed to have healed the son of Rabbi Gamaliel at a distance (cf. Mt. 8.5–13 = Lk. 7.1–10) as well as survived being bitten by a poisonous snake (cf. Mk 16.18; Lk. 10.19; Acts 28.3–5).[130] In these rabbinic miracle stories, however, the emphasis is not on eschatology but rather on the efficacy of prayer, the miracle being seen either as a response to the rabbi's piety, or, as in the Old Testament, legitimating his authority, particularly his interpretation of the Law.

The first of these points is illustrated by Hanina's words after the healing in question: 'I am no prophet, nor am I a prophet's son, but this is how I am favoured. If my prayer is fluent in my mouth, I know that he (the sick man) is favoured; if not, I know that it (the disease) is fatal.'[131] The second is illustrated in the famous story of Rabbi Eliezer ben Hyrcanus, a first-century rabbi, who appealed (in vain) to a host of miracles enacted on his behalf (the uprooting of a carob tree, the reversal of a stream, the inclination of the school walls and even a voice from heaven!) in order to establish his own legal judgment over that of his unimpressed colleagues.[132]

Jerusalem, led his followers from the desert to the Mount of Olives (*B. J.* II.261–3; Loeb, pp. 424–5; see Acts 21.38) and Theudas who persuaded his followers to follow him to the river Jordan in the belief that it would part for them (Josephus, *Antiquitates Judaicae* XX.97–8 and *Jewish Antiquities* (Loeb Classical Library; London: Heinemann, 1963; Cambridge, MA: Harvard University Press, 1965), transl. L. H. Feldman, pp. 440–3; see Acts 5.36). See also his description of the prophets other than Jesus, son of Ananias, who were active during the Romano-Jewish War of 66–70 CE (*B. J.* VI.285–7; Loeb, pp. 458–9). Some of the miracles attributed to Jesus himself (e.g. the feedings in the wilderness, Mk 6.34–44 and 8.1–10 par. (see especially Jn 6.14) and his command over the sea, Mk 4.35–41 par.) may hence have originated in connection with this eschatological prophet tradition.

128 P. Fiebig, *Rabbinische Wundergeschichten des neutestamentlichen Zeitalters* (Kleine Texte für Vorlesungen und Übungen, 78; Bonn: A. Marcus & E. Weber, 1911).

129 Vermes, *Jesus*, pp. 69–72.

130 Vermes, *Jesus*, pp. 72–8; Cartlidge and Dungan, *Documents*, pp. 158–9.

131 Vermes, *Jesus*, p. 75.

132 Vermes, *Jesus*, pp. 81–2; Cartlidge and Dungan, *Documents*, pp. 160–2.

The Gospel miracle stories also have parallels with those of the wider Hellenistic world. Miracles were attributed to the Cynic-Stoic wandering teacher-preachers of Asia Minor and Syria (first and second centuries CE), men whom Lucian of Samosata depicted as tricksters, sorcerers and charlatans.[133] Tales abound of Hellenistic miracle-workers who practised the magical art and produced, it was said, marvellous cures of healing and exorcism. The techniques and magical manipulations which they employed are described in our sources (for example, the use of spittle, the application of touch to the part of the body affected, the incantation of a magic formula, usually in an unknown tongue etc.).[134]

Miracles were also attributed to famous wise men or philosophers (for example, Pythagoras), the most famous of these being Apollonius of Tyana who lived in the first century. Philostratus (born *c.* 170 CE) wrote a biography about him based (the claim was made) on an earlier work by Apollonius' disciple Damis. This work describes the portents surrounding his birth, the belief that he was conceived by a god, his precocious childhood, his preternatural gifts (including clairvoyance, oratory, etc.), his travels, his miracles (including exorcisms and raising from the dead), his confrontation with the Emperor Domitian, his death and return from the dead to his disciples. The portrait was influenced both by the Hellenistic magical tradition (Apollonius is presented as a magician) but also as a divine man (*theios anēr*), a supernatural figure, an 'epiphany' or manifestation of God. This latter feature characterizes many of the miracle stories in the Hellenistic tradition. They are not eschatological but *epiphanic*, that is, they point not to the coming end of the world, as in the Jewish apocalyptic tradition, but to the supernatural status of the miracle-worker.[135]

In short, miracles and miracle-workers were common in the

---

[133] See, for example, Smith, 'Aretalogies', p. 181.

[134] See the magical papyri, Barrett, *Background*, pp. 31–8; J. M. Hull, *Hellenistic Magic and the Synoptic Tradition* (Studia biblica et theologica, 28; London: SCM Press, 1974).

[135] See Philostratus, *Life of Apollonius of Tyana*, I.19; IV.44; VII.38; VIII.7, cited in M. Hadas and M. Smith, *Heroes and Gods. Spiritual Biographies in Antiquity* (Religious Perspectives, 13; London: Routledge and Kegan Paul, 1965), pp. 204, 220, 247, 250–3; Porphyry, *Life of Pythagoras*, 27–9, cited in Hadas and Smith, *Heroes*, pp. 116–17.

ancient Hellenistic and Jewish world. The significance of alleged miracles, however, was variously interpreted. In a Jewish environment, and in line with the Old Testament, they have a *legitimating* function. They are seen to validate the authority of a prophet as God's agent, for example, but they do not indicate that the miracle-worker is in any way divine. Within the apocalyptic tradition, they are *eschatological*, serving as pointers to the coming Kingdom of God. In the rabbinic tradition, they provide moral or *pietistic* demonstrations of the efficacy of prayer, or else function also in a *legitimating* way, either to demonstrate the authority of the rabbi or to confirm his interpretation of the Law. Finally, in the wider Hellenistic world, they can be *magical*, demonstrating the miracle-worker's skill as a magician or revealing him as a sorcerer, or *epiphanic*, revealing the miracle-worker as a 'divine man', the 'epiphany' or manifestation of a god.[136]

This overview of the various estimates which were given to miracles and miracle-workers in the ancient world prompts the following question: How were Jesus' miracles understood at the various levels of the developing tradition about him, namely in the primary tradition (i.e. in his lifetime and in the Palestinian Jewish phase of primitive Christianity), within the Hellenistic Jewish and Gentile communities which in turn transmitted them, and finally by Mark himself?

Let us remind ourselves first of all what source criticism has had to say about the origin of the Markan miracle stories. Attempts have been made to demonstrate that extensive cycles of pre-Markan miracle material were available to the evangelist and subsequently used as sources by him. One such view (P. J. Achtemeier) has it that Mark has incorporated (within 4.35–6.44 and 6.45–8.26) a *double cycle* of pre-Markan catenae which present Jesus as a Hellenistic *divine man*. Each parallel catena, or 'chain', comprises a sea miracle (4.35–41 = 6.45–51),

---

[136] A sharp contrast between characteristically Jewish and Hellenistic reactions is provided, on the one hand, by the narrative in Lk. 7.11–17, where Jesus' miracle is greeted by the response, 'A great prophet has arisen among us!' and 'God has visited his people' (v. 16), and, on the other hand, in Acts 14. 8–15, where that of Paul is met by the Lycaonian acclamation, 'The gods have come down to us in the likeness of men!' (see also Acts 28.6).

three healing miracles (5.1–43 = 8.22–6; 7.24–37) and a feeding miracle (6.34–44 = 8.1–10). These catenae originally formed part of a liturgy celebrating an epiphanic Eucharist whose background is to be sought in Hellenistic-Jewish Moses traditions.[137] Another suggestion which has been made (H. C. Kee) is that Mark has incorporated (within 1.23–2.12) a cycle of four miracle stories which are unified in their language, style and cultural setting (Palestinian/Semitic). What is distinctive about these miracles, among other things, is that they present Jesus as *the eschatological agent of God*.[138] A further hypothesis (L. E. Keck) is that Mark has incorporated (within 3.7–12; 4.35–5.43; 6.31–52, 53–6) a *single cycle* of traditional material which portrays Jesus in the colours of the Hellenistic *divine man* in contradistinction to the remaining Markan miracle material 'which is closely related to the Palestinian scene and message of Jesus in its native setting' and which portrays him as *God's eschatological agent* in defeating Satan, 'the Strong One' (3.23–7).[139]

The dualism and other patterning of the miracle material highlighted by these scholars is suggestive but the nature and extent of Markan redactional work makes such theories difficult to substantiate. While Achtemeier's source-critical hypothesis is the most plausible (although not his suggested *Sitz im Leben* for the material), the observed patterning is better seen, in my view, as a product of Mark's redactional activity rather than that of his sources. In common with many scholars today, therefore, I would hold Mark has taken over isolated miracle stories, for the most part, from the tradition (e.g. 11.12–14, 20–5) or possibly small previously linked units (e.g. 5.21–43?) and is himself largely responsible for their arrangement in the gospel. What is of note, however, is the twofold (and contradictory) presentation of Jesus reflected in these sources and drawn to our attention by

---

[137] See P. J. Achtemeier, 'Towards the Isolation of pre-Markan Miracle Catenae', *JBL*, 89 (1970), pp. 245–91 and 'The Origin and Function of the pre-Markan Miracle Catenae', *JBL*, 91 (1972), pp. 198–221. One should also perhaps note an alternative theory of N. Perrin that Mark has incorporated a *double cycle* of material with a different configuration (comprising the pattern, feeding–crossing of the lake– dispute with Pharisees–discourse on bread, which repeats itself in 6.30–7.23 and 8.1–21; cf. also Jn 6); see Duling and Perrin, *New Testament*, pp. 302–3.

[138] Kee, *Community*, pp. 34–6.

[139] L. E. Keck, 'Mark 3[7–12] and Mark's Christology', *JBL*, 84 (1965), pp. 341–58.

these scholars, namely Jesus as the *eschatological agent of God* and Jesus as the Hellenistic *divine man.*

Before we investigate the interrelationship of these two Christological presentations, it is well to summarize what light has in turn been thrown on the Markan miracle accounts by form criticism. Mark gives us eighteen miracle stories, eight of healing (1.29–31; 1.40–5; 2.1–12; 3.1–6; 5.25–34; 7.31–7; 8.22–6; 10.46–52), four of exorcism (1.23–8; 5.1–20; 7.24–30; 9.14–29), one raising from the dead (5.22–4, 35–43), and five so-called nature miracles (4.35–41; 6.30–44, 45–52; 8.1–10; 11.12–14, 20ff.), as well as four generalized summaries of Jesus' miracle-working activity (1.32–4, 39; 3.7–12; 6.53–6) together with certain other allusions to healing or exorcism (3.15, 22; 6.5, 7, 13; 9.38–9).

Constituting the core of the Synoptic miracle material, these stories have a formal structure common to both Jewish and Hellenistic miracle stories. Bultmann has drawn attention, for example, to their basic threefold structure and conventional features, with the *condition* of the patient being recounted (and often heightened by emphasis on the gravity of the illness, its duration, the futile efforts made in the past to effect a cure, the scorn of the crowd at the appearance of the miracle-worker, etc.), the *healing* described (with magical incantation, the use of touch or other manipulations, the absence of witnesses at the moment of healing, etc.), and the *cure* demonstrated (with an action on the part of the patient – or the demon in an exorcism – a reaction from the crowd, or some other visible effects of the cure). In Mark, this basic pattern can be seen in 1.30–1, and a number of the conventional details in 5.1–43 or 7.31–7.[140]

In common with Bultmann, a number of form critics have asserted that the provenance of individual miracle stories is often capable of being established. While Bultmann claimed that most originated in a Hellenistic milieu, and were designed to prove Jesus' superiority over rival miracle-workers, divine-men and gods, other scholars (as we noted with H. C. Kee) have

---

[140] R. Bultmann and K. Kundsin, *Form Criticism. Two Essays on New Testament Research* (New York: Harper, 1962), pp. 36–9. By way of comparison, see Mk 5.1–20 and the exorcism performed by Apollonius of Tyana (Barrett, *Background*, pp. 83–4).

posited a Palestinian origin for some of the material (1.23–6, 29–31, 40–5; 2.1–12).[141] Given the extent of Hellenization within Palestine itself, however, such certainty is no longer possible, but comments on the respective cultural and religious influences upon the tradition itself can be ventured.[142]

It is clear, for example, that some of the Markan stories reflect the influence of the Hellenistic magic tradition, as J. M. Hull has convincingly demonstrated, especially in the case of 7.32–7 (the healing in privacy, the placing of the fingers in the ears, the use of spittle, the intense emotion, the magic formula 'Ephphatha' in what for the reader would have been a foreign language, etc.) and 8.22–6.[143] While there are too many difficulties in describing the genre of the Gospel of Mark as an 'aretalogy', the similarities between these stories and texts such as Philostratus' *Life of Apollonius of Tyana*, or Porphyry's *Life of Pythagoras* also suggest at the very least the influence of a Hellenistic 'divine man' or 'aretalogical' tradition upon the evangelist (or his tradition), especially in respect of the miracle stories of 4.35–8.26. Here is a being who can calm storms (4.35–41) or walk on water (6.45–52), as Pythagoras is described as doing,[144] or awaken numinous awe in his fearful, bewildered disciples ('Who then is this, that even winds and waves obey him?', 4.41), as does Apollonius of Tyana.[145] As with Apollonius too, he can raise a young person from the dead (5.22–4, 35–43).[146] The haemorrhaging woman need only touch him to be made well (5.28), and his supernatural knowledge makes him

---

[141] See also J. Jeremias, *New Testament Theology. Part One: The Proclamation of Jesus* (The New Testament Library; London: SCM Press, 1971), pp. 89–91 for arguments for a *Hellenistic Sitz im Leben* for 7.32–7 and 8.22–6 and a *Palestinian* one for 10.46–52.

[142] 'Thus, for example, it is impossible to say that what is Palestinian is ancient and what is Hellenistic is more recent, once one realizes how far Hellenism had penetrated Palestine, particularly in frontier regions with a mixed population, like the district surrounding Lake Tiberias' (E. Trocmé, *Jesus as Seen by His Contemporaries* (London: SCM Press; Philadelphia, PA: Fortress Press, 1973), p. 103).

[143] Hull, *Magic*, pp. 73–86 and 'Exorcism' in *IDB(S)*, p. 313.

[144] Porphyry, *Life of Pythagoras*, 27–9 (Hadas and Smith, *Heroes*, pp. 116–17 and Cartlidge and Dungan, *Documents*, p. 155).

[145] Philostratus, *Life of Apollonius of Tyana*, IV.44 (Hadas and Smith, *Heroes*, p. 220 and Cartlidge and Dungan, *Documents*, p. 231).

[146] Philostratus, *Life of Apollonius of Tyana*, IV.45 (Hadas and Smith, *Heroes*, pp. 220–1 and Cartlidge and Dungan, *Documents*, p. 231).

aware that power (*dynamis*) has gone out of him (5.29). Like Apollonius, he is also metamorphosed before his disciples and revealed as a supernatural being, the Son of God (9.2–8).[147] Such parallels have led some scholars to see these stories as originating, or being shaped, in the later Hellenistic phase of the tradition.[148]

Others would object and claim, on the contrary, that they show closer parallels with the Old Testament Moses and Elijah/Elisha miracle traditions, and hence a Palestinian origin may be posited for them. 'Command over the sea' miracles are attributed to Moses (Exod. 14) and Elijah (2 Kgs 2.6–8) and 'supernatural feeding' miracles predicated likewise of Moses (Exod. 16) and Elisha (2 Kgs 4.42–4). Of note, too, is the fact that it is these two figures (Moses and Elijah), both expected to appear again at the end-time, who appear with Jesus in 9.2–8. Jesus, therefore, is being presented in a Jewish vein as God's eschatological agent. The influence of the apocalyptic tradition is clearly also reflected in the exorcisms where Jesus' exorcistic activity is viewed in terms of eschatological warfare, the routing of 'the strong man' by one who is bringing his kingdom to an end (3.22–7).[149]

Here, as we have previously observed, we have reached bedrock in the Jesus tradition. When due allowance is made for embellishments, borrowings and even invention on the part of the early church in respect of the miracle tradition, a historical nucleus remains. These exorcism narratives and the Jewish features they display indicate that we are in touch with the primary tradition (see also the Q passage, Mt. 12.28 = Lk. 11.20). Hence a considerable body of present-day scholarship would now hold that there are sufficient grounds, as I have said, for believing that Jesus was a very powerful, skilled and successful exorcist, and that his exorcisms were originally seen in an eschatological light, that is, as blows struck against the

[147] Philostratus, *Life of Apollonius of Tyana*, VII.38; VIII.7 (Hadas and Smith, *Heroes*, pp. 247, 251 and Cartlidge and Dungan, *Documents*, pp. 235–8).

[148] Betz, 'Jesus' in Trotter (ed.), *Jesus*, pp. 114–33; Smith, 'Aretalogies', pp. 174–99.

[149] O. Betz, 'The Concept of the so-called 'divine Man' in Mark's Christology' in D. E. Aune (ed.), *Studies in New Testament and Early Christian Literature (Fs. A. P. Wikgren)* (Leiden: E. J. Brill, 1972), pp. 229–40; Kee, *Community*, pp. 23–30, 32–8.

:ingdom of Satan and as pointers to the rapidly approaching
Kingdom of God (Mk 1.24).

But, to return to our question, how then did Mark interpret
these miracles of Jesus? Did he share this *eschatological* conception of the miracles, viewing them likewise as the signs of an
apocalyptic prophet proclaiming the coming Kingdom of God?
Did he see them, conversely, in *epiphanic* terms, as secret revela-
tions of Jesus' true identity as a supernatural being? To answer
this question, we need to observe what redaction criticism
reveals about his editorial activity. Seven observations can be
made.

In the first place, the evangelist appears to have grouped the
miracle stories and arranged them in specific sections of the
narrative (1.23–2.12; 4.35–5.43; 6.30–56; 7.24–8.26), reporting
only a few isolated stories (3.1–6; 9.14–29; 10.46–52; 11.12–14,
20ff.) and placing all of them in the first half of the Gospel
(1.1–8.26), except for these last three. Secondly, in two, perhaps
three (2.1–12; 3.1–6; 7.24–30?) of the stories, the emphasis is
more on Jesus' words than his actions, or, in form-critical terms,
they have been conformed more to the category of the
apophthegm or pronouncement story (here a controversy dialogue) than of the miracle story. It is of note, moreover, that in
the first of these examples, the evangelist has introduced a
major plot theme, namely Jesus' conflict with the Jewish authorities, and heightened by his redaction the *Christological* thrust of
the story by emphasizing Jesus' authority as the Son of Man to
forgive sins (2.5b–10a). In the second of these examples (3.1–6),
he has developed the conflict theme, ending the story by
informing the reader of the plot by the authorities to kill Jesus
(3.6). The third story (7.24–30) is introduced by the familiar
Markan secrecy motif (7.24), and develops another of the
evangelist's interests, namely Jesus' dealings with Gentiles.

This brings me to my third observation which is that certain
of the miracles within the second of Mark's double cycle
(4.35–6.44/6.45–8.26), namely, this exorcism (7.24–30), the
following healing miracle (7.31–7) and the second feeding story
(8.1–10), appear to have been deliberately placed by the evangelist on Gentile soil (7.24, 31), so demonstrating to his readers

(but perhaps taking liberties with the tradition as a result) that Jesus' miracles in respect of the Jews were matched by those on behalf of the Gentiles.

A fourth point to note is that Mark has used a number of the miracle stories for symbolic purposes. It is surely no accident that he has selected miracles which lend themselves easily to spiritual or theological interpretation (the cure of the blind, deaf or dumb or the raising of the dead; and not, I might add, the treatment of constipation or piles!). The two stories of Jesus' giving sight to the blind (8.22–6; 10.46–52) are placed suggestively at transitional points in the Markan narrative, the first immediately before the reader is informed of Jesus' attempt to get the disciples to see who he really is, the second immediately after the central section in which Jesus provides teaching on the true nature of his mission and the discipleship arising from it.[150] It has long been held that the feeding miracles too, as well as touching on the delicate question of Jew–Gentile relations, have eucharistic overtones, and even if we were to deny them this symbolic dimension, the invitation to see some deeper significance in them is one that is clearly offered to the reader (6.52; 8.14–21). In the secondary context into which the evangelist has introduced it (the cleansing of the temple), the cursing of the fig tree (11.12–14, 20ff.) likewise performs a symbolic function. The fate of the barren temple is prefigured in that of the withered tree.[151]

Fifthly, as in this last passage (11.22–5), the importance of faith and prayer (as opposed to unbelief) in connection with the miracles can be seen to be a Markan emphasis.[152] Here, in this seemingly pietistic interpretation, we appear to have links with a rabbinic view of the miracles (see also 1.27 where Jesus' miracles are connected in a *legitimating* way with his teaching).

[150] Duling and Perrin, *New Testament*, pp. 304–5.

[151] See Telford, *Barren Temple*.

[152] E. Schweizer, 'The Portrayal of the Life of Faith in the Gospel of Mark', *Int*, 32 (1978), pp. 387–99; M. A. Beavis, 'Mark's Teaching on Faith', *BTB*, 16 (1986), pp. 139–42; S. E. Dowd, *Prayer, Power and the Problem of Suffering: Mark 11:22–25 in the Context of Markan Theology* (SBLDS, 105; Atlanta, GA: Scholars Press, 1988); C. D. Marshall, *Faith as a Theme in Mark's Narrative* (SNTSMS, 64; Cambridge: Cambridge University Press, 1989); M. R. Thompson, *The Role of Disbelief in Mark. A New Approach to the Second Gospel* (New York and Mahwah, NJ: Paulist Press, 1989).

The motif also occurs in 4.40, 6.6 and supremely in 9.14–27 (especially 21–4) where the father of the epileptic boy is a prototype of the believing Christian. Faith for Mark, however, as I have elsewhere argued, is connected with understanding, and understanding with the true significance of Jesus' person and mission.[153] Hence a sixth distinctive feature of Mark's treatment of the miracles is that which we have already encountered, namely the *secrecy* with which the evangelist surrounds his miracle-working activity (e.g. 1.25, 34, 44; 3.11–12; 5.43; 7.36; 8.26).

My final observation is related to this, for, if we can detect an *eschatological* significance in the Markan miracles (3.22–7), then it is equally clear that a number of them have been used for *epiphanic* purposes. In addition to the transfiguration story already discussed, two of the miracle stories in particular bring this out (4.35–41; 6.45–52). Even were one to discount the 'aretalogical' influence in these two sea miracles, and opt for a Jewish background, the 'epiphanic' element is nevertheless still very striking, especially when we consider that in the Old Testament it is God himself who is described as stilling the storm (Ps. 65.7; 107.28–9) and walking on the sea (Ps. 77.19; see also Job 9.8; 38.16)![154]

Having commented on the nature of Mark's redaction, we must now consider its significance. While Mark appears to treat the miracles in a variety of ways, two main perspectives seem to be dominant, the eschatological and the Christological. Three main positions can be, and have, therefore, been adopted. The first would hold that the evangelist saw Jesus (as the earlier

---

[153] Telford, *Barren Temple*, p. 82.

[154] See R. H. Fuller, *Interpreting the Miracles* (London: SCM Press, 1963), pp. 53–4, 58–9. Of 4.35–41, Fuller writes: 'So, despite the strong affinities between this story and the pagan miracles, it is not just the portrait of a wonder-worker; it is the story of a divine revelation. The power of Yahweh is present in Jesus, as it was in the original act of creation. The chaos of the world is being restored to its pristine order' (54). Of 6.45–52, he writes: 'The transformed version has the features of divine revelation, for the words "He meant to pass by them", indicate the mysterious behaviour of a divine Being (Exod. 34.6; I Kings 19.11). Note also the terror of the disciples, who thought it was an apparition; the reassurance, "Take heart ... have no fear"; and finally the word of self-manifestation, "I AM" (RSV: "it is I"). Here is revelation of the Old Testament God in the person of Jesus' (58–9).

Jewish-Christian tradition did) as God's eschatological agent, 'the Strong One', the Son of God (= Messiah) whose miracle-working signalled the rout of Satan and the coming of the Kingdom of God (especially 1.12–13; 1.24; 3.11; 3.22–7). A second would hold that the evangelist saw Jesus (in line with the developing Gentile tradition) as the Son of God, as Gentiles not Jews understood that term, that is, as a divine man whose miracles reveal his supernatural status (especially 4.35–41; 6.45–52; 9.1–8).[155]

My own opinion would incline to the second, since it is not the eschatological elements in the miracle material which need explanation (they derive clearly from the Jewish-Christian tradition which Mark has inherited and with which I believe he stands in creative tension) but the epiphanic ones. In light of the secrecy motif pervading the Gospel, moreover, with its correlated themes of divine revelation (epiphany) and spiritual blindness, it would seem plausible that the evangelist is aware that the position he is adopting, and the perspective on Jesus he is seeking to promote, marks a Christological advance on the tradition that he has taken over. The miracles serve, in other words, his epiphany Christology, and it is for this reason, I believe, that the Markan Jesus is made to reject the signs (8.11–13) which as an eschatological prophet he would have been expected to give.[156]

One further view, however, has been espoused, and this is the view that Mark has taken over miracle stories with a divine man Christology, not because he shares this understanding but precisely because he wished to qualify it by setting it alongside a suffering Son of Man Christology. It is for this reason, it has been suggested, that he places the miracles, for the most part, in the first half of the Gospel (1.1–8.26), and is preoccupied in the second half with teaching on discipleship, the passion predictions and the passion narrative. For the reader, the effect of this

---

[155] For a recent and negative appraisal of this position, see Blackburn, *Theios Anēr*. Cf also Tiede, *Charismatic Figure*; Kingsbury, 'Divine Man', pp. 243–57.

[156] Cf. 'The movement from eschatology to Christology, which can be seen in the case of signs is typical of the transition in early Christianity from an eager expectation of the return of Jesus in apocalyptic glory to a perception of God's glory in or behind his earthly ministry' (D. M. Smith, 'Sign in the NT', *IDB(S)*, p. 825).

juxtaposition is to say: Jesus' true significance is not to be seen
as merely that of a miracle-worker (or teacher or prophet) but
can only fully be appreciated in light of his crucifixion and
resurrection. His true identity, in other words, is not to be
interpreted in his miracle-working alone but must be perceived
sub specie crucis et resurrectionis.[157]

'*The Son of Man must suffer*': eschatology and soteriology

Before going on to explore Mark's eschatology and soteriology,
it might be worth summing up the points we have covered in
our discussion of the mission of Jesus in Mark. We have
examined first of all the nature and function of the miracles in
the Second Gospel. In order to give this study a wider context,
we began by looking at the understanding of miracles and
miracle-workers in the ancient world (in the Old Testament, in
apocalyptic Judaism, in Rabbinic Judaism and within the wider
Hellenistic world). We saw that in a predominantly Jewish
environment, miracles were seen as legitimating the authority
of the miracle-worker as God's agent but were not seen in
general as pointing to his divine or supernatural status. In the
Old Testament, the miracles attributed to Moses, Elijah and
Elisha proved that they were acting on God's behalf. In apocalyptic Judaism, miracles were seen as signs that God's Kingdom
was about to break in and the miracle-worker seen as God's
eschatological agent. In Rabbinic Judaism, the miracles vali-
dated a rabbi's authority, especially his interpretation of the
Law, and demonstrated the efficacy of prayer and piety. In the
wider Hellenistic world, miracles were often seen as the product
of magic and sorcery or as evidence that the miracle-worker
was a god or a manifestation or epiphany of a god, a Son of
God, or a divine man.

We then turned to the question of how Mark understood the
miracle stories he took over from the tradition, and how the
tradition itself understood them. Two theories were mentioned.
The first was that Mark saw the miracles in a Jewish light as the

[157] T. J. Weeden, *Mark – Traditions in Conflict* (Philadelphia, PA: Fortress Press, 1971) and
'Heresy' in Telford (ed.), *Interpretation*, pp. 89–104.

action of God's eschatological redeemer, the Messiah, and that the Markan Gospel should be viewed within the framework of Jewish apocalyptic thought. The second was that Mark saw the miracles in a more Hellenistic light as the action of a divine man, a *theios anēr*, the supernatural Son of God. My own view is that both understandings are found in the traditional material taken over by Mark (and the second particularly in Mk 4.35–8.26) but that the Markan emphasis lies more with the second of these interpretations (the miracle as manifestation of the Son of God as divine man) than with the first (the miracle as manifestation of the Messiah). This Messianic interpretation Mark is seeking, if anything, either to modify or even combat.

Miracles are placed for the most part in the first half of the Gospel and lead to the central passage, viewed by most scholars as the watershed of the Gospel, the confession at Caesarea Philippi (Mk 8.27–9.1). In this climactic passage, as we have already seen, Jesus is made to enquire of the disciples what estimate the Jewish people are placing on him in view of the miracles and teaching which the evangelist has recounted. The popular Jewish estimation, on the basis of these, Mark tells us, is that he is seen as an eschatological prophet, either John the Baptist *redivivus*, Elijah or another of the prophets expected at the end-time. When asked their estimate of Jesus, the disciples, with Peter as their spokesman, say that they believe him to be the 'Anointed One', the Jewish Messiah, the royal, earthly and political figure expected in some circles to usher in the Kingdom of God, the Christ (Mk 8.30), or the apocalyptic figure of heavenly origin expected in certain others. In the carefully constructed section of the Gospel that follows (8.31–10.45), Mark, however, goes on to indicate that this understanding is faulty or inadequate.

Here we may recall N. Perrin's observation[158] that this central section of the Gospel is constructed around three

---

[158] Perrin has discussed this passage in a number of publications; see e.g. 'The Christology of Mark: a Study in Methodology' in Telford (ed.), *Interpretation*, pp. 125–40 (with Duling); *New Testament*, pp. 309–12; 'Son of Man' in *IDB(S)*, pp. 833–6; 'The Literary Gattung "Gospel" – Some Observations', *ExpT*, 82 (1970–1), pp. 4–7; 'The Creative Use of the Son of Man Traditions by Mark', *Union Seminary Quarterly Review*, 23 (1967–8), pp. 357–65.

passion predictions which Mark has composed in which Jesus refers to himself *not* as the earthly, political Messiah or Christ but as the *Son of Man*. The Markan Jesus, however, emphasizes that his immediate destiny is not to be that of the triumphant Messianic warrior-king nor even of a 'Son of Man' who, as a glorious, exalted, victorious figure will ultimately come to execute judgment, but rather to be that of a 'Son of Man' who is to be rejected by the Jews, to suffer, to die and rise again (Mk 8.31; 9.31; 10.33–4). Each prediction, Perrin noted, is preceded by a geographical reference which is redactional (Mk 8.27; 9.30; 10.32). Each is followed by a scene depicting a complete misunderstanding on the part of the disciples with respect to what Jesus is telling them about his true destiny and role (Mk 8.32–3; 9.32, 33–4; 10.35–41). Each misunderstanding scene is followed by a further scene in which Jesus is shown teaching what the true nature of Christian discipleship is in light of a correct understanding of Jesus' person and work (Mk 8.34–9.1; 9.35–7; 10.42–5). The central section then ends with another climactic 'Son of Man' saying (Mk 10.45). What is the significance of Mark's careful redactional work? To understand this, we need to look at the meaning, history and background of the term 'Son of Man' in the Jewish literature of the Hellenistic period.[159]

In the Old Testament, the term 'son of man' is used as a substitute for, or in parallel with the term 'man', and hence to signify 'humankind' ('What is man that thou are mindful of him, or the son of man that thou dost care for him? Ps. 8.4; see also Ps. 80.17; Num. 23.19; Isa. 56.2). In a number of cases, it is an expression denoting the humble creatureliness and mortality of man vis-à-vis his transcendent Creator or God (Ps. 146.3; Job 25.1–6; Isa. 51.12), and thence by extension it serves as a title by which God addresses the prophet or seer (Ezek. 2.1; Dan. 8.17). As we observed when examining the background to the

---

[159] For some important or helpful discussions see S. E. Johnson, 'Son of Man' in *IDB*, pp. 413–20; B. Lindars, 'Son of Man' in *DBI*, pp. 639–42; Perrin, *Kingdom*, pp. 90–111; Perrin, 'Son of Man' in *IDB(S)*, pp. 833–6; H. E. Tödt, *The Son of Man in the Synoptic Tradition* (The New Testament Library; Philadelphia, PA: Westminster Press; London: SCM Press, 1965); Vermes, *Jesus*, pp. 160–91.

Kingdom of God in Mark, the belief that God would act on behalf of his chosen people to defeat the present kingdom or empires of the world and re-establish his reign or kingdom on earth was a prominent one in apocalyptic Judaism (Dan. 7.1ff.). In some cases, we noted, God himself was seen as the sole agent in establishing his Kingdom (*Ass. Mos.* 10). In other cases, a variety of redeemer figures or eschatological agents were seen as acting as his intermediaries. These might be earthly figures such as the earthly, 'anointed' king (Ps. 2), or a descendant of David, the 'root from the stem of Jesse' (Isa. 11.1–5), or the 'Son of David' (*Ps. Sol.* 17). These might also be heavenly figures, such as the archangel Michael (Dan. 12.1ff.) or earthly figures who had been 'translated' to heaven, like Enoch (Gen. 5.24) or Elijah (2 Kgs 2.11; Mal. 4.5; Mk 9.11–13) or Moses, and who were believed to return and play a role at the end-time.

There are three main sources in apocalyptic Judaism in which the expression 'son of man' appears (the passages were cited above). The first is, of course, Daniel 7 itself, where, as we have seen, the seer has a vision involving four great beasts: one like a lion (Dan. 7.4) representing the Babylonian Empire, one like a bear (7.5) representing the Medes, one like a leopard (7.6) representing the Persians, and another great beast with ten horns (7.7) which appears to represent the Greeks. The little horn, with a mouth speaking great things (7.8) represents, it is thought, Antiochus Epiphanes. In the vision, Daniel sees the throne of the Ancient of Days (7.9), the beasts are destroyed (7.11–12) and 'one like a son of man', representing 'the saints of the Most High' (7.18, 22, 27) is presented to the Ancient of Days and given dominion for ever (7.13–14). The passage expresses belief in the vindication of Israel under the oppression of the Seleucid dynasty in the first half of the second century BCE, the 'one like a son of man' being either an angelic being, the nation itself, the future Messiah, or more likely a corporate and symbolic figure standing for the martyrs of the nation who had died in the Maccabean wars.

A further stage in the development of the concept is seen in the Enoch literature whose overall compilation may have begun sometime in the third century BCE but may not have been complete until the first century CE.[160] Here, we recall, a belief is entertained in a heavenly apocalyptic redeemer who has been hidden by God in heaven from the beginning but who will be revealed to the elect at the end-time. He is described as 'the Righteous and Elect One' and 'the [Lord's] Anointed' (Ps. 2.2) and given attributes mentioned in Isaiah 11.1–5. In the previously cited part of 1 Enoch (chapters 37–71) known as the 'Similitudes of Enoch' (which most scholars think are pre-Christian or if post-Christian – on account of their absence from Qumran – show no sign of Christian influence[161]), he is described as 'that Son of Man'. The corporate, symbolic figure of Daniel 7.13, in other words, has now become a transcendent, exalted, supernatural figure. All judgment is given over to him and he will sit on the throne of his glory judging the nations, punishing the wicked and vindicating the righteous. There is no hint that his role will involve any personal suffering, however, and the enigmatic figure is identified by the final redactor of Enoch as Enoch himself (Gen. 5.24).

The third passage comes in 4 Ezra (or II Esdras) 13, a late first-century CE text also previously quoted. Here belief is likewise entertained in a 'man-like' apocalyptic redeemer who will be God's eschatological agent at the end of time. In a dream, the seer, we recollect, sees a figure in the form of a man emerge from the sea and fly with the clouds of heaven. The figure strikes terror in his enemies, slaying them with the breath of his mouth. Daniel 7.13 and Isaiah 11.4 are again the inspiration for the picture painted of this apocalyptic figure, the passage reflecting a combination of the two separate traditions of the 'one like a son of man' and the Davidic Messiah. Once more, however, there is no hint that his apocalyptic role is to be accomplished by means of personal suffering.

Even if we cannot conclude from these three passages alone that there was a normal or even widespread belief or expectation in pre-Christian Judaism of a Messianic agent titled the '(Son of) Man',[162] it is surely reasonable to assume that *in some*

---

[160] See Rowland, *Open Heaven*, p. 266.
[161] See, for example, Rowland, *Open Heaven*, p. 265.
[162] For the view that 'it is not possible to speak with any confidence of a pre-Christian

apocalyptic circles at least speculation on the enigmatic figure of Daniel 7 had given rise to such a concept. While the 'Similitudes of Enoch' may, and 4 Ezra certainly does overlap with the early Christian period, the lack of any otherwise specifically Christian features in these texts suggests that they may reasonably be taken to represent a Jewish Messianic concept substantially uninfluenced by nascent Christianity. In sum, then, the expression 'son of man' can be found as an ordinary Jewish expression for a 'man', 'humankind' or a 'human being' viewed in all his frailty, creatureliness and mortality. At the other end of the spectrum, in the apocalyptic literature, the expression, following Daniel 7 ('one like a son of man') is used in connection with, or even as a designation for, an exalted, transcendent, supernatural apocalyptic redeemer who will appear at the end-time to judge the world, punish the wicked and vindicate the righteous. Apart from Daniel itself, however, there is no suggestion that this figure is to fulfil his Messianic role by suffering, far less by dying and rising again.

When we turn to the New Testament literature we find the self-same enigmatic term used some eighty-two times in the Gospels, sixty-nine of these in the Synoptics, though curiously, apart from Acts 7.56 and Revelation 1.13; 14.14 nowhere else. Outside the New Testament, it appears on one occasion only, on the lips of James, Jesus' brother and leader of the Jerusalem church at his martyrdom.[163] Paul does not use the expression although he does refer to Jesus as the second Adam, and views him within the categories of the 'heavenly Man' idea (Rom. 5. 14–19; 1 Cor. 15.21–3, 45–50; Phil. 2.5–11).[164] In the Gospel

---

Son of Man concept', see Dunn, *Christology*, p. 95, as well as Lindars, 'Son of Man' in *DBI*, pp. 639–42. For an equally cautious evaluation of the evidence, see Rowland, *Open Heaven*, pp. 178–88. While doubting the existence of any coherent , clear-cut or readily understood Jewish Son of Man concept, Rowland nevertheless concludes that 'there is reason to suppose that there were beliefs in a heavenly man figure in Judaism and also an emerging belief that the messianic agent was pre-existent' (p. 188).

[163] See Eusebius, *Ecclesiastical History* II.23.13, Loeb, p. 173.

[164] Philo, it should also be noted, speaks of a heavenly man, the archetype of humanity, who was created in addition to Adam at the beginning of the world and who is also the *Logos*, the first-born Son of God and prototype of Israel. See, for example, Fuller, *Foundations*, pp. 76–8.

tradition (with the exception of Jn 12.34 where it nevertheless picks up a remark of Jesus), it appears exclusively on the lips of Jesus, in many cases as a self-designation.

How then is 'Son of Man' in the Gospels to be understood. Is it to be seen in the apocalyptic sense as a title for the expected apocalyptic redeemer of the Enoch literature, or is its usage much more mundane? Let us consider the Synoptic tradition, apart from Mark, before we go on to look at the term in the Second Gospel. Apart from the Markan Gospel, the earliest attestation of the use of the expression comes in the Q source underlying Matthew and Luke. Here the 'Son of Man' sayings, of which there are some ten examples, divide into two groups. The first group features the use of the expression as a self-designation for Jesus (= 'I') with no apparent apocalyptic connotations (e.g. Lk. 6.22? cf. Mt. 5.11; Lk. 7.34 = Mt. 11.19; Lk. 9.58 = Mt. 8.20; Lk. 12.10 = Mt. 12.32). The second group, however, presents us with the 'Son of Man' as a transcendental, exalted apocalyptic figure, not necessarily always to be identified with Jesus, whose coming in judgment at the end-time will be sudden, dramatic and unexpected (cf. Lk. 11.30 = Mt. 12.40?; Lk. 12.8? cf. Mt. 10.32–3; Lk. 12.40 = Mt. 24.44; Lk. 17.24 = Mt. 24.27; Lk. 17.26 = Mt. 24.37, 39; Mt. 19.28? cf. Lk. 22.29–30).[165]

Matthew takes over a number of the 'Son of Man' sayings in Mark and Q, but he also has eight additional instances of the usage which are peculiar to himself, which seem for the most part to be redactional (though some may be from Q), and which see the 'Son of Man', in most cases, in the apocalyptic sense as the coming heavenly judge (Mt. 10.23; 13.37, 41; 16.13, 28; 24.30; 25.31; 26.2). In some passages, he clearly identifies this figure with Jesus (Mt. 16.13, 28; 19.28; 26.2). Luke has seven additional usages peculiar to himself (again several may possibly be from Q), some bearing the apocalyptic sense (Lk. 17.22, 30; 18.8; 21.36), others with no such obvious reference (Lk. 19.10; 22.48; 24.7). Where Matthew, with his links with Jewish Christianity, emphasizes the coming of the apocalyptic Son of Man,

---

[165] Lk. 12.10 = Mt. 12.32 is perhaps a special case. Here an original generic 'son of man = mankind' (Mk 3.28) may have been misinterpreted in a titular sense. See also Mk 2.10, 28 and Jeremias, *Theology*, p. 261.

Luke, in debt to Gentile Christianity, tends, if anything, to de-emphasize it.[166] John too presents his readers with Son of Man sayings, rendering the expression some thirteen times in all (Jn 1.51; 3.13, 14; 5.27; 6.27, 53, 62; 8.28; 9.35; 12.23, 34 (twice); 13.31), and these also reflect the usage found in the Synoptic Gospels. One important additional feature, however, is that the Son of Man is not only identified with Jesus but is presented as a pre-existent descending/ascending transcendent being, whose glorification is accomplished not at his parousia but on the cross. To sum up, then, both usages, the ordinary, linguistic, non-titular or generic usage of 'son of man' which occurs in the Old Testament (in the Psalms, for example) and the titular, apocalyptic usage met with in the Enoch literature are to be found in the Gospels. All five strata (namely Mark, Q, special Matthew, special Luke and John) place the expression exclusively on Jesus' lips, where he uses it in the third-person form, thereby ostensibly distinguishing himself (where it is not a circumlocution) from this figure.

To account for this puzzling phenomenon, various theories have been suggested. One theory would claim that the non-titular, linguistic or generic usage goes back to the primary tradition and the apocalyptic usage is secondary arising out of a misinterpretation of the use of the expression by Jesus. By a process of mistranslation coupled with misunderstanding the expression 'son of man' used by Jesus as a circumlocutory self-designation (= 'I') came to be viewed as a title for the apocalyptic redeemer 'the Son of Man'.[167] A second hypothesis is that the apocalyptic background to the term is primary, Jesus having shared the same kind of apocalyptic expectation as was entertained in Enoch circles. As part of his Kingdom procla-mation, he may have announced the coming of an apocalyptic redeemer, the 'Son of Man', at the end-time. Alternatively, he may have referred to himself as this apocalyptic 'Son of Man'. Whatever the case, the primitive church, after his resurrection, certainly did identify him as this enigmatic figure.[168] This view,

---

[166] See Perrin, 'Son of Man' in *IDB(S)*, p. 836.
[167] See Vermes, *Jesus*, pp. 160–91.
[168] See Bultmann, *Theology*, Vol. I, pp. 28–32; Tödt, *Son of Man*.

which I myself would share, accepts then that, alongside a more
popular 'Son of David' expectation, the concept of a pre-
existent divine agent of judgment and salvation did exist in pre-
Christian Judaism, albeit in more esoteric circles, and was the
source for the 'Son of Man' as used by Jesus and/or the
primitive church in eschatological proclamation.[169] A third
position is that Jesus used the term 'Son of Man' for himself but
departed from the apocalyptic thought of Enoch by giving the
term his own enigmatic content.[170] Such content, for example,
may have revolved around the themes of suffering, rejection
and vindication and been derived from the nature of the
corporate 'one like a son of man' figure of Daniel 7 combined
with the Suffering Servant of Isaiah 53.

Such variation in scholarly hypotheses points to the ambiguity surrounding the Gospel evidence. However, before we
seek to unravel the nature and significance of the Son of Man
sayings in Mark, it is worth reminding ourselves of the results of
traditio-critical analysis in this complicated area.[171] Where
classification is concerned, the sayings have traditionally been
divided into three categories by virtue of their distinctive (and
only occasionally overlapping) themes. One group, the so-called
present sayings, are united by the fact that Jesus makes reference
to himself as Son of Man in connection with his present, earthly
activity. In the second group, the *passion* or *suffering* sayings,
Jesus, *qua* Son of Man, speaks of his approaching suffering,
death and resurrection. The third group, the *future* or *apocalyptic*

---

[169] In support of this judgment, see, for example, F. H. Borsch, *The Christian and Gnostic Son of Man (Studies in Biblical Theology*, II/14; London: SCM Press, 1970), p. 116; Fuller, *Foundations*, pp. 37–42; Hahn, *Titles*, p. 20; Kee, *Community*, p. 135; Kümmel, *Theology*, p. 78; G. E. Ladd, *A Theology of the New Testament* (Grand Rapids, MI: Eerdmans, 1974), p. 149; Tödt, *Son of Man*, p. 222. For a contrary view, see, for example, M. Casey, *Son of Man. The Interpretation and Influence of Daniel 7* (London: SPCK, 1979), ch. 5; Dunn, *Christology*, pp. 95–6; B. Lindars, *Jesus Son of Man. A Fresh Examination of the Son of Man Sayings in the Gospels in the Light of Recent Research* (London: SPCK; Grand Rapids, MI: Eerdmans, 1983), p. 8; Vermes, *Jesus*, p. 168.

[170] See, for example, M. D. Hooker, *The Son of Man in Mark. A Study of the Background of the Term 'Son of Man' and its Use in St Mark's Gospel* (London: SPCK; Montreal: McGill University Press, 1967); Manson, *Teaching*, p. 227; Moule, *Christology*, pp. 11–22; E. Schweizer, *The Good News according to Mark* (London: SPCK, 1971), pp. 166–71.

[171] See, for example, Bultmann, *Theology*, Vol. 1, pp. 28–30; Fuller, *Mission*, pp. 95–108; Fuller, *Foundations*, pp. 119–25; Jeremias, *Theology*, pp. 258–64.

sayings depict Jesus (or a separate figure) as one to come in judgment and glory at the end-time.

When we turn to Mark, we note that all three categories of Son of Man saying are represented among the fourteen instances of its use. Reflected in the Gospel is the conception of the Son of Man as an exalted, apocalyptic figure who (according to expectation) will return from heaven in glory to judge or save the world (Mk 8.38; 13.26; 14.62). A further and prominent series of sayings emphasizes, however, that this self-same Son of Man (in the person of Jesus) was nevertheless destined (contrary to expectation) to suffer, die and rise again (Mk 8.31; 9.9, 12, 31; 10.33–4; 10.45; 14.21 (twice), 41). A third group (Mk 2.10, 28), if they are not to be interpreted merely in a generic sense (compare Mk 2.10 with Mt. 9.8 or Mk 3.28 and parallels), also informs the reader that the Son of Man (again in the person of Jesus) is already exercising his authority as such on earth.

Comparison with our other early source of Jesus tradition, namely Q, is instructive at this point. Q presents us with material in which both 'future' and 'present' sayings are represented. Since Q therefore has reference to the Son of Man as a transcendental, exalted apocalyptic figure to come in the future (as well as one who in the person of Jesus was already acting as such on earth), then we must assume that, unless Mark has borrowed from Q or vice versa, both are dependent upon a more primitive tradition in this respect. In other words, Jesus' prediction of the coming of this figure (and perhaps too of his present authority) and/or the early church's identification of this figure with Jesus *predates* Mark, and the 'future' sayings incorporated by him (as well as Mark's 'present' ones?) must therefore go back at least to the Jewish-Christian tradition before him.

On the other hand, Q shows no evidence whatsoever of any sayings in the 'suffering' category. While it may be claimed that the notion of rejection is associated with the Son of Man (Lk. 9.58 = Mt. 8.20) or even death (Mt. 12.40; cf. Lk. 11.30), nowhere in the Q tradition is it ever said, or even hinted, that the Son of Man was *destined* to suffer, die and rise again. This emphasis is a distinctively Markan one. Apart from its absence in Q, it occurs elsewhere in the Synoptic Gospels only where Matthew and Luke are borrowing from Mark, or (as in Mt. 26.2; Lk. 22.22; 24.7) editing him. The emphasis, moreover, occurs solely in connection with the Markan passion predictions, the passion narrative or the material otherwise anticipating it. Nowhere do the Markan 'future' sayings speak of 'suffering', and nowhere do the 'suffering' sayings speak of the Son of Man's parousia or future glorification. Q, it is to be noted, significantly lacks any passion narrative, and in consequence any reflection on the significance of Jesus' death and resurrection for the community.

Here then, with N. Perrin, I detect a major contribution on the part of Mark to the developing Son of Man tradition. While rejecting a Jewish-Christian identification of Jesus as the Davidic Messiah, Mark appears to have accepted with qualifications a traditional Jewish-Christian identification of Jesus as the victorious apocalyptic Son of Man about to return (shortly) to bring judgment and salvation. In the circles which produced the Enoch literature or 4 Ezra, the Son of Man or the 'Man' was a triumphal figure with whom the notion of salvific suffering appears not to have been associated. Ideas related to the Suffering Servant of Isaiah, for example, seem not to have been drawn into connection with this figure to produce a Messiah whose role would thus be effected through suffering and death. In early Christian circles, on the other hand, the fact of Jesus' suffering and death at the hands of his enemies was a fact of history, and had therefore to be taken account of in some way in its developing eschatology and soteriology. A crucified Messiah was a novelty ('a stumbling block to Jews and folly to Gentiles', Rom. 1.23) but as long as the resurrection could be seen as God's vindication of his Messiah, his subsequent and imminent parousia would speedily resolve all problems.

The delay of the parousia, however, must have posed a special problem for the primitive community. What could be said for a crucified eschatological prophet raised to the status of Messiah through resurrection (Rom. 1.4; Acts 2.32–6) if he failed to return as promised to inaugurate the new age? Paul himself, in his own way, had grappled with this problem, and his theology of the cross was the result. Jesus was to be considered the divine 'Son of God' and his death itself had brought salvation to the world. The cross, in other words, was pre-ordained, the heavenly one sent for the salvation of the world being fore-ordained to suffer, and through his death achieve that salvation. By virtue of its absence from Q, salvific suffering of this kind does not appear to have been a significant element in the theology of the Q community. What we discern in Mark, by contrast, is the claim that Jesus as Son of Man had not only already begun to exercise his eschatological role on earth, by virtue of the authority demonstrated in his teaching and activity (2.10, 28) but had done so supremely by means of his pre-ordained suffering, death and resurrection (Mk 8.31; 10.45). It is no accident then that Mark 10.45 ('For the Son of Man also came not to be served but to serve, and to give his life as a ransom for many') comes at the climax of the central section of the Gospel (Mk 8.27–10.45), and immediately prior to the start of the passion narrative. While Mark does not cite Isaiah 53, his passion narrative itself, as I have stated elsewhere, is suffused with motifs relating to it (compare Isa. 53.7 'opened not his mouth' and Mk 14.61 and 15.5; Isa. 53.12 'numbered with the transgressors' and Mk 14.48 and 15.27; Isa. 53.9 'made his grave ... with a rich man' and Mk 15.43–6).[172] The fact of Jesus' death has acted back on the Messianic theology of the primitive tradition, and as a result the apocalyptic Son of Man has been transformed into the suffering Son of Man.[173]

The Gospel of Mark represents then a stage in the process by which the apocalyptic Son of Man who saves (or judges)

---

[172] See W. R. Telford, *Mark* (New Testament Guides; Sheffield: Sheffield Academic Press, 1995), p. 107.

[173] Whether the suffering Son of Man is wholly an invention of Mark , or owes a debt to a theological impulse at work already in the pre-Markan tradition is difficult to say. While N. Perrin is of the opinion that 'the evangelist develops into major christological emphases what were previously only tentative uses of the Son-of-man concept' ('Son of Man' in *IDB(S)*, p. 836), he asserts that the Markan passion predictions are entirely Markan creations. Other scholars hold the view that the need to affirm the necessity of the passion was a tendency operative in the (Palestinian) tradition before him. See, for example, Fuller, *Mission*, p. 106; Tödt, *Son of Man*, p. 276.

humankind at his parousia becomes the suffering Son of Man who saves humankind by his redemptive death on the cross. Whether this demonstrates the influence of Paul or Paulinism on Mark is a question we shall consider in chapter 3. Nevertheless, the key to the Markan Gospel is once again to see it as a Christological or soteriological narrative in which its central character is playing out a divine destiny revealed only to those with eyes to see. Through his use of this enigmatic 'Son of Man' Christology, with its associations both transcendent and esoteric, Mark has essentially extended the secrecy motif to the tradition of the death and resurrection of Jesus (Mk 9.9) just as he had to the parables, the Kingdom of God and the miracles. Though expressed in story form, his Gospel is a highly theological document which puts a distinctively religious perspective on Jesus' life and death, and seeks to persuade the reader to see him in the right light. It does so, as I have argued, by taking over traditions already stamped with certain theological understandings, and it seeks in turn to develop, or combat, these earlier, sometimes different understandings. One of the ways it does so is to place these 'correct' or 'incorrect' understandings on the lips of the different characters who feature in the narrative, and it is to two such important groups of characters in the Markan drama, namely, the Jewish leaders and the disciples, to whom we shall now turn.

Before we do so, let me sum up. Thus far, we have discussed the second evangelist's conception of the person, message and mission of Jesus. We have looked at the variety of traditional material Mark has taken over (for example, parables, 'Kingdom of God' and 'Son of Man' sayings, miracles stories) and at the process by which he has selected, arranged, altered or modified this traditional material in order to produce our first connected Gospel. By now, it should be becoming clear that the major thrust of Mark's redactional procedure is to further the evangelist's Christological and soteriological aims. By presenting the traditions at his disposal in the way that he has, he wishes to present Jesus to his readers as the bearer of the concealed dignity or status of God's only Son. This 'Son' is a supernatural figure whose predestined role, while still that of the apocalyptic

Son of Man of the Jewish-Christian tradition, nevertheless differed from that expected of this exalted redeemer figure in that it involved, prior to his ultimate vindication, his preordained suffering and death on the cross. How was this 'Son of God' incognito, this apocalyptic 'Son of Man' of Jewish-Christian faith, this 'divine man' of Gentile-Christian estimation, received by his own people, the Jews? How in particular does Mark treat the Jewish leaders and the disciples and how does such a treatment further serve the evangelist's overall purpose?

SUPPORT AND OPPOSITION: HEROES AND VILLAINS IN THE MARKAN DRAMA

'The leaven of the Pharisees': Mark's treatment of the Jewish leaders

As before, I shall place our examination in context by first offering some background on the Jewish leadership groups as they are presented to us in the Gospels. What, briefly, do they tell us of the Jewish leadership groups active in the time of Jesus? The Gospels speak of the Jewish authorities in respect of six main groups: the Pharisees, the Sadducees, the Herodians, the chief priests, the scribes and the elders. The Pharisees are the most prominent group in the Gospels, but are also known to us from elsewhere in the New Testament, as well as from Josephus and rabbinic sources. As a group, it appears that they were in the ascendancy after the Fall of Jerusalem in 70 CE, and in the nineties practically a para-legal government. They became the main opponents of early Christianity, with power to ban Jewish Christians from the synagogue. Before 70 CE, however, it seems that they were less influential. Some scholars point to the paucity of evidence outside of the Gospels which might suggest that the Pharisees had in fact any substantial presence in Galilee during Jesus' lifetime.[174] In this period they were eclipsed in power and influence by the Sadducees. The most prominent sectarian group before 70, the Sadducees were practically non-existent thereafter. Reference to them in the

---

[174] See M. Smith, *Jesus the Magician* (New York and London: Harper & Row, 1978), pp. 153–7.

Gospels is meagre, with no mention being made of them at all in John's Gospel.

The third group, the Herodians, are obscure to us. No such party is known to have existed in Jesus' lifetime. Some scholars hold them to be officials of the tetrarch, others to be notables won over to the Herodian dynasty.[175] Mark speaks of an alliance between them and the Pharisees (Mk 3.6) but this unlikely conjunction has been viewed with suspicion. The only historical alliance between Pharisees and Herodians we know of occurred in 66–7 CE when moderate Pharisees, in seeking to prevent the holocaust they knew would be the result of war with Rome, joined with the circle around Herod Agrippa II in denouncing to the Romans those groups with apocalyptic and Messianic views or expectations. A similar alliance may have been forged earlier in the period when Herod Agrippa I (41–4 CE) was given the governance of Judaea by Claudius and sought similarly to weave a moderate road between the interests of Rome in this area, and the desire on the part of the Jews for religious autonomy.[176] It is Agrippa I who is held responsible by the writer of Acts (12.1ff.) for the persecution of the primitive Jewish-Christian community.

The three other groups mentioned in the Gospels, chief priests, elders and scribes, are also somewhat obscure to us, and there is considerable scholarly debate as to who exactly they were. Where the scribes are concerned, for example, different opinions prevail. Some hold that the scribes were a sub-group of the Pharisees, an intellectual élite, others that they were a clerical class common to both Pharisees and Sadducees, others still that they were a separate group altogether whose influence declined after 70. These various views are based primarily on the ambiguous interpretation of only a few New Testament verses, namely Mark 2.16 (where, in a disputed reading, the

---

[175] H. H. Rowley, 'The Herodians in the Gospels', *JTS*, 41 (1940), pp. 14–27; *gratia* E. Trocmé, *The Formation of the Gospel According to Mark* (London: SPCK, 1975), p. 91, n. 1.

[176] P. Winter, *On the Trial of Jesus* (Studia Judaica, Forschungen zur Wissenschaft des Judentums, 1; Berlin and New York: Walter de Gruyter, 1961), p. 128.

evangelist speaks of 'the scribes of the Pharisees'); 7.1, 3, 5 and Acts 23.9 ('the scribes of the Pharisees').

It is often assumed that although these groups are obscure to us (apart from the Pharisees), they would have been familiar to the evangelists. This view, however, was challenged in a book by M. J. Cook entitled *Mark's Treatment of the Jewish Leaders* (1978).[177] Since the Gospels were written after 70 CE, and each of these leadership groups, apart from the Pharisees, ceased to be active after then, Cook argues for the probability that the evangelists themselves were not entirely sure who these groups were and had therefore to rely on their sources for information. In the case of Matthew and Luke, their main source was Mark. It is Cook's claim that Matthew and Luke's redaction of Mark reveals that they knew no more about who the Herodians, Sadducees, chief priests, scribes and elders were than their source Mark did, and as a result add little or nothing to our knowledge of them. Where Mark refers to the Herodians, for example, Matthew and Luke drop the reference or substitute another of the groups (e.g. the Sadducees) for them (Mk 3.6 and parallels; 8.15 (variant reading) and parallels). Insensitive to the tensions that existed prior to 70 CE between the Pharisees and the Sadducees, Matthew adds the 'Sadducees' to his source at Mk 8.11, where Mark mentioned only Pharisees, thus showing both groups incongruously in league against Jesus. In other places too he brackets Pharisees and Sadducees together where his sources give him no cause to do so (e.g. Mt. 3.7; 16.6, 11, 12). The most persistent redactional procedure on the part of Matthew and Luke, however, is to add or substitute 'Pharisees' as the opponents of Jesus where the second evangelist has no mention of them or has a different group, usually 'scribes' (Mk 2.6; 3.22; 12.35, 38 and parallels). Matthew also has the Pharisees involved in the proceedings surrounding Jesus' burial (Mt. 27.62, the setting of a guard on the tomb) for which there is again no warrant in his Markan source. As this last example indicates, all these references to Pharisees view them in a hostile light. A similar procedure can be seen with regard to their

[177] M. J. Cook, *Mark's Treatment of the Jewish Leaders* (Novum Testamentum Supplement Series, 51; Leiden: E. J. Brill, 1978).

editing of Q. In all but two of the Q references where Pharisees
are mentioned, the parallel lacks it, and the version mentioning
the Pharisees appears to be secondary.[178]

Matthew and Luke relied, therefore, on their sources for
information regarding pre-70 CE groups other than the Pharisees, and, where the earlier tradition had either unnamed
opponents or mentioned other groups (see especially Lk. 11.16
(Q, 'the crowds') = Mk 8.11 ('the Pharisees') = Mt. 16.1 ('the
Pharisees and Sadducees') = Mt. 12.38 ('the scribes and Pharisees')) tended to exaggerate the role of the Pharisees as Jesus'
opponents. What then of Mark? Did he likewise depend upon
sources, oral or written, for his knowledge of the Jewish leadership groups operative in Jesus' day? Did he know much himself
about such groups? Did he, too, tend to exaggerate the role of
the Pharisees as Jesus' opponents? His knowledge has certainly
been challenged. In Mark 7.3–4, for example, Mark informs his
readers in an editorial aside, that 'the Pharisees, and all the
Jews, do not eat unless they wash their hands, and when they
come from the market place, they do not eat unless they purify
themselves; and there are many other traditions which they
observe, the washing of cups and pots and vessels of bronze'. It
is doubtful, however, if the practice of ritual lustration applied
to any other than priests before 70 CE, yet here it is said to be a
practice not only of Pharisees but of 'all the Jews'. Similarly, in
Mark 10.2ff. the evangelist has Pharisees ask Jesus whether it is
lawful for a man to divorce his wife. Given that the Mosaic law
clearly sanctions divorce (Deut. 24.1–4), some scholars doubt
whether any Pharisee would ever have posed such a question,
or at least in this form.[179]

On the basis of such traditio-critical observations, therefore,
there is now a widespread view that controversies in the
Gospels deemed to represent historical confrontations between

---

[178] Smith, *Magician*, 153–7.

[179] Winter, *Trial*, p. 112. See also Smith, *Magician*, p. 155, who thinks it possible that the
reference to 'Pharisees' in Mark here may be a gloss from Matthew's text. For a
recent view claiming that Mark's knowledge of the Law was not particularly
accurate, see also H. Sariola, *Markus und das Gesetz. Eine redaktionskritische Untersuchung*
(Annales Academiae Scientarum Fennicae Dissertationes Humanarum Litterarum,
56; Helsinki: Suomalainen Tiedeakatemia, 1990).

Jesus and named groups of adversaries during his lifetime reflect more the conflicts that existed between the communities out of which the Gospels sprang and their respective opponents. After 70 CE these opponents were pre-eminently the Pharisees and it was with this now dominant Jewish leadership group that the Matthean, Lukan and Johannine communities of the eighties and nineties were engaged in bitter dispute. Progressively therefore in the Gospel tradition, conflicts with the Pharisees on the part of later Christian communities have been antedated to Jesus' lifetime, or in the words of P. Winter 'enemies of "the Church" are depicted as enemies of Jesus'.[180]

With these caveats in mind, and with the evangelist's *theological* motivations as our primary goal, let us now return to the question of Mark's knowledge and treatment of these Jewish leadership groups. In the Gospel of Mark, all six of the above named leadership groups are mentioned: Pharisees, Sadducees, Herodians, chief priests, scribes and elders. It is instructive to observe how often these groups are mentioned, when and where they appear, the tenor of comments about them, and how they are said to relate to each other.[181]

The Pharisees are the most frequently mentioned group, with eleven references in all (Mk 2.16, 18, 24; 3.6; 7.1, 3, 5; 8.11, 15; 10.2; 12.13). While appearing mostly in the first half of the Gospel, they are shown encountering Jesus in various places (in Galilee, Judaea and Jerusalem). All the references, one notes, are hostile. On two (or three) occasions (7.1, 5; cf. also 2.16),[182] they are linked with the scribes in challenging Jesus on the purity laws, and on two (or three) occasions with the Herodians (3.6; 12.13; see also 8.15)[183] as co-conspirators in a plot to kill Jesus. Curiously they do not appear in the narrative after 12.13 as a named group, and are not involved in the arrest, trial and execution of Jesus. The Sadducees are mentioned only once in Mark's Gospel, appear only in Jerusalem, and act purely on their own (12.18). Although it remains possible that the reader is

---

[180] Winter, *Trial*, p. 120.
[181] For a comprehensive analysis, see Cook, *Jewish Leaders*.
[182] Three times if we count the variant reading 'the scribes *and* the Pharisees' in 2.16.
[183] Three times if we count the variant reading 'the leaven of the Herodians' in 8.15.

meant to include them under the reference to the Sanhedrin in 14.55 and 15.1, they too are not mentioned as a named group in the plot to kill Jesus nor involved in the proceedings over his arrest, trial and execution.

Our third group, the Herodians, take the stage on two, possibly three occasions only (3.6; 12.13; see also 8.15 (variant reading)). Appearing exclusively with the Pharisees, both in Galilee (3.6) and in Jerusalem (12.13), they are linked, as we have noted, with the former in a plot to kill Jesus. It is the chief priests, on the other hand, whom the narrative actually depicts as responsible for the proceedings to arrest, try and execute Jesus. There are thirteen references in all to this group (Mk 8.31; 10.33; 11.18, 27; 14.1, 10, 43, 53, 55; 15.1, 3, 11, 31) and all the references to them are hostile. Appearing in the second half of the Gospel only, and never outside of Jerusalem, they are sometimes mentioned on their own. More often, however, they act in concert with either the scribes, or the elders and scribes, but with no other named group.[184]

The scribes are the most frequently mentioned opponents of Jesus in Mark. There are some twenty-one references in all to them (Mk 1.22; 2.6, 16; 3.22; 7.1, 5; 8.31; 9.11, 14; 10.33; 11.18, 27; 12.28, 32, 35, 38; 14.1, 43, 53; 15.1, 31), the majority occurring in the second half of the Gospel. They are shown encountering Jesus not only in Jerusalem, however, but outside it as well (3.22; 7.1; 9.14). While normally linked with the chief priests and elders, and, on occasion, with the Pharisees (7.1, 5; see also 2.16), they also operate on their own. Presented as hostile for the most part (with the one exception of 12.28ff.), it is they, and not the Pharisees, the Sadducees or the Herodians who are in actuality responsible, together with the chief priests and elders, for Jesus' arrest, trial and execution. Our final group, the elders, appear some five or six times in Mark (Mk (7.5); 8.31; 11.27; 14.43, 53; 15.1). Found only in the second half of the Gospel, and exclusively in Jerusalem, they are a shadowy group, who never

---

[184] According to Trocmé, the *archiereis*, in Mark's eyes, are 'a sort of executive college forming the core of the Sanhedrin without being identical with it (14.55), and enforcing its decisions. It is tempting to think that he takes the title of these people to mean "ruling priests"' (*Formation*, pp. 100–1).

act on their own, but only in conjunction with the chief priests (and scribes).

The references to, actions of, and narrative role exercised by each of the separate leadership groups in Mark is puzzling, to say the least. The narrative critic may be able to discern a literary pattern in such varied comings and goings,[185] but thus far explanations of the textual phenomena have lain for the most part within the province of the tradition critic.[186] It is to source criticism, for example, that the tradition critic has appealed in order to answer the question already raised, namely that of Mark's knowledge of the leadership groups whose activities he recounts.

One influential source theory has been that of M. Albertz who claimed that the evangelist was dependent on two prior controversy collections, one set in Galilee and underlying the conflicts with Jesus' opponents reported in Mark 2.1–3.6, the other set in Jerusalem and detectable beneath the dialogues of Mark 11–12.[187] B. S. Easton in turn reconfigured the pericopae claimed by Albertz to belong to these two pre-Markan controversy collections. By reducing their number, and combining the remainder, he thus posited one main united pre-Markan collection of eight pericopae comprising Mark 2.13–3.6; 12.13–27, 35–40. On the basis of the leadership group designations,

---

[185] For literary approaches to the controversy pericopae and the Jewish leaders, see J. Dewey, *Markan Public Debate. Literary Technique, Concentric Structure, and Theology in Mark 2:1–3:6* (SBLDS, 48; Chico, CA: Scholars Press, 1980); J. Dewey, 'The Literary Structure of the Controversy Stories in Mark 2:1–3:6' in Telford (ed.), *Interpretation*, pp. 141–51; J. D. Kingsbury, *Conflict in Mark. Jesus, Authorities, Disciples* (Philadelphia, PA: Fortress Press, 1989); J. D. Kingsbury, 'The Religious Authorities in the Gospel of Mark', *NTS*, 36 (1990), pp. 42–65; E. S. Malbon, 'The Jewish Leaders in the Gospel of Mark: a Literary Study of Marcan Characterization', *JBL*, 108 (1989), pp. 259–81; Telford, *Mark*, pp. 110–11.

[186] For important or useful traditio-critical discussions, see, for example, J. D. G. Dunn, 'Mark 2.1–3.6: a Bridge between Jesus and Paul in the Question of the Law', *NTS*, 30 (1984), pp. 395–415; A. J. Hultgren, *Jesus and his Adversaries. The Form and Function of the Conflict Stories in the Synoptic Tradition* (Minneapolis, MN: Augsburg, 1979); Kee, *Community*, pp. 38–41; W. R. Telford, 'The Interpretation of Mark: a History of Developments and Issues' in Telford (ed.), *Interpretation*, pp. 19–20; Telford, *Mark*, pp. 138–9.

[187] M. Albertz, *Die synoptischen Streitgespräche* (Berlin: Trowitzsch & Sohn, 1921). For a critique of Albertz, see, for example, J.-G. Mudiso Mbâ Mundla, *Jesus und die Führer Israels. Studien zu den sogennanten Jerusalemer Streitgesprächen* (Neutestamentliche Abhandlungen, Neue Folge, 17; Münster: Aschendorff, 1984).

M. J. Cook, on the other hand, claims that Mark drew upon and combined three main sources for his knowledge of the Jewish leadership groups: an early passion source, set in Jerusalem, in which chief priests, scribes and elders appear as Jesus' opponents (14–16); a source referring to scribes alone, also setting them in Jerusalem; and a source focusing on Pharisees and Herodians which was possibly set in a Galilean context.[188]

Most Markan scholars, however, are less certain that specific written controversy sources can be isolated in this way, and would prefer to detect in the Gospel a variety of controversy pericopae, some of which may have been collected or grouped prior to Mark but most of which were isolated stories which Mark himself arranged in conformity with his own theological purposes. Many, following the insights of form criticism, would prefer then to talk of 'strata' in the tradition rather than of sources. P. Winter, for example, distinguished three strata in Mark on the basis of the diverse and ambiguous leadership group classes appearing in Mark. The earliest stratum of tradition, he maintained, corresponds to those passages which mention the chief priests, scribes (and elders) who appear in the material of the second half of the Gospel, particularly the passion narrative (14–15). Passages mentioning scribes only, on the other hand, correspond to a later stratum, while those mentioning Pharisees are later still.[189]

Form criticism, with its interest in the individual oral units and their *Sitz im Leben* in the pre-Markan communities, has also highlighted the richness and diversity of this controversy material and the range of issues and concerns with which it deals: for example, legal and ethical issues (Mk 10.1–12 (divorce); 12.28–34 (the greatest commandment)); matters of authority (12.13–17 (relation to the state); 11.27–33 (the source of Jesus' authority); 8.11–13 (the demand for a sign)); cultic practice (Mk 7.1–23 (defilement); 2.23–8 (sabbath observance);

---

[188] M. J. Cook, *Mark's Treatment of the Jewish Leaders* (Novum Testamentum Supplement Series, 51; Leiden: E. J. Brill, 1978). For a critique of Cook, see W. R. Telford, *JTS*, 31 (1980–1), pp. 154–62.

[189] Winter, *Trial*, p. 125.

2.18–20 (fasting)); doctrine (12.18–27 (resurrection)) and Christological questions (12.35–7 (Messiah, Son of David)).[190]

Accepting the form-critical model, it is instructive then to consider what redaction critics have said about Mark's editorial procedure.[191] The following are the main passages which concern us: Mk 2.1–3.6; 3.20–35; 7.1–23; 8.11–13; 10.2–12; 11.27–12.40. While Mark's hand is not uniformly or even clearly to be seen in evidence in all of these passages, certain observations can be made. In the first place, Mark, as with Matthew and Luke, appears to redact his sources with the later church situation in mind (e.g. Mk 2.18–20 where the evangelist informs his readers that while Jesus and his disciples did not fast he nevertheless pointed forward to this later church practice, so legitimating it; see also Mk 9.28–9 and the variant readings). The post-dominical situation is often indicated by the fact that it is the disciples' conduct that is challenged, not Jesus', with Jesus being made to answer with a pronouncement which justifies the later conduct of the church (e.g. Mk 2.23–8; 7.1–8). Secondly, Mark reveals a tendency to turn miracle stories in the tradition without any original conflict element into controversies between Jesus and certain named opponents (e.g. Mk 3.1–6 or 2.1–12 where vv. 5a–10a is commonly held to be an insertion which converts the miracle story into a controversy dialogue).[192] Thirdly, he inserts reference to the Pharisees where the underlying tradition perhaps had no such reference.[193] Fourthly, the evangelist can be seen making a piece of isolated tradition refer specifically to Jesus' opponents by supplying it with a particular setting in the Gospel (e.g. Mk 12.1–12 where, by virtue of the Markan context, the wicked tenants of the original parable are identified with the chief priests, elders and scribes).[194]

Such observations, of course, describe individual features of the Markan redaction, but what about the overall purpose and

---

[190] Kee, *Community*, p. 41.

[191] See especially Kee, *Community*, pp. 38–41.

[192] *Ibid.*, pp. 35–7, 38–9.

[193] Most of these references, according to Smith (*Magician*, pp. 154–5), are redactional. Only Mk 2.24; 3.6; 8.15 and 12.13 he claims came to Mark from his source(s).

[194] Winter, *Trial*, p. 112.

effect of the controversy stories? To appreciate the significance of Mark's redaction, a more holistic approach to the Gospel is called for. According to M. Kähler, the Markan Gospel can be described *in toto* as a 'passion narrative with an extended introduction'.[195] This 'extended introduction' prepares the way for the passion narrative by seeking to explain what led up to it (Mk 3.6). By viewing Mark's use of the controversy pericopae in this light, we can see that the evangelist is in fact engaging in Christian apologetic and polemic. What led to the unjust execution of God's only Son, Mark claims, was the overall antagonism, blindness and rejection of the Jewish people, as represented in their various leadership groups, no matter what their complexion, no matter what their differences. Viewed as a whole, the Jewish leaders in Mark act indeed as a single character, their 'flat' characterization and consistently negative attributes built upon their opposition to Jesus.[196]

Some scholars have gone even further. According to S. G. F. Brandon, Mark's presentation amounts to a pronounced campaign of denigration against the Jewish people as well as their representatives.[197] The charge of 'anti-Semitism' implied by this is one which I shall take up in chapter 4. Whatever the nuances in individual passages, it has to be maintained that the Markan Jesus is shown repeatedly throughout the Gospel being misunderstood or rejected by the various Jewish groups, and he in turn is pictured as one repudiating their authority or their doctrine. Presented in a favourable light vis-à-vis the scribes at the beginning of his ministry (Mk 1.22), he is shown confronting and besting in argument each of the representatives of the nation at the end (Mk 12.1ff.). Time and again, their doctrinal beliefs are shown to be in error. The evangelist portrays Jesus as condoning the breaking of the sabbath (Mk 2.23ff.; 3.1–6).

[195] M. Kähler, *The So-called Historical Jesus and the Historic, Biblical Christ* (Philadelphia, PA: Fortress Press, 1964), p. 80, n. 11.
[196] See Kingsbury, *Conflict*; Kingsbury, 'Religious Authorities', pp. 42–65; Malbon, 'Jewish Leaders', pp. 259–81; D. Rhoads and D. Michie, *Mark as Story. An Introduction to the Narrative of a Gospel* (Philadelphia, PA: Fortress Press, 1982), p. 117; Telford, *Mark*, pp. 110–11.
[197] S. G. F. Brandon, *Jesus and the Zealots* (Manchester: Manchester University Press, 1967), pp. 264–73. See also W. A. Johnson, 'The Jews in Saint Mark's Gospel', *Religion and Intellectual Life*, 6 (1989), pp. 182–92.

Jewish lustration practice is disparaged as are other Jewish
practices (Mk 7.1–23). Judaism itself is shown to belong to 'the
old order' (Mk 2.21–2). The Jewish leaders are depicted as 'hard
of heart' (Mk 3.5; see also 2.1ff.) or as 'hypocrites' (Mk 7.6–7).
They are shown as guilty of the unforgivable sin in questioning
the source of Jesus' power (Mk 3.28–30). Tilting against their
insidious influence, Jesus warns his disciples to 'beware of the
leaven of the Pharisees and of Herod/the Herodians' (Mk 8.15).
For rejecting Jesus and the prophets, they are to be viewed as
wicked murderers (Mk 12.1ff.). All the various leadership groups
are shown implausibly plotting his death, the evangelist anticipating the culpability of the chief priests, elders and scribes in
particular in the three passion predictions (Mk 8.31; 9.31;
10.33–4). They are stealthy and devious (Mk 14.1–2), and it is
out of envy, the readers are informed (Mk 15.10), that they
proceed against Jesus. In a final act of rejection, they are shown
cruelly mocking Jesus on the cross (Mk 15.31–2).

This rejection of him, moreover, is presented to the reader as
having been fore-ordained (the passion predictions), and it
extends further than the Jewish leaders themselves (Mk
4.10–12).[198] Not only the authorities, and the Jewish crowd (Mk
15.12–15) but even Jesus' own family and friends are represented
as rejecting him (Mk 6.1–6 or 3.20ff. where scribes and family
are bracketed together as if in the same camp). Jesus in turn is
shown as rejecting them (see Mk 3.31–5 where blood relationship is repudiated and spiritual relationship to Jesus is empha-
sised instead). The overall effect of the Markan presentation,
therefore, is to highlight what is almost a Johannine theme: 'He
came to his own home, and his own people received him not'
(Jn 1.11). To see how Mark reinforces this theme we need next

---

[198] It is worth mentioning here the view of J. M. Robinson, *The Problem of History in Mark*
(Studies in Biblical Theology, 21; London: SCM Press, 1957) that, according to
Mark's eschatological understanding of history, Jesus' debates with his opponents
are simply the continuation of 'the cosmic struggle initiated at the baptism and
temptation and carried into the narrative of Jesus' public ministry first by the
exorcisms' (p. 46). According to Robinson, there is 'an intimate relationship of
meaning between the exorcisms and the debates. Just as there are traces of exorcism
language in the miracle stories, there are equally clear indications in the debates
that they too are the action of Satan' (p. 45).

to consider the picture that Mark presents of Jesus' relation with his own disciples, and they with him.

'Are you also without understanding?': Mark's treatment of the disciples

We begin first by noting the various terms employed by Mark for the original followers of Jesus. One term is the 'twelve' (*dōdeka*; cf. Mk 3.14; 4.10; 6.7; 9.35; 10.32; (10.41–5 'the ten'); 11.11; 14.10, 17, 20, 43), from whom, at intervals, certain named individuals are singled out.[199] Another expression is 'the' or 'his disciples' (*mathētai*; Mk 4.34; 6.35, 45; 7.17; 8.10; 8.34; 9.14, 28; 10.10, 13, 23, 46; 11.1,14; 12.43; 13.1; 14.12, 13, 16, 32; 16.7), a group which may be synonymous with 'the twelve' (R. P. Meye),[200] or indicate a wider circle than 'the twelve' (E. Best).[201] Mark also makes reference to 'those around him' or to 'those who followed him' (Mk 3.32, 34; 4.10; 10.32; 11.9; 15.40–1). In the last cited example, women are included. Frequent reference is also made to the 'crowd' who accompanied him (*ochlos*; Mk 2.4, 13; 3.9, 20, 32; 4.1, 36; 5.21, 24, 27, 30, 31; 6.34, 45; 7.14, 17, 33; 8.1, 2, 6; 9.14, 15, 17; 10.1, 46; 11.18, 32; 12.12, 37, 41; 14.43; 15.8, 11, 15). Curiously the more familiar term 'the apostles' is avoided (except for 3.14 (variant reading) and 6.30).

The use, in often alternate passages, of two distinct designations, the 'twelve' (*dōdeka*) and the 'disciples' (*mathētai*), has suggested to some source critics that the evangelist employed separate sources. E. Meyer, for example, claimed that Mark had used two such sources, one (a Petrine source) using the term *disciples* (*mathētai*), the other (a non-Petrine source) referring to the *twelve* (*dōdeka*).[202] However, of the ten references to the

---

[199] Four are singled out (Peter, James, John, Andrew) in Mk 1.16–20, 29–31; 13.3; three (Peter, James, John) in Mk 5.37; 9.2–8; 14.33; two (James, John) in Mk 10.35ff.; one in Mk 9.38 (John), 14.10, 43 (Judas) and 1.36; 8.29, 32–33; 10.28; 11.21; 14.29; 14.54, 66ff.; 16.7 (Peter).

[200] R. P. Meye, *Jesus and the Twelve. Discipleship and Revelation in Mark's Gospel* (Grand Rapids, MI: Eerdmans, 1968), p. 228.

[201] E. Best, *Following Jesus. Discipleship in the Gospel of Mark* (JSNTSS, 4; Sheffield: JSOT Press, 1981), p. 204.

[202] E. Meyer, *Ursprung und Anfänge des Christentums* (Stuttgart and Berlin: J. G. Cotta, 1921–3).

'twelve', seven are in passages which appear to be Markan constructions (Mk 3.13–19; 4.10–12; 6.6b-13; 9.33–7; 10.32–4; 10.41–5; 14.10–12),[203] one is almost certainly redactional (Mk 11.11),[204] and two others which appear in self-contained narratives (14.17, 43) may also be redactional.[205]

The suspicion, then, that the majority of the references to the 'twelve' may be redactional (*pace* E. Best) indicates that Mark had a special interest in the original twelve appointed as Jesus' intimate followers. This is also shown by the increasing *infrequency* of references to the 'twelve' in the developing tradition.[206] While Mark has ten references to the twelve, as we have noted, Matthew has only nine, Luke only eight, John a mere four, the Acts of the Apostles three, and both Paul and Revelation one. Reference to the 'twelve' is completely lacking in the Pastoral and Catholic Epistles. By contrast, the term 'apostle' is more frequently used outside of Mark for Jesus' appointed followers, a circle, one notes that has widened to include Paul, Barnabas, Andronicus and Junias (Acts 14.14; Rom. 16.7).[207] Mark too, by his use of the expression 'those about him' (e.g. Mk 4.10) or even of the term 'the disciples' (*mathētai*) can be seen to be widening the original circle (indeed even arguing for it; Mk 3.31–5; 9.38–9), although, in a number of cases, by his use of the latter term, he means the 'twelve' (Mk 11.11, 14; 14.12ff., 17, 32).

What is the nature of Mark's treatment of the disciples? In the first place, they are called by Jesus and commissioned (for the period of his ministry) to be 'fishers of men', that is, to evangelize (Mk 1.16–20), to be with him, to preach that people should repent, and to exorcize demons (Mk 3.14–15). While given authority to do these things (Mk 6.7–13), Mark paradoxically does not show them elsewhere (apart from Mk 6.12–13) carrying out the things they were commissioned to do. Indeed, according to Mark 9.18, they are deemed to be failures as

---

[203] I.e. '[N]arratives compiled from fragmentary traditions'. See Taylor, *Mark* , p. 620.
[204] See Telford, *Barren Temple*, pp. 45–6.
[205] See Bultmann, *History*, p. 345. For a contrary view, see E. Best, 'The Role of the Disciples in Mark', *NTS*, 23 (1976–7), pp. 377–401; E. Best, 'Mark's Use of the Twelve', *ZNW*, 69 (1978), pp. 11–35.
[206] Taylor, *Mark*, p. 620.   [207] *Ibid.*, p. 625.

exorcists, and according to Mark 9.38–9, they even seek to prevent other exorcists not of their circle using the authority of Jesus' name. Furthermore, they are not presented by the evangelist as having been given the authority to exercise a leadership role in the post-Easter community (see Mk 10.35–45 and contrast Mt. 16.16ff. and the resurrection narratives in Matthew, Luke and John). They are depicted, on the other hand, as seeking power and status for themselves (Mk 9.33–7; 10.35–45), and, at the same time, as barring others from coming to Jesus or being reckoned as one of their number (Mk 9.38–9; 10.13–14). The Markan author portrays them as having occupied a privileged position, however, in that they had not only witnessed Jesus' miracles and heard his public teaching but had been recipients of private instruction from Jesus himself (Mk 4.10ff., 34; 7.17ff.; 8.14ff.; 9.2ff., 28–9, 30ff.; 10.10–12). Nevertheless, although 'the secret of the Kingdom of God' (namely that Jesus, I have argued, was the 'Son of God', according to Mark) had been given to them together with 'those who were about him' (Mk 4.10–11), Mark shows them to have been remarkably obtuse (Mk 4.13, 40–1; 6.52; 7.18; 8.14–21, 33; 9.10, 32). Before Peter's so-called confession (Mk 8.29) they failed to recognize that he was the Son of God despite every invitation or opportunity to do so (see especially Mk 4.41; 6.52 and 8.21 with 1.24; 3.11; 5.7). After that 'confession', they positively misunderstand the true nature of both Jesus' divine status and mission as well as the true nature of the Christian discipleship springing from it (see especially Mk 8.31–10.45 and the pattern of prediction, misunderstanding and corrective teaching which characterizes this section, according to N. Perrin).

When we look at the treatment of the disciples in the other three Gospels, the differences are striking. Matthew, for example, greatly expands the pre-resurrection mission of the twelve recounted in Mark 6.7–13 (Mt. 10), although he confines it to Jews. He stresses, unlike Mark, that the disciples did understand what Jesus had said to them, and alters Mark accordingly (Mt. 13.16–17, 51; 16.12; 17.13, 23 and parallels). Again in contrast to Mark, the disciples recognize that Jesus was the Son of God and confess him as such during his lifetime.

Accordingly, appropriate alterations have been made to his source (Mt. 14.31–3; 16.16 and parallels). As a result of such a confession, they are given authority over the church that is to come into being after the resurrection, and Peter is the rock on which it will be founded, according to Matthew (Mt. 16.17–19; [18.18] and parallels). They will sit, moreover, upon twelve thrones judging the twelve tribes of Israel (Mt. 19.28 = Lk. 22.30). The disciples are also given a prominent place in the post-resurrection church, being commissioned not only to evangelize but to baptize and teach all nations to observe the law of the 'new Moses' (Mt. 28.18–20). Matthew alters Mark's harsh treatment of the disciples in other ways too. He omits the discussion in Mark 9.33–4 over who is to be the greatest, and makes the mother of James and John, not these disciples themselves, request that her sons should sit at his right and left hand (Mt. 20.20ff. and parallels).

Luke too alters Mark in similar fashion. The third evangelist has Jesus appoint not only twelve, but seventy others as well (Lk. 9.1–6; 10.1–24). He too preserves the Q saying that they would sit on thrones judging the twelve tribes of Israel (Lk. 22.30 = Mt. 19.28). He adds to the Markan source the intimation that Peter would be restored after his denial of Jesus (Lk. 22.31–2). He emphasizes the role of the original disciples as witnesses (Lk. 24.46–9). He also tones down Mark's harsh treatment of the original twelve in other significant ways: for example, by omitting the passage where Jesus denounces Peter as 'Satan' (Mk 8.33 and parallel), curtailing the Gethsemane scene (Mk 14.32–42) where they are shown three times being unable to keep watch with Jesus and giving the reason for their falling asleep as 'for sorrow' (Lk. 22.45 and parallel), and deleting the reference in Mark to the disciples' ignominious flight (Mk 14.50 and parallel). In addition, Luke announces the fact that Jesus had appeared to Peter after his resurrection, although only the (unfulfilled) promise of such an appearance is given in Mark (Lk. 24.34; contrast Mk 14.28; 16.7).

In John's Gospel too, the disciples are treated less harshly than in Mark and credited with more spiritual discernment. Their confession of Jesus' divine status is made right at the start of the ministry (Jn 1.35–51; 6.68–9). After the resurrection, Jesus reveals himself to the twelve, and they are accorded power to remit or retain sins (Jn 20.22–3; see also Mt. 18.18). An appearance to Peter in particular is described, and he is given authority to lead the future church (Jn 21). Where Mark presents Peter making a three-fold denial of Jesus (Mk 14.54, 66–72), the Fourth Gospel shows him offering a threefold declaration of his love and loyalty (Jn 21.15–17; see also Lk. 22.31–2).

In light of all this, Mark's treatment of the disciples of Jesus, and in particular the twelve, does appear significant. In accounting for it, two main types of explanation have been suggested by scholars.[208] The first is the *pastoral* or *pedagogic* explanation, a solution proposed by a considerable number of scholars (e.g. E. Best, R. C. Tannehill).[209] These scholars have held to the view expressed by W. Wrede that 'if anyone for one moment entertained the idea that Mark was ill-disposed towards the disciples he would soon dismiss it again'.[210] Mark's chief concern, it is claimed, was a pastoral one. His purpose was to offer help or encouragement to the congregation to whom he was writing in face of the problems that confronted it: the delay of the parousia, persecution, martyrdom and false Christologies, especially those that bypassed or lacked a theology of the cross with its emphasis on the necessity of suffering as a prelude to glory or vindication.

In the Markan Gospel, the disciples' function is to act as a foil to Jesus, and in two ways. Firstly, by appearing frail, confused, afraid and human by comparison, they make him stand out in all his authority and dignity as the Lord of the church. Secondly, by repeatedly misunderstanding him (a pedagogic device), they offer Jesus (in reality the evangelist) an opportunity to offer

---

[208] For a survey of various approaches to the disciples in Mark, see Telford, *Mark*, pp. 109–10, 141–3; Telford, 'History of Developments' in Telford (ed.), *Interpretation*, pp. 35–7. For a literary approach eschewing the historical context, see Rhoads and Michie, *Mark*, pp. 122–3.

[209] See, for example, E. Best, *Disciples and Discipleship. Studies in the Gospel According to Mark* (Edinburgh: T. & T. Clark, 1986); R. C. Tannehill, 'The Disciples in Mark: the Function of a Narrative Role' in Telford (ed.), *Interpretation*, pp. 169–95.

[210] Wrede, *Secret*, p. 106.

teaching on the true nature of his person and mission, as well as on the discipleship springing from it (e.g. Mk 4.13–20; 7.17ff.; 9.28–9; 10.10–12; 13.3ff.; cf. Jn 14.5, 8, 22ff.). In addressing his disciples in private, the Markan Jesus is in actuality addressing the church, for whom the Gospel was written, and expanding on the tradition in light of the community's contemporary problems and needs. The readers, then, are invited to identify with the disciples, in all their incomprehension, frailty and failure, as prototypical Christians, and so, by such identification, be led to both self-criticism and comfort.[211]

It must be admitted that a pedagogic concern is present in Mark, and that in having Jesus address his disciple, the evangelist is clearly looking beyond them to his readers (see especially Mk 4.10–12; 7.17ff.; 9.28–9; 10.10–12; 13.3ff.). It is said of a certain actor that whereas he believed his performance was elevating the stage, it was merely depressing the audience! Mark's treatment of Jesus vis-à-vis the disciples has been viewed in a similar light. But Mark's treatment in 'elevating' Jesus, it has to be said, is doing more than merely 'depressing' the disciples. A pastoral concern is present but a polemical motive, I would maintain, eclipses it. His treatment of the original twelve indeed goes far beyond the interests of pedagogy (see Jn 14 for an example of normal pedagogic use).

Just as Jesus' family and friends are bracketed together with his enemies the scribes in Mk 3.20ff., the disciples are also

[211] See E. Best, *The Gospel as Story* (Studies of the New Testament and its World; Edinburgh: T. & T. Clark, 1983) ('in the Gospel the disciples play the role of believers; the Christian can identify with them in their failure and in their faithfulness', p. 83); E. S. Malbon, 'Text and Contexts: Interpreting the Disciples in Mark', *Semeia*, 62 (1993), pp. 81–102; E. S. Malbon, 'Disciples, Crowds, Whoever: Markan Characters and Readers', *NovT*, 28 (1986), pp. 104–30; M. A. Powell, 'Toward a Narrative-Critical Understanding of Mark', *Int*, 47 (1993), pp. 341–6 ('What is the effect of inviting empathy with characters who are portrayed so harshly? First, such empathy may enable the narrative's readers to identify their own inadequacies. Second, Mark's readers are expected to notice that, no matter how faithless Jesus' disciples are to him, he always remains faithful to them', p. 344); K.-G. Reploh, *Markus – Lehrer der Gemeinde. Eine redaktionsgeschichtliche Studie zu den Jüngerperikopen des Markus-Evangeliums* (Stuttgarter biblische Monographien, 9; Stuttgart: Katholisches Bibelwerk, 1969); R. C. Tannehill, 'Disciples' in Telford (ed.), *Interpretation* ('The author assumes that there are essential similarities between the disciples and his anticipated readers, so that what he reveals about the disciples may become a revelation about the readers and so enable them to change', pp. 190–1).

bracketed together with the scribes in Mark 9.14, 18–19 in such a way that *both* fall under Jesus' condemnation as belonging to 'this wicked generation'. The description that Mark applies to Jesus' enemies is applied similarly to them. Their hearts have become 'hardened' (Mk 6.52; 8.17 with 3.5; 10.5). The language used to characterize 'those outside' in Mark 4.11–12 is also echoed in Mark 8.17–18 where it is used by Jesus in connection with the disciples. Peter, moreover, is described as 'Satan' (Mk 8.33), a passage omitted, as we have seen, by Luke, and modified by Matthew (see Mt. 16.23 and parallel). The disciples are shown not only to be obtuse, but ridiculously so (Mk 8.4 in light of 6.34–44 or 8.14–21; 9.10, 32). They are revealed as fearful, afraid, even cowardly (Mk 4.40–1; 6.50–51; 9.6, 32; 10.32; 14.50). Exhorted to have faith, they are admonished for not possessing it (Mk 4.40; 9.19; 11.22). For lack of such faith, they are unable to work miracles (Mk 9.18, 19, 23).

A further point to note is that they (and thereby Mark's readers) are taught by Jesus the marks of the true disciple. Such a disciple must be last of all, and servant of all (Mk 9.35). He must be willing to take up his cross and follow Jesus (Mk 8.34). He must not seek to save his own life, but be willing to lose that life for Jesus' sake (Mk 8.35). The true disciple will not deny Jesus but confess him, and whoever is ashamed of Jesus will be denied by the Son of Man at his parousia (Mk 8.38). The true disciple will also keep watch lest his master return and find him asleep (Mk 13.35–7).

Measured against such criteria, the twelve reveal an abject deficiency. By contrast, they are shown to be eager to be first, not last, and to have power and status for themselves (Mk 9.33–7; 10.28–31, 35–45). One of their number, Judas, is shown to betray him, and Mark repeatedly draws attention to the fact that he was 'one of the twelve' – in chapter 14, indeed, no less than *three* times (Mk 3.19; 14.10, 17ff., 43)! Jesus' innermost circle cannot keep watch and their master returns *three* times to find them asleep (Mk 14.32–42). All of them are shown deserting Jesus to save their own lives (Mk 14.27, 50 – a passage, I repeat, which is omitted by Luke). The most prominent of them, Peter, denies his master not once, but again *three* times (Mk 14.54,

66–72). This dramatic treatment, especially in chapter 14, far exceeds what one would expect of someone with mere pedagogic or pastoral concerns (the betrayal of table-fellowship, the threefold inability to keep watch, the threefold return by Jesus, betrayal by a kiss, and by 'one of the twelve', the threefold denial by Peter, etc.).

Furthermore, one cannot help noticing that the other minor characters in the Markan narrative do for Jesus what his original Jewish disciples fail to do.[212] It is the 'crowd' who flock to him, receive his teaching eagerly and gladly hear him (Mk 2.13; 3.9, 20, 32; 4.1; 5.21, 24; 6.34, 45; 7.14, 17; 8.1, 34; 9.14; 10.1, 46; 11.18, 32; 12.12, 37), although they also in the end (stirred up by the chief priests) clamour for his crucifixion (Mk 15.8–15). It is the father of the demon-possessed boy who is shown seeking, and thereby demonstrating faith, not the disciples (Mk 9.23–4 with 9.18–19). It is a woman outside of their circle who comes and anoints him 'beforehand for burial' (Mk 14.3–9). Mark tells us she is reproached for this but has Jesus defend her action and say that hereafter, wherever the gospel is preached throughout the world (namely the Hellenistic world), it will be remembered who it is that has anointed him (Mk 14.9). It is Simon of Cyrene, the father of Alexander and Rufus, Mark informs his readers, and not one of his disciples, who takes up Jesus' cross (Mk 15.21).[213] It is a Gentile, a Roman centurion, not one of the twelve, who is the first human being to recognize and confess him to be the 'Son of God', and hence more than the Jewish Messiah (Mk 15.39). It is Joseph of Arimathaea who obtains his body, and buries him (Mk 15.42–7), again not the disciples, a deficiency in sharp contrast to the conduct of John the Baptist's disciples after his death (Mk 6.29). Finally, it is the women, not the disciples, who come to anoint him after his burial and who receive the message that he has risen (Mk 16.1–8).

In light of these observations, E. Best's judgment that 'the total structure of the second half of the Gospel supports a positive evaluation of the role of the disciples' would appear to

---

[212] See Tannehill, 'Disciples' in Telford (ed.), *Interpretation*, p. 190.
[213] Some have suggested that these were Gentile Christians known to Mark's community; cf. Acts 6.9; 11.19; 13.1; Rom. 16.13.

be a misguided one.[214] If Mark's disciples are merely prototypical Christians whose narrative presence is only meant to
advance pastoral or pedagogic aims, we must surely ask why
Matthew and Luke should have felt it necessary to alter, omit or
otherwise tone down Mark's treatment in order to achieve a
similar aim? Can it be that they recognized the derogatory
nature of Mark's treatment? It is dissatisfaction, indeed, with
the pastoral or pedagogic explanation offered by scholars such
as Best which has led a smaller number of scholars to opt for a
second and more radical form of explanation, namely a *polemical*
one. The unknown author of Mark's Gospel, it is proposed,
was *ill-disposed* towards the leaders of the original Jerusalem
church and saw them, among other things, as representatives
of a Christology and soteriology which he wished to oppose
(see, for example, S. G. F. Brandon, E. Trocmé, J. B. Tyson,
T. J. Weeden).[215]

But what was that Christology and/or soteriology? Two
particularly influential theories have already been mentioned.
The first was that of T. J. Weeden who claimed, we recall, that
Mark's treatment of the disciples reflected an attack on a *theios
anēr* or divine-man Christology which had no place for the
cross, a perspective which (in its blindness) emphasized the role
of Jesus as a Hellenistic miracle-worker without recognizing the
divine necessity of his redemptive suffering and death. Jesus'
disciples are representatives of a divine man Christology which
saw Jesus as a *theios anēr* with paranormal and charismatic gifts
(and imitated him as such), but which placed no theological
significance on his crucifixion. It was Mark's aim to combat
such an estimate of Jesus by juxtaposing the accounts of his
miracles alongside that of his passion and death. While I myself
would concur with Weeden in recognizing a polemic against

---

[214] Best, *Disciples and Discipleship*, p. 122. Best suggests, for example, that Mark's
redactional activity (by widening references to apply to all the disciples) takes the
spotlight off Peter in the tradition (pp. 162–76). Thus the evangelist is actually
responsible for a modification of the tradition's harsh treatment of the twelve, which
Matthew and Luke continue.

[215] See Brandon, *Zealots*, pp. 125–37; Tyson, 'Blindness' in Tuckett (ed.), *Secret*, pp.
35–43; Weeden, *Traditions*; Weeden, 'Heresy' in Telford (ed.), *Interpretation*, pp.
89–104.

the original followers of Jesus in Mark, and further that the Gospel reflects the tension between opposing Christologies in the early church, I am of the opinion nevertheless that he has incorrectly identified the opposing Christologies. As earlier stated, I find it implausible to believe that Jesus' original Jewish disciples should be credited with a Christology which is clearly the product of a Hellenistic outlook. Mark has used the miracle tradition moreover to enhance a 'Son of God' or epiphany Christology and not, I have argued, to combat it.

The second polemical theory, that of J. B. Tyson, was found, on the other hand, to be more plausible. According to Tyson, Mark was attacking the Christology of the primitive Jewish-Christian community which saw Jesus as a royal Messiah, the Son of David, who was shortly to return, and which saw theological significance in his resurrection but not in his crucifixion. It was this community, the Jerusalem church, which wielded authority (or sought to) over the nascent Gentile churches founded before 70 CE by the Hellenistic wing of the *Urgemeinde*, in the person of the Seven (Acts 6ff.)and Paul.[216]

This theory has much to commend it, although one has to add that an equally primitive view of Jesus as the exalted, apocalyptic Son of Man shortly to return in glory is in addition being modified by the evangelist in light of his *theologia crucis*.[217] If this view is correct (and all such historical reconstructions can only remain tentative), then it raises afresh the whole question of the theological purpose of this Gospel, its provenance, addressees, and setting. Before we address this issue in our concluding section, we must take up the question whether Mark

---

[216] It is interesting to speculate whether the Markan Jesus may be speaking in 10.42–4 for Gentile Christians who felt the long arm of the *Urgemeinde* in their communities.

[217] In his article ('Blindness'), Tyson refers to the view of E. Lohmeyer that Mark stood within the tradition of Galilean Christianity which embraced a 'Son of Man' Christology in contradistinction to the 'Son of David' Christology represented by the Jerusalem church (p. 41). This is an intriguing hypothesis, and ties in to some extent with my own view that the evangelist rejects a 'Son of David' Christology while giving qualified acceptance to a 'Son of Man' one. I say 'qualified', however, because of Mark's distinctive emphasis on redemptive suffering. A Jewish-Christian 'Son of Man' Christology may have offered the evangelist a route towards a more transcendent Jesus, but the heart of his Christology remains that of the more Pauline (or at least Hellenistic) suffering 'Son of God'.

saw the twelve as having any leadership role in the early church after the resurrection. Best and others have said that he does, by virtue of Mark 14.28 and 16.7, but this very much depends on our interpretation of these verses. It is to the significance of the Markan ending, therefore, that we shall now turn.

As before, let me sum up. In this section, we have explored Mark's treatment of two principal character-groups, the Jewish leaders and Jesus' disciples. Surprisingly we have found that what unites these two apparently antagonistic groups is a shared blindness to the true status and mission of Jesus, as understood by Mark. Warned to 'beware of the leaven of the Pharisees and the leaven of Herod/Herodians' (Mk 8.15), the disciples in the end appear to share their selfsame hardness of heart, incomprehension and lack of faith. Despite some protests,[218] this 'blindness' motif and its development has been recognized not only as a structural component in the composition of the Gospel,[219] but also as a fundamental element of Mark's Christological perspective,[220] as well as his eschatological world-view.[221] The 'blindness' motif as applied both to the Jewish leaders and the disciples is yet another aspect of the secrecy motif, and Mark uses the concept to enhance his Christology.

THE PURPOSE OF MARK'S GOSPEL

'And they said nothing to anyone': the significance of the Markan ending

In this section, I want to take up the question raised earlier whether Mark saw the twelve as having any significant leadership

---

[218] See C. Focant, 'L'incompréhension des disciples dans le deuxième évangile', *Revue biblique*, 82 (1975), pp. 161–85.

[219] See E. Schweizer, 'Mark's Theological Achievement' in Telford (ed.), *Interpretation*, pp. 63–87. Schweizer charts the motif throughout Mark, and sees it as a thematic element of his now widely accepted outline of the Gospel. 'As Part 1 [Mk 1.14–3.6] ended with the blindness of the Pharisees and Part 2 [Mk 3.7–6.6a] with the blindness of Jesus' fellow-citizens, so Part 3 [Mk 6.6b–8.21] ends with the blindness of the disciples themselves' (p. 74).

[220] Tyson, 'Blindness' in Tuckett (ed.), *Secret*, pp. 35–43.

[221] 'By yielding to Satan's temptation the disciples join the Jewish authorities in the cosmic struggle of Satan against Jesus which began at the temptation in the wilderness, continued in the struggle with demoniacs, advances through the historical context of these debates to right and left, and reaches its climax in the crucifixion and resurrection' (Robinson, *Problem*, p. 51).

role in the early church after the resurrection. If this were so, it would serve to qualify the view that the Gospel is a polemical work directed against them. Best and others have claimed that Mark does envisage such a role, and that by virtue of the two important verses, Mk 14.28 and 16.7 ('Go tell his disciples that he goes before you to Galilee. There you will see him'). These verses anticipate Jesus' post-resurrection reunion with his disciples, and therefore their subsequent rehabilitation. It is to the significance of these verses, therefore, in the context of the Markan ending, that we shall now turn.

Let us consider first of all the nature and content of the empty tomb story. Its main features can be stated as follows. After the burial of Jesus by Joseph of Arimathea (Mk 15.42–7), three named women come to the tomb to anoint Jesus' body (Mk 16.1–5). An announcement is given to them by a young man that Jesus has risen and is not there (Mk 16.6). Jesus, they are told, is to precede them to Galilee and there they will see him. This is accompanied by an instruction that the promise, which has already been given (Mk 14.28), be reported to the disciples and Peter (Mk 16.7). The reader is informed, however, that the message wasn't relayed by the women (Mk 16.8). The Gospel ends abruptly therefore with the women's timid disobedience.[222] No post-resurrection appearances of Jesus to his disciples are recounted.

The Markan ending has attracted considerable scholarly attention.[223] The historical plausibility of the account has been

---

[222] *Pace* D. Catchpole, 'The Fearful Silence of the Women at the Tomb', *JTSouthAfr*, 18 (1977), pp. 3–10. The 'fear', according to Catchpole, is numinous fear, the result of an epiphany, and not cowardly fear.

[223] For some fuller treatments, classic or recent, see, for example, P. L. Danove, *The End of Mark's Story. A Methodological Study* (Biblical Interpretation 3; Leiden, New York and Cologne: Brill, 1993); R. H. Fuller, *The Formation of the Resurrection Narratives* (New York: Macmillan; London: SPCK, 1971), pp. 50–70; R. H. Lightfoot, *Locality and Doctrine in the Gospels* (London: Hodder & Stoughton, 1938), pp. 1–48; R. H. Lightfoot, *The Gospel Message of St Mark* (Oxford: Clarendon Press, 1950), pp. 80–97; J. L. Magness, *Sense and Absence. Structure and Suspension in the Ending of Mark's Gospel* (SBL Semeia Series; Atlanta, GA: Scholars Press, 1986); W. Marxsen, *The Resurrection of Jesus of Nazareth* (London: SCM Press; Philadelphia, PA: Fortress Press, 1968), pp. 25–78; Marxsen, *Mark*, pp. 54–116; N. Perrin, *The Resurrection Narratives. A New Approach* (London: SPCK, 1977), pp. 17–40. For a review of recent approaches, see Telford, 'History of Developments' in Telford (ed.), *Interpretation*, pp. 37–9; Telford, *Mark*, pp. 147–9.

severely questioned by scholars.[224] A number of traditio-critical studies have attempted to determine whether or to what extent it has drawn on previous tradition, and whether or to what degree it is redactional.[225] The key question that we shall pursue, however, is this: why is it that the earliest gospel contains no post-resurrection appearances to the disciples? To appreciate the full significance of the Markan ending one needs to compare and contrast this ending with the other resurrection and post-resurrection traditions of the early church.

Where the pre-Markan tradition is concerned, the earliest recorded claim to post-resurrection appearances on the part of Jesus to his disciples are those reported by Paul in 1 Corinthians 15.3–8. Since Paul states that these claims were passed on to him, we may assume that they pre-date the mid-fifties when Paul was writing his Corinthian correspondence. Paul's statement, it must be noted, does not convey any certain knowledge of the empty tomb story as we have it in Mark, unless (and this is unlikely) 'he was buried' (*etaphē*) has its literal meaning 'he was placed in a sepulchre/entombed' (1 Cor. 15.4). Paul's statement, moreover, only *lists* these alleged post-resurrection appearances (to Cephas, to the twelve, to more than five hundred brethren, to James, to all the apostles, and finally to Paul himself), but offers little in the way of narrative details. We are not told when they occurred, or where they occurred (whether Galilee, Jerusalem or elsewhere), or even what form the appearances took. These reported appearances, furthermore, are difficult to correlate with the narrative accounts in the Gospels. No women, one also observes, are mentioned in the Pauline list. In the case of the appearance to Paul himself (see also 1 Cor. 9.1 and Gal. 1.11–17), the writer of the Acts of the Apostles, writing in the eighties, supplies no less than three such narrative accounts (Acts 9, 22, 26) but each offers a slightly

---

[224] See Fuller, *Formation*, pp. 51–2.
[225] See P. Perkins, *Resurrection. New Testament Witness and Contemporary Reflection* (Garden City, NY: Doubleday, 1984), pp. 114–24, 138–44. For an assessment, see F. Neirynck, 'Marc 16,1–8. Tradition et rédaction', *ETL*, 56 (1980), pp. 56–88. For the view that Mark created the story, see J. D. Crossan, 'Empty Tomb and Absent Lord (Mark 16:1–8)' in W. H. Kelber (ed.), *The Passion in Mark. Studies on Mark 14–16* (Philadelphia, PA: Fortress Press, 1976), pp. 135–52.

different version. In sum, then, we may say that before the writing of Mark's Gospel, the tradition available to Paul knows of certain claims to post-resurrection appearances on the part of Jesus' original disciples, but does not specify their nature, time or location. Narrative details are not supplied by Paul, and the Markan story of the discovery of the empty tomb is apparently unknown to him. The first narrative account of the discovery of the empty tomb, therefore, appears to be Markan, and all subsequent narrative accounts relating to both empty tomb and post-resurrection appearances are post-Markan.

The first of these is that by Matthew, whose account of the finding of the empty tomb is based on that of Mark, that is, up until Mark 16.8 (Mt. 28.1–7). The Markan account, however, has been subject to considerable embellishment by Matthew. The great earthquake, the descent of the angel (replacing the young man), the terrified guards at the tomb, their subsequent report to, and silencing by the authorities are all details not supplied by his source (Mt. 28.2–4, 11–15). The guarding of the tomb in particular is clearly a legendary addition with the apologetic aim of countering a claim, circulating as early as the eighties, that the disciples had stolen the body of Jesus. As in Mark, the women are instructed to inform the disciples of Jesus' promised appearance in Galilee, but, in sharp contrast to Mark, the message this time *is relayed* (Mt. 28.8), with Jesus himself making a brief appearance to them on the way (Mt. 28.9–10). Having altered his source in this manner, Matthew then supplies the promised Galilean appearance to the disciples (Mt. 28.16–20). On 'the mountain to which Jesus (but not Mark!) had directed them' (Mt. 28.16), they are commissioned to 'make disciples of all nations', with evangelism, as well as leadership of the post-Easter church (Mt. 16.17–19; 18.18), their future role.

Luke's resurrection narrative is also based on the empty tomb story of Mark, again, that is, up until Mark 16.8 (Lk. 24.1–7). In common with Matthew, however, Luke informs his readers that the message of the angels (now more than one!) to the disciples was relayed by the women, but in this case *disbelieved* (Lk. 24.8–11). Mention is made of a post-resurrection appearance to Peter (Lk. 24.34), but no narrative account is given. Narrative accounts of post-resurrection appearances, however, are given, although these, it is to be noted, are set in the vicinity of *Jerusalem*, not in Galilee, as given in Matthew (and hinted at in Mark). In consequence, the implied Markan reference to Jesus' appearance in Galilee (Mk 16.7) is deliberately altered by Luke (see also Mk 14.28 which is omitted). The third evangelist's special stories feature an appearance to two disciples on the Emmaus road (Lk. 24.13–35), and a manifestation to the eleven in Jerusalem (Lk. 24.36–49) in which the Lukan Jesus eats before his disciples after inviting them to touch his hands and his feet. Such motifs have an apologetic aim, either to counter the claim that the appearances were hallucinations, or to offset a docetic tendency to view the risen Jesus as a spirit. As with the Matthean account, the disciples are commissioned for their role in the post-Easter church, and, according to Acts, receive a forty-day period of instruction (Acts 1.1–11). This commission is to involve the preaching of repentance, and the forgiveness of sins, 'starting from Jerusalem' (Lk. 24.47). The eleven are also to be witnesses (Lk. 24.48), and a promise of the Spirit is given (Lk. 24.49; Acts 1.4, 5, 8; 2.1ff.). A further special feature of the Lukan account is the climactic ascension scene. This is absent from the Markan and Matthean accounts but present in certain of our textual witnesses for Luke as well as in Acts (Lk. 24.51; Acts 1.9–11). Some manuscripts of Luke also include a passage (Lk. 24.12) in which Peter, following the disbelief with which the women's words are greeted, runs to the tomb, nevertheless, to investigate (Lk. 24.24).

A similar but more developed version of this story is found in John 20 where once again the message is relayed (by Mary Magdalene only) to both Peter and the beloved disciple (a new character) who run to the tomb to check. An appearance to Mary Magdalene is presented (Jn 20.11–18; cf. Mt. 28.9–10) as well as to the disciples in Jerusalem (Jn 20.19–23, 24–9; cf. Lk. 24.36–49). After being commissioned (Jn 20.21), the disciples receive the Holy Spirit directly from Jesus (compare and contrast Lk. 24.49 and Acts 2.1ff.), and are given authority to forgive or retain sins (Jn 20.23; cf. Mt. 16.19; 18.18). In what may be (at least in part) an appendix by a later hand, John 21 presents a further appearance to seven disciples including Peter, this time in Galilee. Here we may be witnessing the combination of the Matthean and Lukan traditions of separate Galilee/Jerusalem appearances. In yet another commissioning scene, the disciples, and in particular Peter, are once again given a role in the post-Easter church. By means of the miraculous draught of fishes allegory, apparently an embellished variant of the earlier 'I will make you fishers of men' story (Mk 1.16–20; Lk. 5.1–11), the Fourth Gospel not only encapsulates the disciples' future task of evangelism but also, after his threefold declaration of love and loyalty (contrast Mk 14.54, 66–72 and his threefold denial), Peter's subsequent leadership role.

A further development in the empty tomb story is reflected in the second century apocryphal *Gospel of Peter* 8.28–14.60.[226] Here there is a highly fanciful account of the resurrection itself (the emergence from the tomb of two giant figures with a third carrying a cross), with the people of Jerusalem coming out to see the sepulchre, and not only the guards (together with a centurion, Petronius) but also the elders and scribes being present for the event. This account, too, has an apologetic aim, and was perhaps created, among other things, to counter the claim that post-resurrection appearances were suspect because they happened to Jesus' disciples only. Further tradition is reflected in the apocryphal *Gospel of the Hebrews*[227] in which Jesus first makes an appearance to his own brother James to whom he passes on his mantle of authority (contrast 1 Cor. 15.7).[228]

Despite all the differences to be discerned in these developing accounts, many of which can be put down to imaginative embellishment or to apologetic or doctrinal factors, certain common and fundamental elements stand out. A major feature (and function) of the post-resurrection appearance traditions,

---

[226] E. Hennecke and W. Schneemelcher (eds.), *New Testament Apocrypha* (London: SCM Press, 1963), Vol. I, pp. 185–7.

[227] The fragment is cited by Jerome, *De Viris Illustribus*, 2; see W. Schneemelcher, *New Testament Apocrypha* (Cambridge: James Clarke; Louisville, KY: Westminster John Knox Press, 1991), p. 178.

[228] For yet further developments, see also *Epistula Apostolorum* and *The Acts of Pilate* (Schneemelcher, *Apocrypha*, Vol. I, pp. 249–84; pp. 505ff.)

indeed perhaps even a generative element, is to show the original disciples as having a leadership role in the post-Easter community in consequence of having been directly commissioned by the risen Jesus. Our brief survey of the trajectory of resurrection and post-resurrection traditions in the early church serves moreover to highlight the distinctive features of the Markan ending. Mark's Gospel offers us our first narrative account of the discovery of the empty tomb. In contrast with the earlier Pauline tradition, our earliest Gospel informs us that a message that he had risen was first delivered to the women, and that the disciples and Peter were to be told (or rather retold) that he would appear (after his resurrection) in Galilee (and not in Jerusalem, as in Luke). In contrast with all the other Gospel accounts, it informs us that this message was not relayed. In contrast to the Lukan or Johannine tradition, there was no visit by Peter or anyone else to the empty tomb (cf. Lk. 24.12 (variant reading); Jn 20.3–10). In contrast with all the pre-Markan and post-Markan traditions, there is no account of any post-resurrection appearances to Peter, to the eleven, to James, to the apostles, to the women, to Mary Magdalene, to the two on the Emmaus road, either in Galilee or in Jerusalem, far less an account of the resurrection itself at which guards and Jewish authorities were present. In consequence, no commission is given to the disciples to play a role in the post-Easter church. No leadership role is granted to them, as in each of the other Gospels. There is no receipt (or even a promise) of the Holy Spirit, as in Luke and John (though see Mk 13.11). There is no restoration of Peter after his denial, as in Jn 21.15–17 or Lk. 22.31–32. There is no ascension scene after a period of teaching, as in Luke–Acts.

It is no wonder then that the Markan conclusion was from a very early time regarded as inadequate or incomplete. As a result, a number of endings were supplied by the early church which were not part of the original text of Mark.[229] One ending, the 'Shorter Ending', adds the following verse after

---

[229] For text-critical comment on these endings, see, for example, C. E. B. Cranfield, 'Mark, Gospel of' in *IDB*, pp. 275–6; J. K. Elliott, 'The Text and Language of the Endings to Mark's Gospel', *TZ*, 27 (1971), pp. 255–62; Fuller, *Formation*, pp. 155–9;

Mark 16.8: 'But they reported briefly to Peter and those with him all that they had been told. And after this, Jesus himself sent out by means of them, from east to west, the sacred and imperishable proclamation of eternal salvation' (Mk 16.9). Present in several uncials of the seventh, eighth and ninth centuries, a few minuscules and several ancient versions, this ending has a high incidence of non-Markan words and a different rhetorical tone to the rest of the Markan Gospel. It is 'gnostic-sounding', according to R. H. Fuller,[230] and the last clause in particular betrays the hand of a later Greek theologian (B. M. Metzger).[231] Again it is to be observed that the text has Jesus commission his disciples for a world-wide mission not confined to Jews alone.

A second ending is the so-called 'Longer Ending' (Mk 16.9–20) which is present in the King James version but lacking in our oldest manuscripts as well as from all Greek manuscripts known to Eusebius and Jerome. It is not attested in Greek manuscripts of the New Testament before the fifth century. Its earliest attestation is by Irenaeus, and so it probably arose in the mid-second century, or shortly before. It was clearly unknown to Matthew or Luke who both sharply diverge, as we have seen, after Mark. 16.8. Lacking Markan style and content (as well as a smooth juncture between Mk 16.8 and 16.9), it presents us with seventeen non-Markan words, or words used in a non-Markan sense. By common consent, it is either an artificial, composite summary of the resurrection traditions in the other Gospels, designed presumably to bring Mark into line with them (W. Marxsen), or a catechetical summary of post-resurrection appearances drawing on some independent elements of the tradition (B. H. Streeter, C. E. B. Cranfield, R. H. Fuller). While the text has Jesus upbraid the disciples for their unbelief and hardness of heart, it has him commission the twelve,

---

B. M. Metzger, *The Text of the New Testament. Its Transmission, Corruption, and Restoration* (Oxford: Clarendon Press, 1964), pp. 226–9.

[230] R. H. Fuller, *A Critical Introduction to the New Testament* (London: Duckworth, 1966), p. 107.

[231] Metzger, *Text*, p. 228.

nevertheless, and give them authority to carry out a mission to all the world, to Jews and Gentile alike.

The third ending, the so-called 'Expanded Longer Ending' consists of an addition after Mark 16.14 (the Freer Logion).[232] Occurring in the fifth century Washington Codex only, it was known to Jerome and was possibly inserted at the end of the second century or beginning of the third to soften the rebuke to the disciples.

Since all these endings are secondary, then, to return to the main question, how do we explain the astonishing fact that our earliest Gospel records no post-resurrection appearances to the disciples? Three possibilities have been suggested. The first is that Mark's Gospel, as we have it, is incomplete, and was not intended to end at 16.8. The second is that Mark's Gospel was intended to end at 16.8, but the evangelist included no narrative accounts of post-resurrection appearances since these were not known to him. A third possibility is that Mark's Gospel was intended to end at 16.8, that Mark did know of these post-resurrection accounts, but that he deliberately chose to omit them. If so, we must ask why?

Is Mark's Gospel incomplete? In support of this first possibility, three main arguments have been advanced. In the first place, it is inconceivable that Mark could have recorded no post-resurrection appearances when claims for such (if not narrative accounts) were in existence prior to the writing of his Gospel (1 Cor. 15.3–8). Mk 14.28 and 16.7 appear, indeed, to indicate knowledge of these. Secondly, the Gospel as it stands ends with the words 'for they were afraid' (*ephobounto gar*). A sentence, paragraph and especially a book cannot end, it has been said, with a conjunction (*gar*). The verb 'to be afraid' (*phobeisthai*), furthermore, cannot be used absolutely, but requires a direct object ('for they feared ...'), an infinitive ('for they were afraid to ...'), or a complementary clause ('for they were afraid that/lest ...'). Thirdly, would Mark have left his readers with this picture of the original Jewish-Christian community's womenfolk, depicting those who had followed Jesus

---

[232] Named after Charles Freer who first obtained it in Cairo in 1906, and deposited it in the Freer Gallery of Art in Washington.

(including his mother) as overcome with fear and, disobedient to the young man's message, telling no one?

To account for the Gospel's abrupt end, various hypotheses have been advanced. Some would hold that the Gospel was never completed by Mark, the work being interrupted by his incapacity, premature death, imprisonment or martyrdom. Others claim that the last leaf of the Gospel suffered unintentional loss or damage, others still that the evangelist had written something which was later regarded as heretical and the last leaf was deliberately removed by an editor who objected to its contents.

The following, however, can be said by way of reply. The first of these objections surely begs the question, although the interpretation of Mark 14.28 and 16.7 poses a special problem to which we shall shortly return. The literary considerations, however, can be easily dispensed with. Since these objections were first raised, the stylistic possibility of a sentence, paragraph and even a book ending with *gar* has now been established without doubt.[233] Mark uses the verb *phobeisthai* twelve times, and apart from 16.8, it occurs in the absolute sense some five times (Mk 5.15, 33, 36; 6.50; 10.32). There is no example of its use in Mark with a complementary clause. The psychological objection also begs the question. The 'fear' motif is a common one in Mark and is often tied up with the notion of unbelief (Mk 4.40–41; 6.50–52; 9.6, 32; 10.32–34). It is entirely appropriate, therefore, that the evangelist should end with such a statement.

Where hypotheses of an incomplete ending are concerned, arguments in respect of the evangelist's alleged incapacity, imprisonment and death are purely speculative, but even if one were to concede these as possibilities, one may question why Mark's community or followers did not immediately afterwards supply the intended conclusion. This never happened as the versions of Mark used by Matthew and Luke indicate (they diverge, as we have observed, after 16.8). Where loss or damage

---

[233] Lightfoot, *Locality*, pp. 10–18; Lightfoot, *Mark*, pp. 85–6; P. W. van der Horst, 'Can a Book End with γάρ? A Note on Mark xvi.8', *JTS*, 23 (1972), pp. 121–4. Cf. also Gen. 18.15 (LXX). For Mark's fondness for explanatory *gar* clauses, see C. H. Bird, 'Some γάρ Clauses in St. Mark's Gospel', *JTS*, 4 (1953), pp. 171–87.

was concerned, this too had to have happened shortly after the Gospel was written (on a codex and not a scroll), and before copies were made, since the copies that reached Matthew and Luke both lacked the supposed original ending. Why did Mark not supply a new conclusion, or if he had suffered incapacity or death in the meantime, why did neither his community nor his disciples supply the conclusion from memory (or tradition?). The notion of suppression is also problematic. It involves three areas of speculation: on the existence of an ending beyond 16.8, on the contents of such, and on an unknown editor prior to Matthew or Luke who disapproved of it and its contents.[234]

For many of the reasons above, the majority of scholars would now hold that 16.8 was the original ending of the Gospel,[235] and this judgment has been reinforced by recent literary studies.[236] These have argued that, in terms of 'closure', Mark 16.8 fulfils textually generated plot patterns or expectations. Indeed the verse itself permits no continuation ('And they said nothing to anyone. For they were afraid')!

If the Gospel ended at 16.8, then, to repeat our question, why are there no post-resurrection appearances to the disciples? Was it because the evangelist knew of no such accounts? Those espousing this second possibility would claim that Mark knows of the resurrection event as such but as with the primitive community could have believed that Jesus had been immediately exalted or 'translated' to heaven like Enoch or Elijah (Mk 16.6), thence to return as the triumphant Son of Man.[237] There is no evidence, apart from Mark 14.28 and 16.7, however, that Mark knew of alleged post-resurrection appearances by the

---

[234] W. Marxsen, *Introduction to the New Testament. An Approach to its Problems* (Oxford: Blackwell, 1968), pp. 139–42.

[235] W. G. Kümmel, *Introduction to the New Testament* (London: SCM Press, 1975), pp. 98–101.

[236] See, for example, T. E. Boomershine and G. L. Bartholomew, 'The Narrative Technique of Mark 16:8', *JBL*, 100 (1981), pp. 213–23; T. E. Boomershine, 'Mark 16:8 and the Apostolic Commission', *JBL*, 100 (1981), pp. 225–39; F. Kermode, 'The Structures of Fiction', *Modern Language Notes*, 84 (1969), pp. 891–915; A. T. Lincoln, 'The Promise and the Failure: Mark 16:7, 8' in Telford (ed.), *Interpretation*, pp. 229–51; N. R. Petersen, 'When is the End not the End? Literary Reflections on the Ending of Mark's Narrative', *Int*, 34 (1980), pp. 151–66; Powell, ' Mark', pp. 341–6.

[237] See N. Q. Hamilton, 'Resurrection Tradition and the Composition of Mark', *JBL*, 84 (1965), pp. 415–21.

risen Jesus to specific people (as listed by Paul in 1 Cor. 15.5–8) prior to his 'translation' to heaven. The two problematic verses, Mark 14.28 and 16.7, which suggest that he does know of such claims, can equally be interpreted as referring not to his resurrection but to his parousia, believed shortly to occur in Galilee (see E. Lohmeyer, W. Marxsen).[238] When the young man declares 'there you will *see* him (Mk 16.7), the verb used here (*horan*) is the same as that used of his parousia in Mark 9.1, 13.26 and 14.62. When Mark was writing, therefore, actual narrative accounts of post-resurrection appearances by Jesus to his disciples prior to his exaltation and parousia were perhaps only beginning to develop and circulate. The early church was prone to extend the tradition at the beginning and at the end of Jesus' life. The separate birth and infancy narratives to be found in Matthew and Luke as well as in the later Apocryphal Gospels testify to this, and one may compare likewise the development in the post-resurrection accounts traced earlier. Such accounts as we have in the later Gospels, then, may be the product of subsequent embellishment and/or invention.

These arguments are compelling, but again certain objections can be raised.[239] The verb used of 'seeing' Jesus (*horan*), while it may be used of his parousia, is also used in the New Testament of the post-resurrection appearances (see 1 Cor. 9.1). The specific reference in Mark 16.7 to 'the disciples and Peter' does seem to suggest the post-resurrection appearances to 'Cephas and the twelve' referred to by Paul in 1 Corinthians 15.5. It would be reasonable to assume, then, that Mark is here betraying his knowledge of the post-resurrection appearances claimed for Peter and the twelve. The later evangelists, Matthew and Luke, certainly interpret their source in this way, taking Mark's words to refer to the promise of a post-resurrection appearance and not to the parousia. Luke, however, as we have seen, alters the reference to 'Galilee' and locates these

---

[238] See E. Lohmeyer, *Galiläa und Jerusalem* (Göttingen: Vandenhoeck & Ruprecht, 1936), pp. 10–14; Marxsen, *Mark*, pp. 83–92, 111–16. Cf. also Fuller, *Formation*, pp. 62–4; Lightfoot, *Locality*, pp. 73–77.

[239] See, for example, R. H. Stein, 'A Short Note on Mark XIV.28 and XVI.7', *NTS*, 20 (1973–4), pp. 445–52.

appearances exclusively in Jerusalem and its environs (Lk. 24.6 and parallel; and note 'beginning from Jerusalem' and 'stay in the city' 24.47, 49). Since Mark 14.28 and 16.7 are redactional (W. Marxsen) and since the Pauline evidence in 1 Corinthians 15 gives no grounds for assuming that the post-resurrection appearances listed there took place in Galilee, it seems, however, that Mark is the first in the developing tradition to claim that Jesus would be seen, or would appear, in Galilee.

Why this stress on Galilee, an interest that appears elsewhere throughout Mark? It is the view of some scholars (for example, E. C. Hoskyns, C. F. Evans, J. Schreiber, G. Boobyer) that references to Galilee in Mark (as with Lukan references to Jerusalem) carry more of a theological significance than a literal one.[240] For Mark, Galilee is a symbol of the Gentile world. Galilee, it is claimed, was notorious in Mark's day for its mixed Gentile–Jewish population. Even in the Old Testament, with which his readers were familiar, it was on several occasions associated with the Gentiles (Isa. 9.1) and Matthew who cites this Isaianic passage certainly understood it in this way (Mt. 4.15). If this is correct, then the significance of the inserted verses 14.28 and 16.7 in Mark is that the evangelist is telling his readers that Jesus promised his disciples that he would appear among the Gentiles, and before them at that!

In Mark's Gospel, then, we have a gospel which ended at 16.8. It records no post-resurrection appearances to Peter and to the twelve. The import of this omission – and this, in our view, has been insufficiently taken account of – is that it fails to present the original disciples as in receipt of a post-resurrection commission from Jesus or of any specific authority, as in the later traditions, to exercise a leadership role in the post-Easter church. While it does anticipate their testimony, and even Spirit-inspired support under persecution (Mk 13.9–13), it offers the reader no restoration of Peter after his denial, promises the

---

[240] See G. H. Boobyer, 'Galilee and Galileans in St Mark's Gospel', *BJRL*, 35 (1952–3), pp. 334–48; C. F. Evans, 'I will go before you into Galilee', *JTS*, 5 (1954), pp. 3–18; E. C. Hoskyns, 'Adversaria Exegetica', *Theology*, 7 (1923), pp. 147–55; Schreiber, 'Christologie', pp. 154–83, esp. 171–2; J. Schreiber, *Theologie des Vertrauens. Eine Redaktionsgeschichtliche Untersuchung des Markusevangeliums* (Hamburg: Furche, 1967), pp. 170–84; see also Fuller, *Formation*, pp. 58–62.

original disciples no authority to forgive or retain sins, nor grants them any promise or receipt of the Spirit in connection with such a commission. Mark intimates, however, by the insertion of 14.28 and 16.7, that he, like Paul, knew of alleged post-resurrection appearances to the disciples and Peter (see 1 Cor. 15.5), although there is no certain evidence that in the tradition before Mark these were associated with Galilee. Luke, for his part, felt free to locate them exclusively in Jerusalem and its environs. Since Mark betrays his knowledge of such alleged appearances, but does not include them, then we are left with no other option than that he deliberately chose to omit them.

In keeping with his treatment of the disciples throughout the Gospel, Mark did so, I suggest, because these stories served to demonstrate the authority of Jewish Christians as the true bearers or interpreters of Jesus' message, and to legitimate their leadership role over nascent Gentile-Christianity. He did so, I further suggest, on account of the particular status these narratives conferred on the twelve, and the support, therefore, that such a post-resurrection commission might have given to their developing hegemony. All the Markan reader is given are two verses inserted into Mark's material (Mk 14.28; 16.7) in which there is a *promise* that Jesus would 'go before' (*proagein*) the disciples to Galilee. If we interpret the reference to Galilee theologically rather than literally, then this is, in effect, a Gentile mission prediction which Mark introduces into a tradition which hitherto knew of no such prediction on the part of the historical Jesus (Mk 13.10; contrast Mt. 10.5–6, 23).

Mark's Gospel ends, therefore, quite appropriately and consistently by proclaiming to the (Gentile-Christian) reader that the risen Jesus is to be found (as the earthly Jesus was)[241] in 'Galilee of the Gentiles', in the Gentile world, but that, as in all else, his original Jewish disciples didn't get the message! The ending is an apposite one, then, if we consider the Gospel of Mark as a Gentile Gospel which may in fact be attacking the primitive Jewish-Christian community for its resistance not only to the 'secret', namely Jesus' divine status as the 'Son of God',

---

[241] See especially Mk 1.14–5.53 (Galilee); 6.1–9.50 (in the Gentile regions within and outside Galilee).

but also for its resistance to the Gentile mission, to contacts with Gentiles, to the sharing of table fellowship etc. This resistance was met by Hellenistic-Jewish Christians such as Paul and is inexplicable if Jesus himself had predicted a Gentile mission. But this raises again the historical questions concerning the aim of Mark's theology and the purpose of his Gospel, and it is to these that we shall turn in the final section.

Parenesis or polemic?: Mark's theology in historical perspective

The subject of Mark's theology in its historical setting was introduced in the first chapter but it is appropriate to return to it now that we have examined the internal evidence of the work. It is time to draw everything together, then, and to assess the question of the Gospel's overall purpose and setting. Before I do so, let me review the major issues which have arisen in the course of the discussion, and the conclusions that have been reached up to this point. We began with some matters of 'Introduction'.

Where the date of Mark is concerned, we noted that most scholars have accepted a time of composition within the period 65–75 CE, that is, just before or just after the Romano-Jewish War in 66–70. Crucial for a dating specifically before or after this event is the interpretation of Mark 13, and in particular the question whether the writer composed this passage in light of the fall of Jerusalem and the destruction of the Temple. In my opinion such a knowledge is presupposed, and I have therefore placed the Gospel in the early seventies. It is unlikely that the Gospel writer is to be identified with the John Mark of the New Testament. The Papias evidence which supports this attribution is unreliable, I have maintained, and the internal evidence weighs against it. This evidence indicates, however, that our unknown author was in touch with the Palestinian Jesus tradition, even if he was, at the same time, unfamiliar with Palestinian geography and Jewish customs. Where the Second Gospel's provenance is concerned, Galilee, Rome or Syria (Antioch or rural, small-town southern Syria) have all been suggested, but, while Rome remains the strongest contender,

certainty in this area is not possible. The internal evidence of
the Gospel, however, would offer support for the view that
Mark's audience consisted of Greek-speaking Christians of
Gentile origin who were in some tension with their Jewish
heritage.

We also observed in passing the problem of history in Mark.
An extremely optimistic view of the historical reliability of the
Markan Gospel has traditionally been defended on the basis of
the hypothesis that John Mark was the author and that, as
Peter's *hermeneutēs*, he drew on the eye-witness testimony of this
prominent figure in the primitive Jewish-Christian community.
Apart from Papias, this theory was based almost entirely on the
prominence given to Peter and the twelve in the Gospel, but, as
we have seen, other explanations can account for this interest.
This traditional picture has also come to be seriously challenged
by the findings of source, form and redaction criticism.

In the introduction, we considered what the traditio-critical
methods had contributed to our knowledge of the Gospel's
theology in its historical setting. We enquired whether Mark
had incorporated distinct and extensive written sources into his
Gospel, but here the results were negative. We did, however,
recognize that different types of material are to be found
arranged in rough groupings within the Gospel and linked
together with summary passages. These include miracle stories,
for example, in Mark 1.21–2.12; 4.35–5.43; 6.31–52 and
7.24–8.10, 22–6; controversy pericopae (mostly apophthegms)
in 2.1–3.6, 7.1–23, 11.27–12.40; parables in 4.1–34; sayings
complexes in 3.22–30; 8.34–9.1; 9.33–50; 10.2–45 and 11.22–5;
an apocalyptic discourse in 13 and a passion narrative in 14–15.
Mark was probably responsible for the overall arrangement of
this material, but there exists a distinct possibility that some of
the material in these groupings had already been linked together before the evangelist took it over.

Form and redaction criticism, tempered by the insights of
literary criticism, have been the other fundamental tools on
which reliance has been placed. Adhering in the main to the
basic axioms and results of form criticism on Mark, I have
throughout regarded the Gospel as a product not of direct eye-

witness testimony but of community traditions compiled, arranged and interpreted by a creative redactor. The Gospel is
the compilation of a number of single, isolated, easily memor-
ized traditions or pericopae (or small clusters of such pericopae)
which circulated in oral form before being written down. The
traditions with which the evangelist operated had been retained
and transmitted in response to the practical needs of the
Markan community (preaching, teaching, exhortation or parenesis, controversy, etc.), and by virtue of constant repetition had
taken on a stereotyped form which is clearly recognizable.
These traditions, moreover, reflected the faith of the communities that preserved them and were stamped with their own
particular estimate of the significance of Jesus' person and
activity. The evangelist first provided the framework in which
these diverse narrative and sayings traditions were brought
together into our first connected Gospel, but, as redaction
criticism has shown us, he did far more than this. One of my
consistent emphases has been that the evangelist was not a
mere compiler, collector or editor of traditions but one who was
to a large degree responsible for the final form of the Gospel. In
this, moreover, he has revealed himself to be a theologian of not
inconsiderable skill.

From a consideration of Mark's sources, oral or written, we
proceeded, therefore, to examine the *creative* editorial work
conducted by Mark on his sources – his redaction – and from
thence to determine his theological outlook and motivation. We
saw that redaction critics had isolated at least seven key redactional features, emphases or motifs in the Gospel. It is worth
reminding ourselves what these were:

(a) the *secrecy* motif and the writer's interest in the true but
hidden *identity of Jesus*.

(b) an interest in the *passion* of Jesus (his suffering, death and
resurrection) and its significance for Christology.

(c) an interest in the nature and coming of the *Kingdom of God*
and in the question of Jesus' return as *Son of Man*.

(d) an interest in *Galilee*.[242]

---

[242] According to W. Marxsen, *Mark*, pp. 54–116, all references to Galilee in the Gospel
(except Mk 6.21) are to be considered redactional. Jesus' proclamation of the gospel

(e) his use of the term 'gospel' (*euangelion*).[243]

(f) an interest in *Gentiles* and the Gentile mission.

(g) an interest in *persecution, suffering* and *martyrdom* and the true nature of *discipleship*.

(h) his harsh treatment of the *Jewish leadership groups,* Jesus' *family* and especially his original *disciples*.

Any valid theory of the Gospel's overall theological purpose must take into account all of these distinctive features and assess them accordingly, as I have attempted to do.

In chapter two, we began our examination of Markan theology. Two emphases have guided the study. On the one hand, the scope of the enquiry has been narrowed to focus especially on Mark's Christology, soteriology and eschatology. On the other hand, our perspective on Mark's theological treatment of his traditions has been widened by the attempt to place these traditions within their broader cultural and religious context. We first looked at Mark's Christology and the nature and function of the so-called 'Messianic secret' in particular. By means of this motif Jesus is presented as acting – in respect of his teaching and miracles – in the capacity of the concealed and unrecognized 'Son of God' (unrecognized, that is, except by the supernatural world and by a Gentile centurion).

Of special importance was the question of the interpretation of the crucial titles 'Son of God' and 'Son of Man' in Mark. I argued that the term 'Son of God' was not a common designation or title for the Messiah as such and hence that what we have in Mark is not strictly a 'Messianic' secret but a 'Son of God' secret.[244] In Mark the term has moved in the direction of being understood in the Hellenistic sense of a pre-existent, supernatural or divine being present in human form, as an

---

of the Kingdom of God begins in Galilee (Mk 1.9, 14), a report about him first spreads throughout Galilee (Mk 1.28), his subsequent activity is centred on Galilee and the surrounding Gentile regions (e.g. Mk 1.39 *et passim*), and, contrary to Luke, Galilee is the location for his promised appearance (Mk 14.28; 16.7).

[243] This again, according to Marxsen, is redactional (*Mark*, pp. 117–50). The term is used by Hellenistic Christianity, particularly by Paul, for the 'proclamation of a message of salvation'. This message has as its content the death and resurrection of Jesus and the salvation effected thereby. If employed in some such sense by Mark, then it is clearly anachronistic. See Telford, *Mark*, pp. 120–1.

[244] See Schulz, 'Markus', pp. 184–97.

epiphany of God, and not in the Jewish sense of a human figure appointed by God, the obedient agent of his will. The primitive Jewish-Christian community saw Jesus in this latter sense, I submit, but by virtue of a belief in his resurrection and exaltation to heaven viewed him thereafter as God's eschatological agent about to return in glory and power either as the Davidic Messiah, the Son of David or as the apocalyptic Son of Man. In such a capacity he would bring in the Kingdom of God whose imminent coming he had proclaimed in his lifetime as a prophet.

Mark in part rejects, in part modifies these earlier triumphalist Jewish-Christian estimates and does so in two ways. Christologically, he presents Jesus as he was seen by Gentile Christians, namely as the divine Son of God, and not as the Jewish Messiah, the Son of David. By means of the secrecy motif, the Jesus of the Jewish-Christian tradition is presented to the reader as the bearer in his earthly life of the more exalted (but concealed) status of the (divine) Son of God. Soteriologically, he presents Jesus' suffering and death as not only predestined but as fundamental to salvation (e.g. Mk 10.45). By means of the passion predictions (Mk 8.31; 9.31; 10.33–4), the other suffering 'Son of Man' sayings (Mk 9.9, 12; 10.45; 14.21 (twice), 41) and the passion narrative, the *suffering, death and resurrection* of the returning (apocalyptic) Son of Man is presented as a pre-ordained part of the divine plan for redemption.

The case for considering these suffering 'Son of Man' sayings as redactional is, as we have seen, a strong one. In emphasizing the pre-ordained suffering, death and resurrection of the Son of Man, they serve to bind the passion and resurrection narrative of chapters 14–16 to the miscellaneous traditional material presented beforehand. With these emphases, therefore, Mark reflects a shift away, I believe, from an earlier Jewish-Christian apocalyptic tradition towards one reflecting the influence of the Hellenistic kerygma of the cross, particularly that of Paul, for whom the 'Proclaimer' of the coming Kingdom of God of the Jewish-Christian tradition has become the one whose saving death, as well as resurrection, is the content of the message of salvation, the 'gospel' proclaimed among the Gentiles, the 'mystery' or 'secret' now being made manifest to them.

This shift in emphasis from apocalyptic eschatology to Christology and soteriology we traced also in Mark's redaction of the parables and the Kingdom sayings of the tradition. Originally elucidating Jesus' proclamation about the coming Kingdom of God, the parables are seen by Mark as cryptic utterances whose meaning is only open to those who recognize that Jesus is the 'Son of God' and who, as believers therefore, see the gospel message prefigured in them. The Kingdom of God which is viewed as a future apocalyptic event in the pre-Markan tradition is now a mystery or secret revealed to the initiated and that secret is again bound up with Jesus' identity (and presence) as 'Son of God'(on earth). The Gospel of Mark in its eschatology, I therefore concluded, represents an early stage in the transformation of the apocalyptic hope of both Jesus and primitive Jewish Christianity. Jesus 'the Proclaimer' of the coming eschatological Kingdom of God is in process of being seen as 'the Proclaimed' in whose person and ministry the Kingdom was (in another sense) already present. This is the 'the secret (or 'mystery') of the Kingdom of God' (Mk 4.11). Eschatology, in other words, is on the way to being eclipsed by Christology and soteriology.

A similar movement is to be seen in Mark's treatment of the miracle tradition. Here I distinguished between an eschatological understanding of the miracles (the miracles as 'signs' or manifestations of the Messiah) and an 'epiphanic' or Christological one (the miracles as manifestations of the Son of God as divine man), the former Jewish, the latter more Hellenistic. While both understandings appeared to be attached to the miracles of Jesus in the different strands of the pre-Markan tradition, I inclined to the view that Mark saw the miracles in an *epiphanic* light, that is, as the action of a divine man, a *theios anēr*, the supernatural Son of God. They therefore enhanced his epiphany Christology.[245]

Finally, we examined Mark's treatment of the Jewish leader-

---

[245] See K. Kertelge, 'The Epiphany of Jesus in the Gospel (Mark)' in Telford (ed.), *Interpretation*, pp. 105–23.

ship groups, Jesus' family and the twelve. In each case, I remarked on the denigration to which each of these is subject in the Markan Gospel. Uniting these two apparently antagonistic groups is a shared blindness to the true status and mission of Jesus, as understood by Mark. Both groups are shown to have rejected Jesus and his way of the cross and to have failed, despite every invitation, to recognize him as Son of God, as Gentile Christianity was later to confess him. In turn, Jesus is shown rejecting them, so appearing to the Markan reader as one who no longer has Jewish roots, as one no longer to be seen through Jewish eyes, as one no longer to be accorded a Jewish identity. Speaking and acting as though with a Hellenistic Christian community in mind, the Markan Jesus begins to emerge then as a universal saviour figure, one whose very ministry, according to Mark (but not according to Jewish-Christians), was conducted with Gentiles in mind. Appropriately then, he 'goes before' his original disciples to Galilee, leaving them behind. The reader is left therefore with no account of any reunion which offered them rehabilitation after failure or a commission to lead the post-Easter church.

The nature of Mark's redactional activity hence answers one of the questions which was posed at the beginning of this book, namely whether a coherent theology can be seen to be operating on the pastiche of traditions taken over by the evangelist. Here an affirmative answer must be given, for a consistent theological perspective does appear to inform the Gospel at its redactional level. Our examination has emphasized in particular the significance of the secrecy motif, and, in the course of the discussion, we have observed links between all five aspects of this motif: the Christological secret, the 'parables' secret, the secret of the 'Kingdom of God', the 'miracles' secret and the 'Son of Man' secret. It is worth observing, for example, how in Mk 3.20ff. (a Markan construction), a number of these Markan themes all come together: the incomprehension of Jesus' family and the Jewish leaders, the veiled significance of Jesus' miracles (in this case the exorcisms), Jesus' reply (and self-disclosure) in parables, the kingdom imagery, the Christological undertones (Jesus as the 'strong' or rather 'stronger man'). The evangelist's claim is that in the exorcisms of Jesus the kingdom of Satan is being usurped and (by implication) that of God being established through the agency of his Son (see the Q saying Mt. 12.28 par.). Jesus, through his supremacy over Satan, is, by implication, 'the strong(er) man' of the parable but the true secret of his identity has already been disclosed for the Markan reader earlier in the passage (Mk 3.11–12) where the exorcised demons recognize that he is in fact the 'Son of God'.

What then was the Gospel's purpose in its historical setting? A number of theories regarding the purpose of the Gospel and its setting have been proposed, some of which have been touched on here.[246] These theories have often been divided by virtue of their opposing views as to whether parenesis[247] or polemic[248] was the primary motive for the Gospel's composition. According to V. Taylor, for example, the evangelist was a simple editor or compiler rather than a creative theologian (far less one swinging any theological axes!). He faithfully brought together elements of the Jesus tradition and combined them with the longer passion narrative in order to produce what is essentially a tract encouraging a predominantly Gentile-Christian church at Rome in the face of persecution or martyrdom for the sake of the Gospel in Nero's reign. For E. Best likewise, Mark 'writes as a pastor for his community which he is concerned to deepen in its understanding of the Gospel'.[249] His

---

[246] For a fuller review of these, see Telford, *Mark*, pp. 149–52; Telford, 'History of Developments' in Telford (ed.), *Interpretation*, p. 39.

[247] See, for example, E. Best, 'The Purpose of Mark', *Proceedings of the Irish Biblical Association*, 6 (1982), pp. 19–35; Best, *Gospel as Story*, pp. 51–4, 93–9; C. E. B. Cranfield, *The Gospel according to St. Mark: an Introduction and Commentary* (Cambridge Greek Testament Commentary; Cambridge: Cambridge University Press, 1959), pp. 14–15; N. A. Dahl, 'The Purpose of Mark's Gospel' in Tuckett (ed.), *Secret*, pp. 29–34; Marxsen, *Mark*, pp. 54–116; Taylor, *Mark*, pp. 26–32, 130–5.

[248] See, for example, S. G. F. Brandon, *The Fall of Jerusalem and the Christian Church* (London: SPCK, 1951), pp. 185–205; S. G. F. Brandon, 'The Apologetical Factor in the Markan Gospel' in *Studia Evangelica II: Papers Presented to the Second International Congress on New Testament Studies held at Christ Church, Oxford, 1961* (Berlin: Akademie Verlag, 1964), pp. 34–46; Brandon, *Zealots*, pp. 221–82; W. H. Kelber, *The Kingdom in Mark. A New Place and a New Time* (Philadelphia: Fortress Press, 1974), pp. 129–47; Trocmé, *Formation*, pp. 87–137; Schreiber, 'Christologie', pp. 154–83; Tyson, 'Blindness' in Tuckett (ed.), *Secret*, pp. 35–43; Weeden, *Mark*; Weeden, 'Heresy' in Telford (ed.), *Interpretation*, pp. 89–104.

[249] Best, *Gospel as Story*, p. 95.

Gospel is a work of parenesis which sought to address the church at large suffering persecution by presenting it with the figure of its suffering Messiah and using the pedagogic device of the disciples' misunderstanding to present teaching on the true nature of discipleship under such circumstances.

These theories account for certain of Mark's redactional emphases such as his use of the word 'gospel', his interest in Gentiles and the Gentile mission, his preoccupation with persecution, martyrdom and the true nature of discipleship, and his accent on the passion predictions, but they inadequately explain the interest in Galilee (unless this is taken *theologically* to refer to the Gentiles or the Gentile mission), the harsh treatment of Jesus' family and disciples and the Christological motivation behind the secrecy motif.

One very different parenetic theory is that of W. Marxsen who claims that the Gospel was written to the Jewish-Christian community in Jerusalem round about 66 CE. Living between the crucifixion and the parousia, the Gospel exhorted them in the light of current political events to flee to Galilee, there to await Jesus' parousia. Linking the Gospel with the tradition of the Jerusalem church's flight to Pella, this theory explains Mark's special (*literal* and not theological) interest in Galilee, and in the twelve, but it has been criticized in other ways. Apart from doubts that Pella can legitimately be located in Galilee, scholars have questioned why, if the situation was so very urgent for Mark and the Markan community, the evangelist needed to address it by writing a book.[250]

Dissatisfaction with parenetic factors as the sole explanation for the work have led some scholars, as we have seen, to consider polemic as a motivating force. Polemical theories have the advantage of offering more convincing explanations for the harsh treatment of the Jesus' opponents, family and disciples as well as for the secrecy motif and its Christological motivation.[251] These theories see the author as the representative of a

---

[250] See H. Conzelmann, *An Outline of the Theology of the New Testament* (The New Testament Library; London: SCM Press; Evanston, IL: Harper & Row, 1969), p. 144; *gratia* Martin, *Mark*, pp. 70–5.

[251] For an analysis and critique of such views, however, see, for example, H. Anderson,

particular early Christian tradition and one who is engaged in a struggle against what he regards as false doctrine, especially false Christology. One interesting suggestion is that Mark was combating Gnosticism or more particularly docetism (see E. Schweizer, R. P. Martin).[252] The evangelist drew on a mainly Jewish-Christian tradition which preserved Jesus' words about the approaching end-time. He also drew on a mainly Hellenistic-Christian tradition of his miracles in which he was regarded as a wonder-working divine man. These traditions he combined with a Pauline emphasis on the cross and resurrection, so preventing a gnosticizing emphasis on the figure of Jesus as the divine Christ becoming detached from the figure of the historical Jesus as reflected in the Jesus traditions he had collected (and to which Paul himself, I may add, had little or no access). This line of approach accounts for the combination of the separate strands or traditions apparent in Mark but it does not adequately explain Mark's attack on the twelve.

Another line of approach is that taken by T. J. Weeden, as we have seen. Mark attacks the twelve because for him they are the representatives of the Christology he is seeking to combat. That Christology, Weeden claims, was a divine-man Christology (recognizable in part in the miracle stories) against which Mark pits the conception of the suffering Messiahship of Jesus. This position, however, fails to explain adequately why Jesus' original Jewish disciples should be held up as representatives of a Christology with a strongly Hellenistic flavour. *Pace* Weeden, the miracles, I have maintained, serve to enhance Mark's Christology rather than to contradict it. Closer to the target, in my opinion, are those views which claim that the evangelist uses the twelve as a target for attacking the Jewish-Christian community which they more appropriately represent (see

The Gospel of Mark (New Century Bible Commentary; Grand Rapids: Eerdmans, 1981), pp. 40–58. The disadvantage of polemical theories is that they have to rely perforce on speculative factors extrinsic to the text, or on appeal to a putative historical event or situation as the occasion for the Gospel. As a result they often tend to present too specific or too ambitious a reconstruction of the presumed situation.

252 Schweizer, *Good News*, pp. 380–6; R. P. Martin, 'A Gospel in search of a Life-Setting', *ExpT*, 80 (1968–9), pp. 361–4; Martin, *Mark*, pp. 156–62.

J. Schreiber, S. Schulz, J. B. Tyson). In the case of Tyson, the disciples are seen as the representatives of a nationalistic and militant, royal Messianic Christology which unlike Paul placed no great emphasis on the saving efficacy of Jesus' death.

A further classic exemplar of this position is that of S. G. F. Brandon. In general, he claimed, this Gospel is a polemic against the Jewish Christianity which held such power and influence in the tunnel period between 40 and 70 CE and which did so much either to discourage the Gentile mission or to lay down strict rules about the inclusion of Gentiles within their community (for example, circumcision, the keeping of the law, abstinence from food offered to idols, chastity, etc.). In particular, Mark is an apologetic for the Gentiles Christians at Rome who were embarrassed at the Jewish origins of their faith. Written in 71 CE following the Romano-Jewish War, it attempted to put a different complexion on these origins. Writing of the Caesarea Philippi episode (Mk 8.27ff.), Brandon states:

Accordingly, we find the author of Mark, in effect, declaring here that the original disciples of Jesus, who formed the nucleus of the Jerusalem Church, conceived of Jesus as the Jewish Messiah, but they balked at accepting him as the divine Saviour of mankind. In other words, this first of the apologists writes from the Pauline viewpoint, and he is concerned here to inform his readers of the limitations of the Christology of the Jerusalem Christians.[253]

Of all explanations for the purpose of Mark's Gospel, this one places the sharpest emphasis on the evangelist's harsh treatment of the Jewish leaders, the family of Jesus and his disciples, as the following indicates:

There can, accordingly, be traced throughout the Markan Gospel a consistent denigration of the Jewish leaders and people, and of the family of Jesus and his original Apostles, which adds up to a truly damning indictment of the Jews for their treatment of Jesus. The Jewish leaders and people are responsible for his death, his family regard him as insane, and his Apostles fail to understand him and finally desert him. In turn, Jesus is shown as rejecting those of his nation who reject him, as making the serving of God, not blood-relationship, the basis of communion with himself, and as vehemently

---

[253] Brandon, *Zealots*, p. 278.

rebuking his chief Apostle's obsession with a nationalistic conception of his own status and mission. Consequently, in Mark, despite the lively depiction of his essentially Jewish environment, Jesus is portrayed as essentially independent of his Jewish origin and relationships.[254]

Sadly, we know very little, however, about the original Jewish-Christian community at Jerusalem. Its influence and power, strong in the years before the Romano-Jewish war, waned with the deaths of James, the son of Zebedee in 44 CE (Acts 12.1–2), of James, the brother of Jesus in 62 CE (Josephus, *Ant.* xx.197–203; Eusebius, *Eccl. Hist.* II.23), of Peter (reputedly) in the Neronian persecution (*1 Clement* 5.4), and, of course, with the cataclysmic effects of the war itself. We have traditions that indicate that it attempted to reassert its influence after 70 CE, and to lay claim to the legitimate tradition about Jesus. Eusebius, quoting Hegesippus, refers to the family of the Lord, the so-called *desposynoi* who laid claim to special authority as being descendants of Jesus and of the house of David (*Eccl. Hist.* I. 7.14; III.11–12, 19–20; IV.22). We are told in particular of the grandsons of Jude, brother of Jesus, who were alive in the reign of Domitian and who were questioned by him in connection with claims to their being of the house of David and about their apocalyptic beliefs (*Eccl. Hist.* III.19–20). Hegesippus' traditions also refer to the cousin of Jesus, Simeon, who holds the dynastic succession to the church in Jerusalem up until Trajan's reign when he was martyred (*Eccl. Hist.* III.11; IV.22).

Jewish Christians are also mentioned in connection with Bar Cochba's Second Revolt in 135 CE, where they are said to have been persecuted by their fellow Jewish Messianists, presumably for their belief in the coming of another Messiah, Jesus (Justin, *Apologia*, 1.31). Jewish Christianity also survived in the form of Jewish-Christian sects, the Ebionites and the Nazoraeans, who produced Gospels such as the *Gospel of the Hebrews*, the *Gospel of the Nazoraeans*, the *Gospel of the Ebionites* and the *Pseudo-Clementines* (which attack Paul as the perverter of Christianity). They were themselves regarded as heretics by the Paulinist and now predominantly Gentile churches and their writings and beliefs

[254] *Ibid.*, p. 279.

suppressed in favour of an emergent Gentile Christianity. Does the Gospel of Mark represent then an early (literary) step in the process which eventually saw the triumph of a Paulinist Gentile Christianity over a Jewish Christianity which laid claim both to a legitimate tradition about Jesus (the eschatological prophet/royal Messiah/apocalyptic Son of Man) and a legitimate succession from Jesus?

CHAPTER 3

Mark and the New Testament

I have completed my historical profile of the theology of the Gospel of Mark and it is now my task to relate that theology to the rest of the New Testament. Mark's Gospel and the Pauline Epistles are the earliest extant writings of early Christianity that we possess. It is fitting therefore that I should begin by commenting on the relationship between Mark and Paul. The question has entered into our enquiry at a number of points hitherto, and a positive connection between the two has in fact been one of the conclusions towards which I have leaned. It is time, therefore, to give more systematic attention to it.

There are clearly a number of affinities between Mark and Paul, a state of affairs which intriguingly (but no doubt co-incidentally) mirrors the external tradition that connects the apostle with the John Mark of the New Testament. Both exhibit a tension with the Jerusalem church. Paul, in a number of (admittedly disputed) passages, can barely disguise his impatience with these 'pillars' of the establishment (e.g. Gal. 2.6ff., 11–12; 2 Cor. 11.4–6, 22–3; 12.11), and, not averse to calling down a curse on anyone preaching a different gospel (Gal. 1.8–9), accuses Peter as one who 'stood condemned' (Gal. 2.11). Implying that they are outsiders, Mark too imputes the charge of blindness against them (Mk 4.10–12 in light of 8.17ff.),[1] a hapless Peter being likewise cursed by the Markan Jesus for his lack of perception (Mk 8.33), and the major threesome (Peter,

---

[1] See M. D. Goulder, 'Those Outside (Mk. 4:10–12)', *NovT*, 33 (1991), pp. 289–302.

James and John) accorded a revelation on the Mount of Transfiguration which – like Paul's Israelites before Moses (2 Cor. 3.7ff.) – taxes their powers of comprehension even more (Mk. 9.2–8, 9–13).[2]

In each case, too, this tension with the original bearers of the Jesus tradition seems to derive from a similar attitude to the Law, one that exalts Jesus over the Jewish tradition (Mk 7.1–23 and Rom. 10.4), which has an overarching concern for Gentiles, Jew–Gentile relations and the Gentile mission (Mk 13.10 and Gal. 1.15–16),[3] and which, as a result, is concerned with such issues as table fellowship and the food laws (Mk 2.15–17, 7.1–23, especially 19, and Gal. 2.11–21). Mark certainly demonstrates an interest in 'food and eating' imagery, as well as in the shared meal (e.g. Mk 2.26; 5.43; 6.37ff.; 7.27–8; 8.1ff., 14ff.). Behind the dual feeding stories, as we observed in chapter two, a deeper significance has been detected.[4] If not prefiguring the Christian Eucharist itself (compare the use of *eucharistein* in Mk 8.6 as well as in 14.23),[5] then these stories may at least symbolize the extension of the Christian mission to Jew and Gentile alike. The symbolism of the 'one loaf' in Mark 8.14–21 has been linked, by some, to Paul's teaching in 1 Corinthians 10.1–5, 17, and Mark's words of institution, 'This is my blood of the (new) covenant, which is poured out for many' (Mk 14.24) to Paul's 'This cup is

---

[2] For a link between Mk 9.1 and the triumvirate about whom Paul speaks, see D. Wenham and A. D. A. Moses, "There are some standing here ...": Did They Become the 'Reputed Pillars' of the Jerusalem Church? Some Reflections on Mark 9:1, Galatians 2:9 and the Transfiguration', *NovT*, 36 (1994), pp. 146–63.

[3] See G. H. Boobyer, 'Galilee and Galileans in St Mark's Gospel', *BJRL*, 35 (1952–3), pp. 334–48 and F. G. Lang, '"Über Sidon mitten ins Gebiet der Dekapolis": Geographie und Theologie in Markus 7,31', *Zeitschrift des Deutschen Palästina-Vereins*, 94 (1978), pp. 145–60. Lang argues that the implausible route described in Mk 7.31 served a theological purpose for Mark. The places mentioned represent *in toto* the Gentile regions lying to the north and east of Galilee. The three stories in Mk 7.24–8.10 are hence included in this journey, and have a theological unity in that they are concerned with the Gentile–Jew question, and the mission to the Gentiles. The details all contribute to this theme: Jesus is shown blazing a trail in Gentile regions which the church was later to follow.

[4] See W. R. Telford, 'The Interpretation of Mark: a History of Developments and Issues' in Telford (ed.), *The Interpretation of Mark* (Edinburgh: T. & T. Clark, 1995), pp. 34–5.

[5] For a negative judgment, see G. H. Boobyer, 'The Eucharistic Interpretation of the Miracles of the Loaves in St. Mark's Gospel', *JTS*, 3 (1952), pp. 161–71.

the new covenant in my blood' (1 Cor. 11.25).[6] A common strategy in regard to dealings with the Roman state may also be discerned in both Mark 12.13–17 and Romans 13.1–7.[7]

It is not only in matters of praxis, however, that Mark and Paul have been compared, but also in terms of a common ideology. J. C. Fenton has identified a number of *themes* which unite Mark's Gospel and the Pauline Epistles,[8] and numerous *ideas* also relate them to one another in terms of theology. These shared conceptions have mostly to do with Christology and soteriology. Where Mark rejects a pre-Markan 'Son of David' Christology, Paul too appears to do so in favour of a higher 'Son of God' Christology. While acknowledging its priority in Romans 1.3–4, he thereafter disowns it by sheer neglect. Paul, as we have noted, does not use the title 'Son of Man' for Jesus as such, but he does speak of the resurrected Christ as 'the last Adam' or 'the man of heaven' (see 1 Cor. 15.20–50, especially 21–2, 45–9; Rom. 5.12–21; Phil. 2.5–11). He, too, then, like Mark, may have taken over but qualified a Jewish 'heavenly man' Christology, perhaps, as M. Black suggests, combining the *eschatological* Son of Man (Dan. 7.13) with the *ctisiological*[9] or 'heavenly Adam' figure of which Philo speaks.[10]

Apart from a shared use of the title 'Lord' for Jesus (Mk 11.3 and 1 Cor. 12.3), both the apostle and the evangelist regard the title 'Son of God' as of supreme importance (Mk 1.1, 11; 3.11; 5.7; 9.7; 15.39 and Gal. 4.4; Rom. 1.3–4; 8.3). This 'Son of God' for Paul is a pre-existent figure (Gal. 4.4; 1 Cor. 8.6; 10.4; 2 Cor. 5.21; 8.9 Rom. 8.3; Phil. 2.6–7; Col. 1.15–17)[11] and although doubts have been raised that 'pre-existence' as such underlies

[6] See B. W. Bacon, *The Gospel of Mark: its Composition and Date* (New Haven, CT: Yale University Press; London: Oxford University Press, 1925), pp. 180, 269. For a contrary view, see V. Taylor, *The Gospel According to St Mark* (London: Macmillan; New York: St Martin's Press, 1966), pp. 127–8.

[7] See W. R. Herzog, 'Dissembling, a Weapon of the Weak: the Case of Christ and Caesar in Mark 12:13–17 and Romans 13:1–7', *PerspRelSt*, 21 (1994), pp. 339–60.

[8] J. C. Fenton, 'Paul and Mark' in D. E. Nineham (ed.), *Studies in the Gospels. Essays in Memory of R. H. Lightfoot* (Oxford: Blackwell, 1955), pp. 89–112.

[9] From *ktisis* = creation.

[10] M. Black, 'The Pauline Doctrine of the Second Adam', *SJT*, 7 (1954), pp. 170–9.

[11] For a dissenting (minority) view, see J. D. G. Dunn, *Christology in the Making. A New Testament Inquiry into the Origins of the Doctrine of Incarnation* (London: SCM Press, 1989), pp. 33–46.

the Markan use of the title, the case has been made by a number of scholars who cite such evidence as the 'sending/coming forth of the Son' language of Mark 12.6 (compare Mk 1.38 and Rom. 8.3), the miracles as epiphanies, the transfiguration (Mk 9.2–8), the Markan Jesus' identification with the heavenly Son of Man (e.g. Mk 2.10; 8.38) or even pre-existent 'Kyrios' (Mk 12.35–7).[12] According to Bultmann, Mark's very purpose was '*the union of the Hellenistic kerygma about Christ*, whose essential content consists of the Christ myth as we learn of it in Paul (esp. Phil. 2.6ff.; Rom. 3.24) with *the tradition of the story of Jesus*'.[13] One element in that myth was the self-emptying or *kenōsis* of the heavenly figure, and, in keeping with Isaiah's suffering Servant, his willingness to endure humiliation and anguish in order to carry out his redemptive task.

It is this soteriological emphasis, then, this theology of the cross, the *salvific death* of Jesus (Mk 10.45 and Rom. 3.23–5; 5.8–9, 18–19) and the universality of salvation engendered by it (Mk 13.10; 14.9 and Rom. 15.14–21), which bring Mark and Paul into the same theological orbit. According to U. Luz, it is only in Paul and Mark, indeed, that a *theologia crucis* is placed in opposition to a *theologia gloriae* (Mk 15.31–2 and 1 Cor. 1.18–25).[14] In both writers, too, it is *faith* in Jesus, in the context of discipleship, which enables the believer to appropriate his divine power (Mk 9.20–4 and Rom. 1.16–17; Phil. 4.13).

This common Christology and soteriology extends even to the technical vocabulary used to express it. Both writers make the distinction between the 'flesh' and the 'spirit' (Mk 14.38 and Gal. 5.16–17), and where the flesh is weak, concur in their

---

[12] See, for example, R. H. Fuller, *A Critical Introduction to the New Testament* (London: Duckworth, 1966), p. 111; J. Schreiber, *Die Markuspassion. Eine Redaktionsgeschichtliche Untersuchung* (BZNW, 68; Berlin and New York: Walter de Gruyter, 1993), pp. 210–59.

[13] R. Bultmann, *The History of the Synoptic Tradition* (Oxford: Blackwell, 1968), pp. 347–8. See also W. Marxsen, *Mark the Evangelist. Studies on the Redaction History of the Gospel* (Nashville, TN and New York: Abingdon Press; London: SPCK, 1969), p. 216; J. Schreiber, 'Die Christologie des Markusevangeliums', *ZThK*, 58 (1961), pp. 154–83; S. Schulz, 'Mark's Significance for the Theology of Early Christianity' in Telford, *Interpretation*, pp. 197–206.

[14] U. Luz, 'Theologia crucis als Mitte der Theologie im Neuen Testament', *EvTh*, 34 (1974), pp. 116–41.

catalogue of vices (Mk 7.21–3 and Rom. 1.29–31).[15] Each employs the *pōrōsis* or 'hardening' motif, 'hardness of heart' being applied by Mark to Jesus' Jewish disciples and enemies (Mk 3.5; 6.52; 8.17) and by Paul to his Jewish compatriots (Rom. 11.7, 25; 2 Cor. 3.14). The word 'gospel' (*euangelion*) is the term used by each to denote the proclamation of the message of salvation, or 'good news' as preached by Paul,[16] or by Jesus (e.g. Mk 1.1, 14, 15; 8.35; 10.29; 13.10; 14.9). Two other favourite Pauline expressions for the Christian message or the content of God's revelation, the 'word' (*logos*) and the 'mystery' (*mystērion*), also occur in Mark (e.g. Mk 4.16 and 1 Thes. 1.6; Mk 4.11 and Rom. 11.25; 16.25; Col 1.26; 2.2; 4.3).[17]

The parallels, then, are striking, and a variety of interpretations have been placed on them.[18] Some have argued that the Gospel is a defence of the authority of Paul and the Pauline churches against the claims of the Jerusalem church (G. Volkmar, A. Loisy). B. W. Bacon argued more modestly that a Paulinist perspective could be detected in Mark and that 'the reduction of all soteriological teaching to the doctrine of the Cross and Resurrection, cannot be explained without reference to Paul'.[19] Mark is then, in the words of R. H. Fuller, 'a powerful reassertion, in terms of a "life of Jesus", of the Pauline kerygma of the cross'.[20] Others have denied a specific Pauline influence, preferring to view the Gospel as the product of the same Hellenistic church out of which Paul emerged, and the second evangelist as an heir therefore to the general tradition of Gentile Christianity.

In a classic study published in 1923, M. Werner presented the case that 'there cannot be the slightest idea of an influence of Pauline theology in the Gospel of Mark'.[21] Comparing the

---

[15] For a number of the common words, see Taylor, *Mark*, p. 127.

[16] Paul uses the term, according to Taylor, no less than fifty-six times (*ibid.*, p. 126).

[17] After the occurrence of the term 'mystery' in Col. 4.3, Taylor notes Paul's use of the expression 'those outside' (*tous exō*) in 4.5 and compares this with Mk 4.11 (*tois exō*) (*ibid.*).

[18] See Fenton, 'Paul and Mark' in Nineham (ed.), *Studies*, p. 91.

[19] Bacon, *Mark*, p. 262.   [20] Fuller, *Introduction*, p. 110.

[21] M. Werner, *Der Einfluss paulinischer Theologie im Markusevangelium* (BZNW, 1; Giessen: Alfred Töpelmann, 1923), p. 247.

Gospel with the Epistles, Werner argued that the resemblances between the two could be put down to the common tradition of primitive Christianity. A number of distinctively Pauline ideas, moreover, were either absent in Mark (for example, justification by faith, faith union with Christ, life in the Spirit) or presented from an opposing standpoint. Werner's study, which has been, and still remains, extremely influential, was produced, however, before the advent of redaction criticism and the newer literary criticism. W. Marxsen, for example, has criticized Werner for comparing Pauline thought with the Markan Gospel *as a whole* and not with the Markan *redaction*, that is, with the distinctively *Markan* contribution to the pre-Markan tradition.[22]

When we recall that among these redactional features are to be included the secrecy motif in respect of Jesus' true identity (the 'Son of God' Christology), the emphasis on Jesus' death and resurrection, the use of the term 'gospel', the interest in Gentiles and the Gentile mission, the accent given to persecution, suffering and martyrdom and the true nature of discipleship, and finally the harsh treatment accorded to the Jewish leadership groups, Jesus' family and his original disciples, the links with Paul are easier to see. When due allowance, furthermore, is made for the differences in the way each writer has chosen to express his theology – Paul in the *direct* form of an epistle, Mark in the *indirect* form of a story – the second evangelist may be seen to have taken up, in Marxsen's words 'the Pauline fundamentals'. The use of pre-Markan Jesus traditions as well as the narrative form, then, would not lead us to expect more in the way of distinctively Pauline theological ideas and vocabulary than we in fact find in the Gospel. With the development, moreover, of narrative-critical tools and an increasing sensitivity on the part of scholars to the nuances of narrative theology, Volkmar's original suggestion that Mark's Gospel is an allegorical presentation of Pauline teaching in the form of a narrative may be due, therefore, for a comeback.

[22] Marxsen, *Mark*, p. 213.

MARK AND Q

The affinities between Mark and Paul should not lead us, however, to undervalue Mark's individual and distinctive contribution to the theological history of early Christianity. What distinguishes Paul is the Christological and soteriological significance that he places on the death and resurrection of Jesus. The apostle shows little interest, however, in the Palestinian Jesus traditions which were grist for the evangelist's theological mill (the parables, the Kingdom of God and Son of Man sayings, the miracles, etc.). Mark's genius was to wed these traditions, by means of the secrecy motif, to a theological perspective on the death and resurrection of Jesus that unites him, as we have seen, with Paul. Since their respective writings represent the only surviving documents from the earliest period of Christianity, is their proximity in time alone sufficient to account for these affinities, as some have suggested? Here we must turn to a comparison between Mark and Q, for the latter source, although it is hypothetical and has to be reconstructed, gives evidence of a Jewish-Christian tradition concerning Jesus which predates the fall of Jerusalem. Examination of Q, therefore, may throw into further relief the distinctive Markan contribution to the theological history of early Christianity.[23]

Q was compiled between 40 and 70 and passed through various editorial stages, according to current scholarship. In terms of genre, it is a 'sayings' collection, although there is dispute whether, as such, it is to be characterized as primarily 'prophetic' or 'sapiential' (showing affinities with either the prophetic or the Wisdom writings).[24] Beginning with the preaching of John the Baptist, his testimony to Jesus, and Jesus' temptation, it presents Jesus' public teaching and responses to it, the mission of the twelve, Jesus' instructions about prayer, his controversies with the scribes and Pharisees, his teaching about

---

[23] For some scholarly treatments of Q, see, for example, D. R. Catchpole, *The Quest for Q* (Edinburgh: T. & T. Clark, 1993); J. Delobel (ed.), *Logia. Les Paroles de Jésus – The Sayings of Jesus (Memorial Joseph Coppens)* (BETL, 59; Leuven: Leuven University Press/Peeters, 1982); C. M. Tuckett, *Q and the History of Early Christianity. Studies on Q* (Edinburgh: T. & T. Clark, 1996).

[24] See Tuckett, *Q*, pp. 325ff., esp. 353–4.

discipleship, sayings about the Law, and prophecy concerning the parousia of the Son of Man.[25] Some of the material contained in Q overlaps with Mark (see especially Mk 8.12 with Mt. 12.39 = Lk. 11.29; Mk 8.38 and Mt. 10.33 = Lk. 12.9; or Mk 11.23 with Mt. 17.20 = Lk. 17.6), and so scholars are divided on the question whether the evangelist knew Q or whether these common sayings circulated independently within their respective communities.[26]

Careful analysis of the Q source has enabled scholars to construct a profile of the community whose concerns it reflects. What emerges is a group who, in terms of praxis, differed from the Markan community in their continuing commitment to the covenant, the Law and the Temple. Conservative in their attitude to the Law, they were in close touch with the Pharisees, with whom they were nevertheless at odds. Cherishing their own Jewishness, and therefore their separateness from Gentiles, they were conscious of having a mission to fellow-Jews with whom they identified but from whom they were experiencing rejection, if not persecution. According to C. M. Tuckett, they are to be understood as 'more of a "reform movement" working within Israel than a "sect" separated from its Jewish contemporaries by a rigid line of demarcation'.[27] A similar judgment is given by D. R. Catchpole whose picture of the Q community is of one 'whose outlook was essentially Jerusalem-centred, whose theology was Torah-centred, whose worship was temple-centred, and which saw (with some justice) no incompatibility between all of that and commitment to Jesus'.[28] In terms of ideology, analysis of the Q source (and its redaction) has revealed a number of distinctive ideas and motifs.[29] The

---

[25] For a helpful, if dated, summary of the contents and structure of Q, see F. C. Grant, *The Gospels: their Origin and their Growth* (London: Faber & Faber, 1957), pp. 59–60. Also in F. C. Grant, 'Matthew, Gospel of' in *IDB*, p. 305.

[26] See W. R. Telford, 'Pre-Markan Tradition in Recent Research (1980–1990)' in F. van Segbroeck *et al.* (eds.), *The Four Gospels 1992* (Leuven: Leuven University Press/ Peeters, 1992), p. 701.

[27] Tuckett, *Q*, p. 436.   [28] Catchpole, *Quest*, p. 279.

[29] Tuckett includes among these 'the phrase "this generation" as the object of Q's preaching, the theme of the violent fate suffered by the prophets, and the theme of Wisdom as the sender of the prophets' (*Q*, p. 166).

study of the theology of Q is still in progress,[30] but where comparison with Mark is concerned, an examination of Q in respect of Christology, eschatology and soteriology is instructive.[31] A witness other than Mark to the primitive Jewish tradition of Jesus as teacher, prophet and exorcist (e.g. Lk. 11.20 = Mt. 12.28), Q also offers independent attestation, as we have seen, of the Jewish-Christian identification of Jesus with the present and coming apocalyptic Son of Man. Evidence of a 'Son of David' Christology, however, is absent, and there is no trace of the so-called 'Messianic secret' (Q does not use the title 'Christos'/Messiah), far less of Mark's epiphany Christology. Jesus is seen, on the contrary, in the category of the authoritative teacher,[32] 'eschatological prophet' or 'the final messenger of Wisdom, the last in the line of Wisdom's envoys, these envoys being regarded as prophets who experience rejection and violence'.[33]

A major accent in Q is the eschatological one. Where the Markan tendency is to de-eschatologize the life and message of Jesus,[34] a futurist eschatology permeates the Q material from John the Baptist's opening words of judgment (Lk. 3.7b-9 = Mt. 3.7b–10) to the Son of Man's imminent parousia (Lk. 17.26–30 = Mt. 24.37–9). Despite setbacks and opposition, the Kingdom of God is drawing near (Lk. 10.2–12 = Mt. 10.5–15), and in that Kingdom, moreover, a leadership role will be reserved for the twelve who will sit on thrones judging the twelve tribes of Israel (Lk. 22.28–30 = Mt. 19.28).

What is apparent, then, is that, while Q has a place in its divine scheme for rejection of, and even violence against Wisdom's envoy, it has no passion narrative, no soteriology connected with the death and resurrection of Jesus, no theology

---

[30] Cf., however, R. A. Edwards, *A Theology of Q. Eschatology, Prophecy, and Wisdom* (Philadelphia, PA: Fortress Press, 1976).

[31] See Tuckett, *Q*, pp. 209–37 (Q's Christology), 139–63 (Eschatology in Q).

[32] See Tuckett, *Q*, pp. 214–18. It is in this sense, according to Tuckett, that the occasional and otherwise Christologically insignificant title 'Lord' (Kyrios) is used in Q.

[33] Tuckett, *Q*, p. 221.

[34] See U. Luz, 'Das Jesusbild der vormarkinischen Tradition' in G. Strecker (ed.), *Jesus Christus in Historie und Theologie. Neutestamentliche Festschrift für Hans Conzelmann zum 60. Geburtstag* (Tübingen: Mohr–Siebeck, 1975), pp. 347–74.

of the cross. In H. E. Tödt's words, 'the one who is rejected is seen not as the redeemer who gives his blood for many but as the authoritative teacher who by means of his word summons men to follow him'.[35] To draw significance from this situation for the theological history of early Christianity is of course to indulge in argumentation from silence. It is possible that, given its function, perhaps as a manual of teaching or a guide to catechists, a kerygma of the cross was presupposed by Q, as some have argued.[36] This too, of course, would be an argument from silence, as would the claim that Paul likewise presupposed the Jesus traditions known to Q and Mark. The fact remains, however, that 'Mark's originality', in R. P. Martin's words, 'is thrown into relief by our admission that no pre-Markan tradition which united both Jesus' words and Jesus' Passion is attested'.[37] The nature of the Q evidence, therefore, gives us one more reason for recognizing Mark's literary and theological creativity and for regarding his Gospel as the 'Gentilization' of originally Jewish-Christian traditions under the influence of a Paul-inspired theology of the cross.

MARK AND THE GOSPELS

If Q was a 'sayings' collection without a passion narrative, and Paul's was a death and resurrection kerygma with little connection to, or need for a Jesus tradition, then, Mark, we have seen, represents a combination of the two. Let us now turn to the later evangelists to see how they relate to the example set by Mark.[38] In essence, both Matthew and Luke represent a further combination of tradition, this time that of Mark with Q, and this configuration in turn had its theological repercussions.

By common consent, Matthew took over Mark's Gospel,

---

[35] H. E. Tödt, *The Son of Man in the Synoptic Tradition* (The New Testament Library; Philadelphia, PA: Westminster Press; London: SCM Press, 1965), p. 266; *gratia* R. P. Martin, *Mark – Evangelist and Theologian* (Exeter: Paternoster, 1979), p. 147.

[36] Cf. T. W. Manson, *The Sayings of Jesus* (London: SCM Press, 1949), pp. 15–16; *gratia* Martin, *Mark*, p. 147; Grant, *Gospels*, pp. 60–1.

[37] Martin, *Mark*, p. 147.

[38] For background to the Gospels, see the standard Introductions, e.g. Fuller, *Introduction*; W. G. Kümmel, *Introduction to the New Testament* (London: SCM Press, 1975).

subjecting the Markan framework to substantial editorial *expansions* at the beginning (the birth narratives in 1–2) and the end (the post-resurrection appearances in 28); major *insertions* (comprising Q/Special Matthew/editorial material) throughout, largely in the form of sayings material (see the five or six main teaching or 'discourse' blocks of 5–7, 10; 13; 18; 23/24–5, each marked out by a special formula in 7.28; 11.1; 13.53; 19.1; 26.1) and OT quotations (over sixty, including fourteen 'formula quotations'; see Mt. 1.22–3; 2.5–6; 2.15; 2.17–18; 2.23; 3.3; 4.14–16; 8.17; 12.17–21; 13.14–15; 13.35; 21.4–5; 26.56; 27.9–10);[39] some limited *rearrangements* (the miracle stories found in Mk 1, 2, 4–5, 10, for example, are combined into a single block in Mt. 8–9) and a number of stylistic (e.g. the improvement of Mark's Greek) and theological *modifications*.

The significance of Matthew's redaction for his theology lies in a number of areas.[40] Matthew produced, as we noted in chapter two, a more reverential portrait of the original disciples. They understand Jesus' words (Mt. 13.16–17, 51; 16.12; 17.13 and par.; contrast Mk 6.52 par.), recognize and confess him as 'Son of God' (Mt. 14.31–3; 16.1b–18 and par.) and are given a prominent role to play, especially in the post-Easter church (Mt. 10; 16.16–20; 19.28; 28.18–20 and par.). While scathing in his attack on the Jewish authorities, and especially on the scribes and Pharisees (e.g. Mt. 23), Matthew, in contrast to Mark, demonstrates an affirmative attitude to the Law (e.g. Mt. 5.17–20; 16.27b; 22.11–14; 23.2–3; 28.18–20, especially 20 and par.; contrast Mk 7.1–23),[41] and, while accepting the Gentile mission (Mt. 21.43; 28.18–20), albeit reluctantly, a certain disparagement of Gentiles (Mt. 7.6; 10.5–6, 23; 15.24; 18.17).

Matthew's Christology and eschatology bear close comparison with that of Mark. Heir, like Mark, to the primitive

---

[39] For a convenient treatment of Matthew's OT quotations, see Grant, 'Matthew' in *IDB*, pp. 307–11.

[40] See, for example, G. Bornkamm, G. Barth and H. J. Held, *Tradition and Interpretation in Matthew* (London: SCM Press, 1963); U. Luz, *The Theology of the Gospel of Matthew* (New Testament Theology; Cambridge: Cambridge University Press, 1995).

[41] See D. Hill, *The Gospel of Matthew* (New Century Bible; London: Oliphants, 1972). 'Matthew's teaching on the Law to which all disciples are to be obedient is striking and significant. The enduring validity of the Law is affirmed' (p. 66).

tradition of Jesus as teacher, prophet and healer, Matthew enhances this picture by the addition of teaching material derived from Q combined with a more reverential portrayal of Jesus' miracles.[42] Where Christological titles are concerned, the most fundamental of these, as for Mark, is 'Son of God'.[43] Mark's secrecy motif, and his epiphany Christology is to an extent retained, therefore, although in contrast to the second evangelist, he is shown being recognized and confessed as 'Son of God' (and as 'Lord'; Mt. 8.25 and par.) by the disciples already in his lifetime (Mt. 14.33; 16.16 and par.).

On the other hand, where Mark rejects a Jewish-Christian Son of David Christology, Matthew clearly and emphatically affirms it (Mt. 1.1ff.; 1.20; 9.27; 12.23; 15.22; 20.30, 31; 21.5; 21.14–17 and par.), although it is softened by pacific motifs (Mt. 11.28–30; 21.5; 26.52ff.) as well as by reference to Isaiah's Servant (Mt. 8.17; 12.17–21).[44] In further tension, it seems, with Mark, Matthew reflects his Jewish-Christian orientation by presenting Jesus as the new Moses: see, for example, the birth narrative (especially Mt. 2.13ff.); the five teaching blocks (= the five books of the Law?); the teaching on a mountain (Mt. 5.1ff.; cf. Exod. 19ff.); the new lawgiver (Mt. 5.17–20, 21–2, 27–8, 31–2); the commission to the disciples, also on a mountain (Mt. 28.16–20; cf. Deut. 31–4, especially 34.1ff.).[45] Matthew's Christology, like that of the Q community, is inextricably connected not only with his understanding of the 'church' as 'the true Israel' (Mt. 5.20; 23.2–3) but also with his eschatology,[46] and his tendency to restore, rehabilitate, or simply to give due weight to the Jewish-Christian tradition before him is further reinforced not only by his preservation and enhancement of the 'Son of Man' sayings of Mark and Q, but also by a pronounced

---

[42] Note, for example, the heightening of Jesus' miraculous powers in Mt. 8.13; 9.22; 15.28; 17.18 and par. (*from that very hour/instantly*); 8.16; 12.15 and par. (*many* becomes *all*); 20.30 and par. (*one* blind man becomes *two!*); 4.23 etc.

[43] See J. D. Kingsbury, *Matthew. Structure, Christology, Kingdom* (London: SPCK, 1975), esp. p. 83.

[44] See Fuller, *Introduction*, p. 118.

[45] *Ibid.* For a contrary view, see Kümmel, *Introduction*, p. 106.

[46] Hill, *Matthew*, p. 66.

apocalyptic emphasis (e.g. Mt. 13.24–30; 16.27b; 22.11–14; 24 especially 30, 37–51; 25).

Luke, on the other hand, displays an opposite tendency. While employing two of the same sources as Matthew, Luke managed, by virtue of his redaction, to create a different theological impression for his readers. He too subjected the Markan framework to a number of changes. These consisted of the following: substantial (but very different) editorial *expansions* at the beginning (the birth and infancy narratives in 1–2) and at the end (the post-resurrection appearances in 24); major *insertions* (comprising Q/Special Luke/editorial material) throughout (e.g. the two main 'discourse' blocks of 6.20–8.3 and 9.51–18.14), largely in the form of sayings material, especially parables; *omissions* (especially of Mk 6.45–8.26); some limited (but intriguing) *rearrangements* (e.g. the placing of John the Baptist's arrest by Herod in Mk 6.14–29 *before* Jesus' baptism; cf. Lk. 3.18–20, 21–2; the transfer of Jesus' visit to his home town in Mk 6.1–6 to the beginning of his ministry *immediately after* the temptation pericope; cf. Lk. 4.16ff. and par.; his alternative order for the temptations in Q, with Jesus' final temptation before beginning his ministry taking place in the *Temple*; cf. Lk. 4.9ff. and par.) and a number of stylistic (again the improvement of Mark's Greek) and theological *modifications*, some of which I have already remarked upon in chapter two.

More faithful to the inherent direction of Mark's redaction, Luke nevertheless can be seen to have a distinctive theology.[47] Toning down Mark's harsh treatment of the disciples, as we have observed, though somewhat ambiguous in his attitude to the Jewish people and their leaders,[48] Luke is sympathetic to Gentiles (Lk. 7.1–10; 23.47) and welcomes the Gentile mission

---

[47] See, for example, J. B. Green, *The Theology of the Gospel of Luke* (New Testament Theology; Cambridge: Cambridge University Press, 1995). Cf. I. H. Marshall, *Luke. Historian and Theologian* (Exeter: Paternoster, 1988). 'Our study, however, has suggested that Luke was basically faithful to the traditions which he was using; he was drawing out motifs already present in them rather than radically reshaping the material and adding to it from his own ideas' (p. 217).

[48] See Green, *Luke*, pp. 68–75.

(Lk. 14.16–24 and par.).[49] While faithfully transmitting the Christological traditions of his sources, imbued as they are with their varying estimates of Jesus as teacher, prophet, exorcist, 'Son of David', 'Son of Man', 'Son of God' and 'Lord', in terms of Christological emphasis, Luke is generally regarded as having a 'lower' Christology than the other evangelists,[50] lacking in this respect the 'innovative' thrust of Mark, the 'reactionary' emphasis of Matthew, or the 'sublime' quality of John. Although he incorporated the Q source into his Gospel, Luke writes, where eschatology is concerned, at a greater remove from the apocalyptic urgency of Jewish-Christianity. For the third evangelist the delay of the parousia is more serious than for Mark, so he further qualifies the imminent parousia expectation of his source, by, for example, omitting Mk 1.14–15, emending Mk 9.1 and 14.62 (note the omission of 'come with power' in the former, and the emphasis on Christ's *present* glory in the latter) or altering the Markan apocalypse in subtle ways (e.g. Lk. 21.8, 9, 20, 24 and par.).

According to H. Conzelmann, Luke, by means of such redaction, transmuted the eschatology of his sources into a threefold 'salvation history' scheme, namely *the time of Israel* ('the law and the prophets') before Jesus (e.g. Lk. 3.23–38; 16.16; 24.13–27, 44–9); *the sacred time of Jesus* (from baptism to ascension; e.g. Acts 1.21–2; 10.36–43, especially 37, 38) and *the time of the church* or *Holy Spirit* (e.g. Acts 1.6–9).[51] While this may be too schematic for some, most scholars would agree that in the Lukan perspective, redemptive history has been prolonged through the delay of the parousia, and the interim period

---

[49] Of the infrequency with which Gentiles are mentioned in the Gospel, Green writes:

> In the Third Gospel, 'Gentiles' may be understood as members of a more encompassing category of persons generally understood to be outside the boundaries of divine graciousness. This list would include lepers, Samaritans, the sick, women, 'sinners', toll-collectors, children, Gentiles, and others – that is, persons normally excluded from the religious circles of the pious, but, in Luke's depiction, welcome in the community of Jesus' followers. That is, in the Third Gospel, Luke's treatment of 'the problem of the Gentiles' is foremost a subset of his more general concern with the universalism of grace proffered through Jesus' mission (*ibid.*, p. 126).

[50] See J. Drury, 'Luke, Gospel of' in *DBI*, pp. 413.

[51] H. Conzelmann, *The Theology of St Luke* (London: Faber, 1960). Cf. also Fuller, *Introduction*, p. 120; Kümmel, *Introduction*, pp. 144–5.

theologically legitimated with the inauguration of the church's mission. On the other hand, while 'the Son of Man came to seek and to save the lost' (Lk. 19.10), signs of a Markan (or Pauline) *theologia crucis* are not apparent in Luke. Luke borrows and embellishes the Markan passion narrative, but the climactic ransom logion of Mark 10.45, by which Jesus' death is interpreted, and which is therefore so pivotal for the second evangelist, is simply omitted by the third.[52]

When we turn to John,[53] the situation is somewhat more complicated, since the lack of certainty in the source-relations between the Second and the Fourth Gospels means that it is not clear where John's theological debt lies, and if to Mark whether it was direct or indirect. Some scholars would hold that John knew the Synoptics, or at least Mark (compare Jn 5.8 with Mk 2.11; Jn 6.7 with Mk 6.37; Jn 12.3 with Mk 14.3 for alleged evidence of literary relationship), others that he was merely acquainted with the tradition they contain, others still (following P. Gardner-Smith) that he drew upon an entirely independent tradition.[54] Whatever view is taken (and I myself incline to the first), a comparison between their respective presentations reveals that the Fourth Gospel marks a further advance in the theological direction taken by Mark and followed by the other Synoptists.

The recipients of extensive private revelatory discourses on the part of the Johannine Jesus (see the 'Farewell Discourses' in 13–17), the disciples are nevertheless shown to have recognized the 'true' (i.e. 'divine') status of Jesus from the very beginning (Jn 1.35ff.; 6.66–9). Where the Jewish leaders and, by implication, the Jewish people are concerned, however, the 'hardening' motif, has intensified (e.g. Jn 12.37–43). The 'Jews', the Johannine reader is informed, cannot hear the words of God because they 'are not of God' (Jn 8.47) but of their 'father the devil' (Jn 8.44). Alluded to under the figure of the 'other sheep

---

52 See Green, *Luke*, p. 125.
53 For a recent treatment of John's theology, see D. M. Smith, *The Theology of the Gospel of John* (New Testament Theology; Cambridge: Cambridge University Press, 1995). See also R. Bultmann, *Theology of the New Testament* (London: SCM Press, 1952/1955), Vol. II, pp. 3–92.
54 For discussion of the evidence, see Kümmel, *Introduction*, pp. 200–4.

that are not of this fold' (Jn 10.16), and prefigured in the Greeks who wished to see Jesus (Jn 12.20ff.), the future mission to the Gentiles is now clearly a *fait accompli*, a fact of redemptive history.

Accredited with a veritable array of Christological titles, whether 'Messiah' (*Messias/Christos*; Jn 1.41; 4.25, 26, 29, 30; 7.25–31, 40–3; 9.22; 10.24, 25; 11.27; 20.31), 'King of Israel' (Jn 1.49; (6.15); 12.13; [18.33ff.]), 'Son of Man' (Jn 1.51; 3.13, 14; 5.27; 6.27, 53, 62; 8.28; 9.35; 12.23, 34; 13.31), 'Lord' (*Kyrios*; Jn 4.1; 6.23; 11.2; 20.2, 13, 18, 25, 28), 'Saviour' (*Sōtēr*; Jn 4.42), 'Son of God'/'Son' (Jn 1.34, 49; 3.16ff.; 5.18ff.; 10.36; 11.4, 27; 20.30–1) or, supremely, the 'Word' (*Logos*; 1.1–18), the Johannine Jesus is a being whose supernatural status is now no longer in doubt. More divine revealer than teacher, his (epiphanic) healing and nature miracles – there are no exorcisms in John – either 'manifesting', to his disciples, 'his glory' (e.g. Jn 2.11) or merely proclaiming, to the people, 'the prophet who is to come into the world' (Jn 6.14), the Johannine Jesus confidently displays attributes which are merely presented as clues for the Markan characters. Sent from God (Jn 5.37; 7.28–9; 15.21; 17.25) and invested with his authority (Jn 5.22, 27 (to execute judgment); 17.2 (to confer eternal life); 20.22 (to impart the Spirit)), he, like the Markan Jesus, is endowed with God's Spirit (Jn 1.32–3). In perfect union with God (Jn 8.46 (sinless); 10.30; 14.9), on terms, indeed, of equality with him (Jn 5.17, 22ff., 26; 8.16, 58; 14.6–11; 15.23; 16.15; 17.5 contrast 5.30; 14.28c), the Johannine Jesus issues impressive 'I Am' (*Egō Eimi*) sayings which throw into sharp relief the reluctance towards self-disclosure of the Markan Jesus: (Jn 6.35 (the bread of life); 8.12 (the light of the world); 10.7 (the door); 10.11 (the good shepherd); 11.25 (the resurrection and the life); 14.6 (the way, the truth and the life); 15.1 (the true vine)).

Underlying the Johannine presentation, then, is the conception of a divine Being (Jn 8.23), a divine man, one who possesses supernatural knowledge of men and of events (Jn 1.47–51; 2.23–5; 4.16–19; 6.64; 13.18–19), who is clairvoyant (Jn 13.11, 24–26), who effortlessly works miracles (Jn 2.1ff.; 4.46ff.; 5.2ff.; 6.1ff., 16ff.; 9.1ff.; 11.1ff.), who is in command of his own destiny (Jn 10.17–18; 18.4–6), a pre-existent Being (Jn 1.1–18; 8.56–8; 17.5), a divine 'Revealer' (Jn 1.18; 5.37ff.; 6.46; 7.28–9; 8.19, 54–8; 14.6–11; 15.21ff.; 16.3; 17.25–6). With his status as such no longer a secret,[55] Mark's epiphany Christology has been carried to new heights. In E. Käsemann's celebrated words, 'John changes the Galilean teacher into the God who goes about on earth'.[56]

It is to be observed, therefore, that there are no parables in John, such as we find in Mark, and only two references to the Kingdom of God (Jn 3.3, 5). Radically transforming the apocalyptic ideology which Mark was engaging, John presents a more fully developed 'realized' eschatology which gives a *present* emphasis to traditional apocalyptic categories: the expected *tribulation* is *now* (Jn 16.32–3); the *glory* of God's eschatological agent is *already manifested* and given to his followers (Jn 1.14; 2.11; 17.22); the glorification of the *Son of Man* takes place in the *cross*, not at the *parousia* (Jn 3.14–15; 6.62; 7.39; 8.28; 12.23–4, 27–33; 13.31–2; 17.1ff.); the Father/Son come *privately* to the individual believer in mystical fashion and not *publicly* to the world in apocalyptic fashion (Jn 14.21–3); *resurrection* from the dead is a spiritual reality *now* (Jn 5.25; 11.23–6); separation/division (judgment or *krisis*) between righteous and wicked occurs *now* as does the *final judgment* (Jn 3.18–19; 7.43; 9.39; 12.31); the righteous/believers are *not* removed from this world (Jn 17.15); the eschatological *rewards* for believers are a fact of present experience (*eternal life* (Jn 3.36; 5.24; 6.47, 54; 17.3), *adoption as God's Sons* (Jn 1.12), *joy, peace, glory* (Jn 1.14; 14.27; 15.11; 16.33; 17.13, 22ff.)). If not insertions by an ecclesiastical redactor (R. Bultmann),[57] some vestiges of a futurist eschatology can be seen to remain (Jn 5.28–9; 6.39–40, 44, 54; 12.48) but the major thrust of John's presentation is to replace traditional apocalyptic eschatology with 'Christ-mysticism' (see the Son's union with the Father, Jn 5.18; 10.18, 30; 14.6, 7; 17.20ff.; the mutual

---

[55] Cf., however, M. D. Hooker, 'The Johannine Prologue and the Messianic Secret', *NTS*, 21 (1974–5), pp. 40–58.

[56] See E. Käsemann, *The Testament of Jesus. A Study of the Gospel of John in the Light of Chapter 17* (The New Testament Library; London: SCM Press, 1968), p. 27.

[57] See R. Bultmann, *The Gospel of John. A Commentary* (Oxford: Blackwell, 1971), pp. 218ff.

intercommunion of believer, Christ and Father, Jn 1.12; 11.25; 14.17, 23; 15.1–6; 17.20ff.).

The Johannine soteriology is likewise more 'sublime' than that of Mark. John's soteriological vocabulary is full of the dualisms of existence: God (*theos*)/the world (*kosmos*)/the ruler of this world (Jn 3.16; 12.31; 15.18–19; 16.11; 17.24); light/darkness (*phōs*/*skotia*; Jn 1.4–9; 3.19–21; 8.12; 12.46); truth/falsehood (*alētheia*/*pseudos*; Jn 1.14; 8.31–3, 43–7; 14.6); freedom/bondage (*eleuthēria*/*douleia*; Jn 8.31–8); life/death (*zōē*/*thanatos*; Jn 5.24–7; 11.25–6). For those in sin (*hamartia*; Jn 8.21–4, 34), or who are perishing (*apolyein*; Jn 3.16; 10.28; 11.50), there is wrath/judgment (*orgē*/*krisis*; Jn 3.19, 36; 5.22–9), but for those who believe (*pisteuein*; Jn 3.16, 18, 36; 5.24; 7.38; 10.37–8; 20.31) or who know (*ginōskein*; Jn 1.18; 8.32; 17.3; 17.26), glory (*doxa*; Jn 1.14; 2.11; 11.4, 40; 13.31; 17.22, 24), love (*agapē*; Jn 13.34–5; 15.9–10) or eternal life (*zōē aiōnios*; Jn 3.16, 36; 5.24; 6.40, 68; 10.28).

Mark's theology of the cross has also reached new heights. Salvation is effected through the personal agency of the Son, the divine Word, or Revealer (Jn 1.17; 5.39–40), who reveals his glory not only through his miracles or 'signs' (Jn 2.11) but through his crucifixion. It is not for the Johannine Son of Man to come 'in the clouds with great power and glory' (Mk 13.26), nor to suffer and *then* enter into his glory (Lk. 24.26). The cross itself, for John, is the *glorification*, the route by means of which the descending 'Son of Man' ascends again to his heavenly Father' (Jn 3.14, 15; 7.39; 8.28; 12.16, 23; 13.31–2; 17.1, 5). The crucifixion, therefore, is the final sign. In John, an epiphany Christology has been so united with soteriology that the distinction between them has become blurred. Salvation for the fourth evangelist, furthermore, is understood in individualistic terms rather than as a collective experience (as in apocalyptic eschatology). It is for the elect rather than for the world (Jn 6.44, 64–5; 8.47; 10.26–9; 17.9; 18.37). It is theocentric rather than anthropocentric (Jn 6.44, 65). It is appropriated, by the Spirit's agency, through knowledge or truth (Jn 8.32; 14.16–17, 26; 15.26; 16.13; 17.3, 7, 8, 14, 24, 25), by faith (Jn 3.16, 18, 36), and in the present rather than the future (Jn 3.18, 19, 36).

In John, then, we have advanced a long way, in terms of

Christology, eschatology and soteriology, from the first bold step taken by Mark in suggesting that the Jesus of his inherited traditions was other than what he seemed, more than the Jewish teacher, prophet and exorcist, more indeed than the Jewish Messiah, whether Son of David or apocalyptic Son of Man. John represents the ultimate triumph of a Hellenistic Christian Jesus on his way eventually to Gnosticism. More confident in his theology, John completes the movement initially begun by Mark, partially resisted by Matthew, faithfully continued by Luke. While the wedding of Q's apocalyptic and nomistic sayings to Mark's narrative framework ensured the survival of a Jewish-Christian emphasis, it was eclipsed by the Markan 'story' of Jesus' which in turn led to the 'story' of his church in the world.[58] It is to this story, the Acts of the Apostles, that we now turn.

MARK AND ACTS

The second volume of Luke's two-volume work, the Acts of the Apostles, begins, as we have seen, with a radical rewriting of the Markan ending. Furthermore, in contrast to the single day scenario of the Gospel's epilogue (Lk. 24.1, 13, 33, 36, 50–2), the prologue to Acts (1.1–11) presents its readers with a commissioning scene which ends a forty-day period of instruction given to the disciples by the risen Jesus prior to his ascension (Acts 1.3, 8–9). Replete with Lukan themes and redactional motifs (the Jerusalem setting, the promise of the Holy Spirit, the delay of the parousia, etc.), this programmatic passage (see especially Acts 1.8) prepares the disciples, and the reader, for the world-wide mission to come, a mission which will carry the redemptive history of Jesus into the period of the church, leaving the final consummation of all things for a more distant future. Ostensibly history, the Acts of the Apostles,[59] like the Gospel of Mark, is

---

[58] See Schulz, 'Mark's Significance' in Telford (ed.), *Interpretation*, pp. 197–206. 'When the Q *halacha* was subsumed under the Gospel, and not Mark's Gospel under the Q *halacha* – in this copernican revolution the victory in principle of hellenistic Christianity over the apocalyptic-nomistic linguistic area of Jewish Christianity becomes evident' (p. 201).

[59] For introduction, background and history of interpretation, see, for example,

now being increasingly regarded as a product of theology, and its author, long thought of as a historian, as in fact more of a theologian, albeit of a 'narrative' rather than a 'systematic' kind.[60]

Writing with the needs of his contemporaries in mind, Luke, it is generally agreed, addressed two major theological concerns of the post-apostolic generation, namely eschatology and ecclesiology.[61] Two particular questions receive special attention, namely 'the expectation of the imminent end of the world, and the mission to the Gentiles without the law'.[62] By refusing to answer the disciples' question whether he would presently restore the Kingdom to Israel (Acts 1.6, 7) – a question appropriate to a triumphalist Son of David Christology – by promising them the Holy Spirit in lieu of that Kingdom (Acts 1.8a), and by decreeing a progressive evangelism (Acts 1.8b), the Lukan Jesus not only silences speculation about the delay of the parousia, and not only compensates for it, but effectively gives it theological legitimation. Taking his cue perhaps from Mk 13.10, Luke informs his readers that a world mission is to fill the space between the resurrection and the parousia. Whether the writer of the Acts of the Apostles himself expected the parousia to occur in his lifetime is as difficult a question to answer as for the writer of Mark (Mk 13.30, 32),[63] but the enterprise itself, a

H. J. Cadbury, 'Acts of the Apostles' in *IDB*, pp. 28–42; P. Esler, 'Acts of the Apostles' in *DBI*, pp. 2–5; D. Juel, *Luke–Acts* (London: SCM Press, 1983); L. E. Keck and J. L. Martyn (eds.), *Studies in Luke–Acts* (London: SPCK, 1968); Kümmel, *Introduction*; R. Maddox, *The Purpose of Luke–Acts* (Studies of the New Testament and its World; Edinburgh: T. & T. Clark, 1982); I. H. Marshall, *The Acts of the Apostles* (New Testament Guides; Sheffield: Sheffield Academic Press, 1992); W. C. Robinson, 'Acts of the Apostles' in *IDB(S)*, pp. 7–9.

[60] Esler, 'Acts' in *DBI*, p. 4; E. Haenchen, *The Acts of the Apostles. A Commentary* (Oxford: Blackwell, 1971), p. 91; W. C. van Unnik, 'Luke–Acts, a Storm Center in Contemporary Scholarship' in Keck and Martyn (eds.), *Luke–Acts*, pp. 23–4; P. Vielhauer, 'On the "Paulinism" of Acts' in Keck and Martyn (eds.), *Luke–Acts*, pp. 33–50.

[61] See Maddox, *Luke–Acts*, esp. p. 183.   [62] See Haenchen, *Acts*, p. 94.

[63] See Vielhauer, 'Acts' in Keck and Martyn (eds.), *Luke–Acts*, pp. 33–50. 'The expectation of the imminent end has disappeared and the failure of the parousia is no longer a problem; Luke replaces the apocalyptic expectation of the earliest congregation and the christological eschatology of Paul by a redemptive historical pattern of promise and fulfillment in which then eschatology *also* receives its appropriate place' (p. 47). For an opposing view, see E. Franklin, *Christ the Lord. A Study in the Purpose and Theology of Luke–Acts* (London: SPCK, 1975). '[W]e would suggest that Luke stood within the main eschatological stream of the early Christian

(theological) history of the early church for posterity, testifies to the waning of his eschatological expectation.

Initial responsibility for this worldwide mission is given to the apostles whose status in Acts is noticeably more elevated than that in the Gospel of Mark. Where Mark fails in narrative terms to present them as witnesses of the risen Jesus, Luke emphasizes the point (e.g. Acts 1.3 'to them he presented himself alive ... by many proofs'), making such witness indeed the *sine qua non* of apostleship (Acts 1.22). Whereas in Mark they are unable to work miracles (see the exorcism of Mk 9.14ff., especially 18–19), in Acts they perform, in Jesus' name, many of the 'wonders and signs' (including exorcisms), which also legitimated their Lord's 'divine man' status and mission (e.g. Acts 2.22, 43; 3.16; 4.30; 5.12). Their role has also been extended from that assigned to them in Mark. According to H. C. Kee 'The apostles are pictured in Acts as not only messengers ... but also as agents of supervision, confirmation and commissioning.'[64] Peter, in particular, is given a prominent leadership role, and is credited, surprisingly, in view of the evidence of Galatians (e.g. Gal. 2.6–9, 11–12), with the first major breakthrough to the Gentiles (Acts 10.1–11.18; 15.6–11). The leadership role, too, of James, the brother of Jesus, is acknowledged, and it is under his benign chairmanship and encouragement (contrast Gal. 2.12) that the Jerusalem church gives its approval to the admission of Gentiles (Acts 15). While he is not called an apostle (except Acts 14.4, 14),[65] even greater prominence is given to Paul, his speeches being presented as the mouthpiece of sub-apostolic theology,[66] and his exploits made to occupy the major part of the work.

The emphasis in Acts, as in Mark, on Gentiles and the Gentile mission, and the respective roles assigned to the Jeru-

---

expectations, and that salvation history in his two volumes, though present, is used in the service of his eschatology rather than as a replacement of it' (p. 6).

[64] See H. C. Kee, *Good News to the Ends of the Earth. The Theology of Acts* (London: SCM Press; Philadelphia: Trinity Press International, 1990), p. 74.

[65] See Fuller, *Introduction*, who comments: 'But here the title is shared with Barnabas, and probably means envoys commissioned by the Antioch community, not apostles of Jesus Christ' (p. 128).

[66] *Ibid.*, p. 129; Vielhauer, 'Acts' in Keck and Martyn (eds.), *Luke–Acts*, pp. 33–50. '[T]he author of Acts is in his Christology pre-Pauline, in his natural theology, concept of the law, and eschatology, post-Pauline' (p. 48).

salem apostles, especially Peter, as well as to Paul, in the initiation and promulgation of that movement, is clearly significant. It has led many to see reflected therein, if not a Hegelian synthesis between (historically antithetical) Petrine and Pauline Christianity (F. C. Baur), then at least 'some sort of dialectic between what are often assumed to be clearly demarcated Jewish and Gentile modes of Christianity'.[67] Where Mark represents a less confident Gentile Christianity in the face of the still prevalent influence of Jewish Christianity, the Christianity of Acts represents a viewpoint which looks back on the tensions of a earlier period and attempts to reconcile these in the warm and more edifying glow of a radically rewritten 'myth of Christian origins'. Luke's understanding of this Christianity's relation to the Judaism out of which it emerged, however, is still a matter of debate. Does the author of Acts see the church as the 'true' Israel or the 'new' Israel? Does he envisage the Gentiles being incorporated into an existing Israel, so *fulfilling* the OT prophecies,[68] or does he think that they, together with believing Jews, comprise a reconstituted Israel, so *replacing* the old (Israel)?[69] This ambiguity also extends to the author's treatment of the Jewish people, as we saw in the case of the Gospel. While some would highlight Luke's 'ecumenism', noting, for example, his acknowledgment of the place of Pharisees in the early church (Acts 15.5), others would maintain that the portrait he paints of the Jews and their leaders – as obstreperous, as hostile to Jesus (e.g. Acts 4.25–8; 13.27–9) and to the nascent Christian community (e.g. Acts 12.1–5), and as predestined to reject the Gospel (e.g. Acts 28.17–28 and the use of Isa. 6.9–10 and the 'hardening' motif at the climax of the second volume) – is one that amounts to nothing less than anti-Semitism.[70]

The Gospel's Christology and soteriology, in relation to Mark, have already been commented upon. What is striking about the Acts of the Apostles is the wide range of functions

---

[67] Kee, *Good News*, p. 2.   [68] See Franklin, *Christ the Lord*.

[69] See Vielhauer, 'Acts' in Keck and Martyn (eds.), *Luke–Acts*, pp. 33–50. Cf. Marshall, *Luke*, pp. 231–2.

[70] See J. T. Sanders, *The Jews in Luke–Acts* (London: SCM Press, 1987).

assigned to Jesus (e.g. healer and exorcist, Acts 2.22; 10.38; eschatological prophet, Acts 3.20–3) or his 'name' (Acts 2.38; 8.12; 10.48; cf. Mk 9.38–9) and the diversity of the Christological titles used of him, some familiar (e.g. 'Christ'/'Messiah', Acts 2.31, 36; 3.18; 4.26; 5.42; 'Son of Man', Acts 7.56; 'Son of God', Acts 9.20; 'Lord', Acts 2.36 *et passim*), others less common (e.g. 'Servant'/*pais*; Acts 3.13, 26; 4.27, 30; 'Saviour'/*Sōtēr*; Acts 5.31), some distinctively Lukan (e.g. 'the (holy and) righteous one', Acts 3.14; 7.52; 13.35; the 'Author'/'Leader'/*archēgos*; Acts 3.15; 5.31)).[71] Reflecting Gentile Christianity's basic confession (1 Cor. 12.3), Luke uses the term 'Lord' for Jesus on frequent occasions (Acts 10.36; 11.16; 16.31; 20.21; cf. Mk 1.3; 2.28; 5.19; 7.28; 11.3). Curiously, the title 'Son of God', so crucial for Mark, is used only once in Acts, but nevertheless appropriately (Acts 9.20), for it is given as the essence of Paul's Christological kerygma (see also Acts 13.33). The title 'Son of Man' also occurs only once (Acts 7.56) and here, as in Lk. 22.69 (contrast Mk 14.62), his present position of power at God's right hand (and *not* his parousia) is emphasized. Important in the Gospel, the title 'Son of David' is, surprisingly, not present in Acts at all. David himself, H. C. Kee points out, 'is portrayed in Acts not so much as a prototype of the eschatological king but as a prophet who foresaw that one of his descendants would ascend this glorious throne as promised by God' (see, for example, Acts 2.25–35).[72] Luke's distinctive term for Jesus, the *archēgos* (Acts 3.15; 5.31) is found elsewhere only in Hebrews (Heb. 2.10; 12.2). Its significance in relation to Markan theology will be commented on later.

This smorgasbord of Christological estimates has placed a question mark therefore over any notion that Luke harboured a uniform Christology.[73] A more recent study by D. L. Bock,[74] nevertheless, has argued for a more unified conception on the part of Luke. Using the Old Testament in the service of his

---

[71] See Kee, *Good News*, pp. 10–27.   [72] *Ibid.*, p. 16.

[73] See C. F. D. Moule, 'The Christology of Acts' in Keck and Martyn (eds.), *Luke–Acts*, pp. 159–85.

[74] D. L. Bock, *Proclamation from Prophecy and Pattern. Lucan Old Testament Christology* (JSNTSS, 12; Sheffield: JSOT Press, 1987).

Christology, Luke, he claims, presents Jesus as the 'Messiah-servant' whom the reader is gradually led to see as 'Lord'. If Bock is right, Luke would be similar to Mark, then, in that his redactional enterprise served to further the interests of what is perceived to be a 'higher' Christology. A number of scholars, however, have not only argued that the author's Christology was a composite one, but, following P. Vielhauer, that it was pre-Pauline. 'Luke himself', Vielhauer declared, 'is closer to the Christology of the earliest congregation, which is set forth in the speeches of Peter, than he is to the Christology of Paul.'[75] Analysing the self-same speeches in Acts, C. H. Dodd had also concluded that '[t]he Jerusalem *kerygma* does not assert that Christ died *for our sins*. The result of the life, death, and resurrection of Christ is the forgiveness of sins, but this forgiveness is not specifically connected with His death.'[76] Whether the Lukan speeches reflect the Christology or soteriology of the Jerusalem church, the sub-apostolic church or that of Luke himself, then, is a moot point.

The issue also impinges upon the disputed question, already touched upon, whether Luke or his sources in Acts, had a distinctive soteriology, and, in particular, following Paul and Mark, a 'theology of the cross'. The case has had its ardent supporters,[77] but also its powerful detractors.[78] While foreseen in scripture, according to Luke (Acts 4.25–8 and Ps. 2.1–2), Jesus' death is 'the outcome of a coalition of evil powers – Gentile and Jewish – who were hostile toward the one who had been chosen and empowered by God'.[79] '[T]he Cross of Jesus', then, according to E. Käsemann, 'is no longer a scandal but only a misunderstanding on the part of the Jews which the

---

[75] Vielhauer, 'Acts' in Keck and Martyn (eds.), *Luke–Acts*, p. 45.

[76] C. H. Dodd, *The Apostolic Preaching and its Developments* (London: Hodder & Stoughton, 1936), pp. 48–9.

[77] See, for example, C. K. Barrett, 'Theologia Crucis – in Acts?' in C. Andresen and G. Klein (eds.), *Theologia Crucis – Signum Crucis. Festschrift für Erich Dinkler* (Tübingen: Mohr–Siebeck, 1979), pp. 73–84; P. Doble, *The Paradox of Salvation. Luke's Theology of the Cross* (SNTSMS, 87; Cambridge: Cambridge University Press, 1996).

[78] For a review, see J. A. Fitzmyer, *The Gospel According to Luke I–IX* (Anchor Bible, 28; New York: Doubleday, 1986), pp. 22–3.

[79] Kee, *Good News*, p. 8.

intervention God at Easter palpably and manifestly corrects'.[80]
For Käsemann, indeed, Luke's rewriting of Christian origins,
and in particular his triumphalist theology of history, with 'the
Church itself ... the willed and intended end-product of this
history,' means that '[a] *theologia gloriae* is now in process of
replacing the *theologia crucis*'.[81] If Käsemann is correct, then
there is a certain irony in the fact that Luke, otherwise relatively
faithful to the redactional direction of Mark's Gospel, should
have placed in reverse gear one major thrust of his presentation
(as well as Paul's), namely his theology of the cross. Luke was
not deemed by Käsemann, however, to be a 'late pupil of Paul,
but the first representative of nascent early catholicism'.[82] This
judgment has, of course, been challenged,[83] but since this takes
us away from our subject, let us turn to other exemplars of the
literature of early Catholicism, namely, the Letters of Peter, and
then the Epistle to the Hebrews, to see how their theology
relates to that of the Gospel of Mark.

MARK AND THE LETTERS OF PETER

In comparing the theology of the Second Gospel with 1 and 2
Peter, due allowance must be made for the differences between
these writings, especially in respect of their genre and purpose.
The first, it should be remembered, is a narrative, while 1 Peter,
even if forged, like the Gospel, in the crucible of suffering and
persecution (or the threat of it) is a letter of encouragement to
Christians in Asia Minor. According to W. G. Kümmel, 1 Peter
is 'a hortatory writing formed from traditional paraenetic and
possibly liturgical material, which by recalling the gift of
baptism and the eschatologically grounded universality of these
sufferings serves to present to the consciousness of these Christians in a convincing way the necessity of enduring suffering

---

[80] E. Käsemann, 'Ministry and Community in the New Testament' in *Essays on New
Testament Themes* (London: SCM Press, 1964), p. 92.
[81] *Ibid.*
[82] E. Käsemann, 'New Testament Questions of Today' in *New Testament Questions of
Today* (London: SCM Press, 1969), p. 21.
[83] See Kümmel, *Introduction*, pp. 145–6, 172–3; Maddox, *Luke–Acts*, pp. 185–6; Robinson, 'Acts' in *IDB(S)*, p. 8.

and the strength to do so'.[84] Combining parenesis and polemic, 2 Peter too is clearly a work of exhortation whose purpose is 'to admonish the church to be steadfast and to warn it against deceivers'.[85] Both types of literature present their theology in an indirect way, the Gospel's theology embedded in its story form, the theology of the Letters over-ridden by their practical concerns.[86]

All three writings, nevertheless, are linked in tradition, not only by virtue of their deemed connection to Peter, but also, in the opinion of some, by a common Roman provenance. The two letters claim to have been written by the apostle (1 Pet. 1.1; 5.1; 2 Pet. 1.1, 16–18; 3.1, 15), who speaks of himself as 'a witness of the sufferings of Christ' (1 Pet. 5.1), as present at the transfiguration (2 Pet. 1.16–18), and as being in harmonious relations with 'our beloved brother Paul' (2 Pet. 3.15). While some scholars have accepted the authenticity of 1 Peter, with Silvanus acting as Peter's amanuensis (1 Pet. 5.12), most would view it, along with 2 Peter, as pseudonymous.[87] There is little in the way of detail here that would lead one to assume the apostle's own testimony, Jesus' sufferings, for example, being described not in the realistic terms of an eye-witness but in the stereotyped language of the Old Testament (compare 1 Pet. 2.21–25 with Isa. 53). If we were to press 1 Peter 5.1, indeed, then Peter, according to Mark's Gospel, did not in fact witness Jesus' sufferings since he disappears from the scene after the denial (Mk 14.66–72), leaving the women alone 'looking on from afar' (Mk 15.40). A traditional connection between Peter and Mark himself, as well as the case for a Roman provenance, has also rested on 1 Peter 5.13 where 'Peter' sends greetings from 'she who is at Babylon (= Rome?)' and from 'my son Mark' (= 'John Mark'?).[88] The difficulties of this verse were

---

84 Kümmel, *Introduction*, p. 421.

85 B. Reicke, *The Epistles of James, Peter, and Jude* (Anchor Bible, 37; New York: Doubleday, 1985), p. 147.

86 See F. W. Beare, *The First Epistle of Peter* (Oxford: Blackwell, 1947), p. 31; J. N. D. Kelly, *The Epistles of Peter and of Jude* (Black's New Testament Commentaries; London: A. & C. Black, 1969), p. 26.

87 See Kümmel, *Introduction*, pp. 421–4.

88 See Martin, *Mark*, p. 59. For the idea of a Petrine circle in Rome, including Mark and Silvanus, see J. H. Elliott, 'Peter, Silvanus and Mark in 1 Peter and Acts. Sociological-

discussed in chapter one, and the conclusion reached was that this pseudonymous work merely witnesses at most to a late first-century or early second-century tradition that associated the apostle with a 'Mark' (even perhaps *the* John Mark) but does not make of itself a connection between this 'Mark' and the writer of the Gospel.

The Letters of Peter belong, then, as previously stated, to the literature of early Catholicism, 1 Peter, according to R. H. Fuller 'showing the crystallization of liturgy in the early sub-apostolic age as one of the institutions through which the apostolic tradition was perpetuated after the death of the apostles',[89] while 2 Peter, according to E. Käsemann, 'was written as an apologia for primitive Christian eschatology' and 'is from beginning to end a document expressing an early Catholic viewpoint'.[90] On this view, therefore, the former is to be dated (in light of the persecution references) towards the end of Domitian's reign, 90–5 CE, or even as late as 113 CE in the reign of Trajan,[91] and the latter *c.* 150 CE, which would make it hence the latest of the NT writings.[92]

For purposes of theological comparison, however, the deter-mination of authorship and precise dating is less important than the source- or tradition-critical relations between the three documents, the nature of the theological emphases they embody, and the theological development they evince. 1 Peter was known to the author of 2 Peter, as 2 Peter 3.1 indicates. Some have also detected theological affinities between 1 Peter

---

Exegetical Perspectives on a Petrine Group in Rome' in W. Haubeck and M. Bachmann (eds.), *Wort in der Zeit. Neutestamentliche Studien. Festgabe für Karl Heinrich Rengstorf zum 75. Geburtstag* (Leiden: E. J. Brill, 1980), pp. 250–67; J. H. Elliott, 'The Roman Provenance of 1 Peter and the Gospel of Mark. A Response to David Dungan' in B. Corley (ed.), *Colloquy on New Testament Studies. A Time for Reappraisal and Fresh Approaches* (Macon, GA: Mercer University Press, 1983), pp. 181–94.

[89] Fuller, *Introduction*, p. 159.

[90] E. Käsemann, 'An Apologia for Primitive Christian Eschatology' in *Essays*, pp. 169–95. See also Kümmel, *Introduction*, pp. 430–4. For an opposing view, cf. R. Bauckham, *Jude, 2 Peter* (Word Biblical Commentary, 50; Waco, TX: Word, 1983), pp. 151–3. '[F]or Käsemann "early Catholicism" is not so much a historical category as a theological accusation' (p. 151).

[91] Kümmel, *Introduction*, p. 425. For an opposing view, Reicke, *Epistles*, p. 71.

[92] Kümmel, *Introduction*, p. 434; Käsemann, 'Apologia' in Käsemann, *Essays*, p. 172. Contr. Reicke, *Epistles*, p. 144 ; Bauckham, *2 Peter*, p. 158.

and the sermons in Acts discussed in the last section.[93] By far the greatest theological influence on the author of 1 Peter is Gentile Christianity, and in particular Paul, whose letters offer abundant parallels to the language and ideas of this letter.[94] The Pauline letters themselves, now elevated to the status of 'scripture', are appealed to by the author of 2 Peter (2 Pet. 3.15–16). He acknowledges also that they are 'hard to understand' and bemoans the fact that they are now subject to misinterpretation by those he deems false teachers (see also 2 Pet. 1.20). Typical of early Catholicism, both letters represent, then, 'a rapprochement between the two leaders',[95] with Peter and his theology being presented in Pauline terms, and with both apostles acting in the capacity of guarantors of the one apostolic tradition.[96] This picture of Peter as 'authentic apostolic teacher and source of tradition', whose 'image is so strong that [his] name can be invoked to correct those who are misinterpreting the Pauline letters',[97] can be clearly contrasted with that in the Gospel of Mark.

Pursuing the question of source or tradition relations, we might ask if either author knew the Gospels, and particularly the Gospel of Mark. Parallels do exist, although mostly with Matthew (compare 1 Pet. 1.10–11 and Mt. 11.13; 13.17; 1.17 and Mt. 6.9; 2.7 and Mt. 21.42, though see also Mk 12.10; 2.12 and Mt. 5.16; 3.9 and Mt. 5.44; 3.14 and Mt. 5.10),[98] the closest of these, according to E. Best, being 1 Peter 3.14 and Matthew 5.10 and 1 Peter 1.18 and Mark 10.45.[99] In general, the lack of verbal agreement indicates that knowledge of the Synoptic tradition, especially that contained in Matthew 5.10–16, Mark 10.45, Luke 6 and 12,[100] rather than direct dependence upon the

---

[93] See E. Best, *1 Peter* (New Century Bible; London: Oliphants, 1971), p. 60; G. E. Ladd, *A Theology of the New Testament* (Grand Rapids, MI: Eerdmans, 1974), p. 595; E. G. Selwyn, *The First Epistle of St Peter* (London: Macmillan, 1947), pp. 33–6.

[94] See Beare, *Peter*, p. 25; Reicke, *Epistles*, p. 70.

[95] J. L. Houlden, 'Peter' in *DBI*, p. 534.

[96] J. C. Beker, 'Peter, Second Letter of' in *IDB*, p. 771.

[97] R. E. Brown, 'Peter' in *IDB(S)*, p. 657.   [98] See Kelly, *Epistles*, pp. 11–12.

[99] E. Best, '1 Peter and the Gospel Tradition', *NTS*, 16 (1969–70), pp. 95–113; Best, *1 Peter*, p. 53.

[100] See P. H. Davids, *The First Epistle of Peter* (The New International Commentary on the New Testament; Grand Rapids, MI: Eerdmans, 1990), p. 27.

Gospels themselves is in view, and that such knowledge on the part of the author was of the more developed rather than of the more original form of the tradition.[101] Although a common provenance within the Roman church accounts, according to Best, for the use in 1 Peter of the 'ransom' image in connection with the death of Christ, his highlighting of this important Markan parallel is one to which we shall return. Similarly, with 2 Peter, a knowledge of the Gospel tradition, if not of the Gospels themselves,[102] is presupposed by parallels such as 2 Peter 1.14 and John 21.18, 1.16–18 and Mark 9.2–8 par., 2.20 and Matthew 12.45 = Luke 11.26, 3.10 and Matthew 24.43 = Luke 12.39 (see also 1 Thes. 5.2).[103] Where the Gospel of Mark is concerned, the author's reference to and use of the Transfiguration tradition is also to be noted.

If we cannot be certain, however, of a direct influence of Mark on the letters of Peter, then in what ways may the theology of their respective texts be compared?[104] As with other early Catholic writings, ecclesiology is important. While employing the language of Diaspora Judaism in addressing 'the exiles of the Dispersion in Pontus, Galatia, Cappadocia, Asia, and Bithynia' (1 Pet. 1.1; see also 1.17; 2.11), the writer of 1 Peter had, by common consent, Gentile Christians in mind.[105] Unlike the Gospel of Mark, or the Pauline Epistles before it, the letter shows little evidence of a tension between Jewish and Gentile Christianity.[106] This dispute has been left behind, and the church is now viewed as the true people of God, the *new* Israel, whose calling it is to be separate, whose duty it is to be holy, and

---

[101] See Best, *1 Peter*, p. 53. For a contrary view, see R. H. Gundry, '*Verba Christi* in 1 Peter: their Implications Concerning the Authorship of 1 Peter and the Authenticity of the Gospel Tradition', *NTS*, 13 (1967), pp. 336–50.

[102] However on 2 Pet. 1.16–17, see Beker, 'Peter' in *IDB*, p. 771, and on 2 Pet. 3.2, Käsemann, 'Apologia' in *Essays*, p. 173.

[103] See Bauckham, *2 Peter*, p. 148. Bauckham also gives as possible echoes 2 Pet. 1.16 and Mk 9.1 par. Mt. 16.28 (but if so an independent form of this saying), 2.9 and Mt. 6.13, 2.21 and Mk 9.42; 14.21 par. (see also 1 Clem. 46.8) and 3.4 and Mk 9.1 par.; Mk 13.30 par.

[104] For a recent theological treatment of the letters, see A. Chester and R. P. Martin, *The Theology of the Letters of James, Peter, and Jude* (New Testament Theology; Cambridge: Cambridge University Press, 1994). For standard treatments, see Beare, *Peter*; Kelly, *Epistles*; Selwyn, *St Peter*.

[105] See Best, *1 Peter*, p. 19.   [106] *Ibid.*, p. 45.

whose real home is in heaven (1 Pet. 1.15; 2.4–5, 9–10).[107] The corollary of this *theologoumenon*, however, is that the 'hardening' motif where the Jews are concerned, has been intensified. Where Mark (or the tradition before him) appended the 'cornerstone' logion of Psalm 118.22–3 to the parable of the Vineyard (Mk 12.10–11), so indicting the Jewish leaders for their rejection of Jesus, the author of 1 Peter employs the same logion to more universal effect (1 Pet. 2.7). Where Mark, in presenting his 'parables secret,' employed Isaiah 6.9–10 to explain the 'outsiders' rejection of Jesus' word (Mk 4.11–12), the writer of 1 Peter employs Isaiah 8.14–15 to even more telling effect so that the old Israel 'stumble because they disobey the word, *as they were destined to do*' (1 Pet. 2.8; *italics mine*). The role given to the church by the Letters of Peter is also reflected, as we have seen, in the view taken of its leaders. Where Mark entertained a negative attitude in respect of the original followers of Jesus, the apostles, especially Peter, have now become the essential guardians of the truth (e.g. 2 Pet. 3.2). Writing of the role of Peter in 2 Peter, Käsemann declares: 'The messenger of the gospel has become the guarantor of the tradition, the witness of the resurrection has become the witness of the *historia sacra*, the bearer of the eschatological action of God has become a pillar of the institution which dispenses salvation, the man who is subject to the eschatological temptation has become the man who brings *securitas*.'[108]

Where sharp contrast, then, can be seen between Gospel and Letters in the respective status accorded to Jesus' original Jewish disciples, the Christology of the Letters may be seen to reflect the Gentile orientation already adopted, though more tentatively, by the Markan evangelist. The Christology is high, focusing on Christ's sufferings and death, as well as his exaltation. While the Gospel incorporates, though seeks to supersede, the tradition of Jesus as teacher, prophet and exorcist, the

---

[107] See Kümmel, *Introduction*, p. 418; Ladd, *Theology*, pp. 597, 599. 'So far as the Church is concerned, Christians are the new Israel, the people of God who were once no people, strangers and sojourners in the world awaiting their heavenly inheritance', Kelly, *Epistles*, p. 26.

[108] Käsemann, 'Apologia' in *Essays*, p. 177.

Letters have little interest in the historical Jesus other than in his passion. Similarly, Jewish-Christian Messianic Christologies which the evangelist did his best to engage – Jesus as the royal 'Son of David' or as the apocalyptic 'Son of Man' – have also been left far behind. The recipients of 1 Peter are instructed to 'reverence Christ (now virtually a second name) as Lord' (1 Pet. 3. 15), a title also used with reference to God (e.g. 1 Pet. 1.25; 2 Pet. 2.9, 11; 3.8, 9, 10). Both writers correspondingly refer to Jesus in devotional terms as 'the Lord Jesus Christ' (1 Pet. 1.3; 2 Pet. 1.8, 14, 16) or, in the case of 2 Peter, as 'our Lord and Saviour Jesus Christ' (2 Pet. 1.11; 2.20; 3.18). Although 1 Peter does not use the title 'Son of God', some commentators think that his status (e.g. 1 Pet. 1.2–3) and even his pre-existence as such (1 Pet. 1.20) is presupposed.[109] In citing the Transfiguration story, with its heavenly declaration of Jesus' Sonship, the writer of 2 Peter, however, is clearly recapitulating a tradition which, in its original form in Mark, functioned, as we saw, to reinforce such a Christology.

A distinctive element of 1 Peter is its presentation of Christ as the suffering Servant of Isaiah 53 (1 Pet. 2.22–4).[110] Although this is deemed by some not to be a prominent feature of Mark,[111] the influence of Isaiah 53 is to be detected, I have argued, in Mark's transformation of the apocalyptic Son of Man into the suffering Son of Man, in the pivotal 'ransom' saying of Mark 10.45 in particular, and in the narrative of the passion itself (see also Mk 9.35 where true discipleship is defined in terms of the 'servant' role). It is significant, then, that the evangelist's portrait of Jesus, in its emphasis on his suffering and death, is presented also by the writer of 1 Peter, the former holding this portrait up to his readers for its Christological implications, the latter (presupposing these) for its ethical ones. For the one, Christian *belief* is the focus, and it resides in penetrating the 'secret' of Christ's sufferings. For the other, it is

---

[109] See Selwyn, *St Peter*, p. 249. Cf. Ladd, *Theology*, p. 599.

[110] See Kelly, *Epistles*, pp. 25, 30; S. Laws, 'Peter, First' in *DBI*, p. 534.

[111] See, for example, E. Best, *The Temptation and the Passion: the Markan Soteriology* (SNTSMS, 2; Cambridge: Cambridge University Press, 1965), pp. 140ff.; Best, *1 Peter*, p. 60; M. Hooker, *Jesus and the Servant* (London: SPCK, 1959), pp. 62–102.

Christian *behaviour* that matters, and it resides in the *imitatio Christi*, the imitation of that suffering.

In placing an emphasis on the salvific implications as well as the exemplary nature of the suffering and death of Jesus, the writer of 1 Peter may be said to stand in a soteriological tradition which owes much to the influence of Paul and Mark. Like theirs, his soteriology is a *theologia crucis*. The essence of Christian salvation lies in the death of Christ, and his subsequent glorification (1 Pet. 1.11), and this death is 'sacrificial, vicarious, and redemptive'.[112] Although the Gospel offers no parallel to the remarkable descent of Christ into hell (1 Pet. 3.19–20), nor any claim that he was sinless (contrast 1 Peter 2.22 and Mk 1.4, 9; 10.18), the particular use by both Mark and the writer of 1 Peter of 'ransom' imagery (Mk 10.45 and 1 Pet. 1.18–19) to express the significance of Christ's death is, as we have noted, a striking feature, contrasting, as it does, with other soteriologies which see Christ's death as a victory over evil powers (e.g. Col. 2.15),[113] or which view that death itself as his glorification (e.g. Jn 12.23ff.).

Eschatology is an important feature in the Letters of Peter as it is in the Gospel of Mark. There is in both writers the notion that the death of Christ is in itself an eschatological event. According to the writer of 1 Peter, Christ's death was prophesied (1 Pet. 1.10–11), was predestined before the foundation of the world (1 Pet. 1.20) and has inaugurated the end-time (1 Pet. 1.20).[114] In the Gospel, links exist between the passion narrative and the apocalyptic discourse which precedes it, with eschatological signs attending the death of the Son of God (the prediction of the Temple's demise, Mk 13.1–2 and 15.38; the cosmic darkness, 13.24 and 15.33; the summons to watchfulness, 13.33, 35–7 and 14.32–42, 66–72; see also the anticipation of Elijah, 1.2–3; 9.11–13; 15.35–6).[115] As in Mark, watchfulness in light of 'the end of all things' is advocated in 1 Peter 4.7. An

---

[112] Beare, *Peter*, p. 34.   [113] Best, *1 Peter*, p. 60.

[114] See Ladd, *Theology*, p. 595.

[115] For a discussion of the links between Mk 13 and the passion narrative, see R. H. Lightfoot, *The Gospel Message of St Mark* (Oxford: Clarendon, 1950), pp. 48–59. See also T. J. Geddert, *Watchwords. Mark 13 in Markan Eschatology* (JSNTSS 26; Sheffield: JSOT Press, 1989), pp. 89–111.

eschatological emphasis, indeed, permeates the entire letter.[116] While references to the Kingdom of God are lacking, the eschatological hope is strongly declared both at the beginning (1 Pet. 1.3–13) and at the end (1 Pet. 5.10).

By virtue of the author's emphasis on the salvific death of Christ, however, a 'realized' element, as with Mark, qualifies this future hope.[117] At the individual level, salvation comes to the believer with conversion (1 Pet. 1.22) and 'baptism now saves you' (1 Pet. 3.21). At the cosmic level, Christ has been manifested (1 Pet. 1.20), was resurrected, has ascended into heaven, and is now 'at the right hand of God, with angels, authorities, and powers subject to him' (1 Pet. 3.22). At the social or political level, however, believers must be subject to these earthly powers, as well as to all human institutions (1 Pet. 2.13–17). Despite the sufferings of Christian communities, Rome itself, though described as 'Babylon' (1 Pet. 5.13) must, in the form of the Emperor, be honoured. Although the emphasis is on a realized eschatology, therefore, the future hope, as with Mark (Mk 13) has clearly not been abandoned (1 Pet. 1.5, 9, 13; 4.13), and, in this respect, 1 Peter can be said to retain a primitive feature.

This unwillingness to abandon the future hope is seen even more strongly in 2 Peter's 'apologia for primitive Christian eschatology' (see especially 2 Pet. 3. 3–13). While sharing Mark's view that the second coming will be sudden in appearance and dramatic in nature (Mk 13. 24ff., 33, 35 and 2 Pet. 3.10), the writer departs from the Gospel's traditional apocalyptic claim that God would shorten the days (Mk 13.20) and speed its coming (Mk 13.30). Instead, God lengthens the time of the end 'not wishing that any should perish, but that all should reach repentance' (2 Pet. 3.9).[118] Notwithstanding this provi-

---

[116] See Davids, *Peter*, p. 15; W. C. van Unnik, 'Peter, First Letter of' in *IDB*, p. 765.

[117] 'The Messiah has been revealed and the End has already begun (i. 20); redeemed and regenerated, Christians have the promised salvation already within their grasp. Although the full glory is yet to come (i. 4f.; iv. 13), their temporary sufferings are themselves proof that it is just round the corner (iv. 7; 17: cf. v. 10); the final conflict of God and His saints with the Devil has been effectively won, so that they can face every sort of ill-treatment with confidence, even exultation', Kelly, *Epistles*, p. 26.

[118] See Beker, 'Peter' in *IDB*, p. 771.

dential delay, fiery judgment for the ungodly will be inevitable, and 'entrance into the eternal kingdom of our Lord and Saviour Jesus Christ' (2 Pet. 1.11) the reward for Christian allegiance and fortitude. In this somewhat crude way, then, 2 Peter 'has provided the church with a rationale to deal with the delay of the Parousia while retaining a doctrine of the destruction of the world at the time of the Last Judgment'.[119]

These primitive Christian convictions are also buttressed, however, in another remarkable way. 'Standing' with those in the Gospel who would 'not taste death' before they saw 'the Kingdom of God come with power' (Mk 9.1), the 'Peter' of the Second Letter, himself about to taste death (2 Pet. 1.12–15) makes an appeal to his experience of the Transfiguration (compare Mk 9.2–9 par. and 2 Pet. 1.16–19). Where the evangelist used this account to reinforce his epiphany Christology, however, the writer of the Second Letter uses it, along with Old Testament prophecy, emphatically to reassert the primitive parousia expectation. On the other hand, the removal of imminence, the breaking of the link between Christ's death, resurrection, ascension and parousia in the primitive kerygma, and the unsophisticated use of the second coming both as a carrot to reward the godly and as a stick to punish the wicked,[120] all contribute to Käsemann's criticism that 2 Peter is 'perhaps the most dubious writing in the canon'.[121] Having 'a relatively autonomous existence alongside the other articles of Christian doctrine', he declares, '... it would arouse no interest at all if its help were not needed in giving a clear-cut solution to the problem of theodicy and in encouraging Christian morality by directing the eye towards reward and punishment ... [C]oncerned only with the hope of the triumphal entry of believers into the eternal kingdom and with the destruction of the ungodly', this latest writing in the New Testament sadly demonstrates, then, that a '[t]heologia gloriae triumphs all along the line'.[122]

[119] *Ibid.*, pp. 767.   [120] See Fuller, *Introduction*, p. 165.
[121] Käsemann, 'Apologia' in *Essays*, p. 169.   [122] *Ibid.*, pp. 185, 187.

MARK AND HEBREWS

Few comparisons appear to have been made between the Gospel of Mark and the Epistle to the Hebrews,[123] yet such comparison can be illuminating, especially where the history of NT theology is concerned.[124] Both writings, as with 1 Peter, are preoccupied with the theme of suffering, persecution and martyrdom, and seek to bolster faith in face of it (e.g. Heb. 10.32–9 and Mk 10.29–30; 13.9–13). As with 1 Peter, too, both hold up for the reader the example of Jesus' own sufferings and draw implications from it, both practical and theological.[125] As with the Letters of Peter, Rome too has been claimed as a possible provenance for the Epistle, hence bringing it into the same orbit as that traditionally suggested for the Gospel.[126] With regard to its date of composition, the Epistle was probably written between 80 and 90 CE,[127] but an earlier date – perhaps just before 70 CE (if Heb. 9.9–10; 13.13–14 imply that Jerusalem and the Temple are still standing) would make it almost contemporary with Mark.

---

[123] Cf., however, Bacon, *Mark*, pp. 331–4; A. A. K. Graham, 'Mark and Hebrews' in F. L. Cross (ed.), *Studia Evangelica 4,1. Papers Presented to the Third International Congress on New Testament Studies held at Christ Church, Oxford, 1965: Part 1. The New Testament Scriptures* (Berlin: Akademie Verlag, 1968), pp. 411–16.

[124] For general background, see the standard introductions, commentaries or dictionary articles: e.g. H. W. Attridge, *The Epistle to the Hebrews* (Hermeneia; Philadelphia, PA: Fortress Press, 1989); F. F. Bruce, *The Epistle to the Hebrews* (The New International Commentary on the New Testament; Grand Rapids, MI: Eerdmans, 1964); F. F. Bruce, 'Hebrews, Letter to the' in *IDB(S)*, pp. 394–5; D. C. Duling and N. Perrin, *The New Testament. Proclamation and Parenesis. Myth and History* (New York: Harcourt Brace College, 1994), pp. 282–93; P. Ellingworth, *The Epistle to the Hebrews. A Commentary on the Greek Text* (The New International Greek Testament Commentary; Grand Rapids, MI: Eerdmans; Carlisle: Paternoster, 1993); Fuller, *Introduction*, pp. 144–50; J. Héring, *The Epistle to the Hebrews* (London: Epworth Press, 1970); Kümmel, *Introduction*, pp. 388–403; H. Montefiore, *The Epistle to the Hebrews* (London: A. & C. Black, 1964); R. Williamson, 'Hebrews' in *DBI*, pp. 273–6; R. M. Wilson, *Hebrews* (New Century Bible Commentary; Grand Rapids, MI: Eerdmans; Basingstoke: Marshall, Morgan & Scott, 1987). More specialized theological discussion can be found in Ladd, *Theology*, pp. 571–87 and B. Lindars, *The Theology of the Letter to the Hebrews* (New Testament Theology; Cambridge: Cambridge University Press, 1991).

[125] See Bacon, *Mark*, pp. 333–4.

[126] *Ibid.*, esp. p. 331; W. Manson, *The Epistle to the Hebrews* (London: Hodder & Stoughton, 1951), esp. pp. 23–4.

[127] See Kümmel, *Introduction*, p. 403.

Before making a specific comparison between their respective theologies, we might again consider the source or tradition relations existing in general between Hebrews and other NT documents, especially the Gospels. Although there are clear echoes of Pauline ideas in the Epistle,[128] it is generally agreed that the author's theology is to be clearly differentiated from that of the apostle.[129] Affinities have been detected between Acts and Hebrews, especially Acts 6–7. Here the expression 'the Hebrews' (probably Hebrew- or Aramaic-speaking conservative Jewish Christians, see Acts 6.1) is found. Ideas attributed to Stephen (e.g. the supersession of the Temple cultus, the wandering people of God) also find their place in the Epistle.[130] The Epistle, or 'word of exhortation', as it describes itself (Heb. 13.22) has its strongest links, however, with 1 Peter, especially in terms of soteriology.[131] References to the Synoptic tradition, on the other hand, are scarce.[132] Hebrews 7.14 remarks that 'our Lord was descended from Judah' rather than from priestly Levi, a tradition that the writer's High Priest Christology has to overcome. Hebrews 4.15 may allude to the Temptation (cf. Mk 1.12–13 par.) and 5.5 to the Baptism (cf. Mk 1.9–11 par.).

---

[128] Kümmel lists these as 'Christ the Son, the preexistent agent of creation; the redemptive death of Christ as the central message of salvation; the idea of the New covenant of God (καινὴ διαθήκη), cf. I Cor 11:25; II Cor 3:6, 14; Gal 4:24; the decisive importance of faith; the use of the same quotations in scriptural proofs: 10:38 and Rom 1:17; Gal 3:11; Hab 2:4–2:6 ff and I Cor 15:27; Ps 8; echoes of Pauline exposition (cf. 5:12 ff with I Cor 3:1 ff)' (*ibid.*, p. 395).

[129] *Ibid.*, p. 395; Montefiore, *Hebrews*, p. 5; E. F. Scott, *The Epistle to the Hebrews* (Edinburgh: T. & T. Clark, 1922), pp. 58–9.

[130] See Duling and Perrin, *New Testament.*, pp. 284–5; Manson, *Hebrews*, esp. pp. vi, 23–4.

[131] These are summarized by H. W. Attridge as follows: 'Both focus on the Christ who was "manifested" at the end of days. His "once for all" death is a central salvific event, and that death is portrayed in cultic terms, as the sacrifice of a sinless victim. The death of Christ is not the end of his story and both texts highlight his exaltation, relying on Ps 110. The application of Christ's sacrifice, imaged as a "sprinkling of blood" and connected with baptism, removes sin, affects conscience, provides access to God, and sanctifies. This soteriological event was announced in the scriptures through which the spirit spoke', *The Epistle to the Hebrews* (Hermeneia; Philadelphia, PA: Fortress Press, 1989), pp. 30–1. See also Montefiore, *Hebrews*, p. 5.

[132] Bacon, *Mark*, p. 331; E. Grässer, 'Der historische Jesus im Hebräerbrief', *ZNW*, 56 (1965), pp. 63–91; G. Hughes, *Hebrews and Hermeneutics. The Epistle to the Hebrews as a New Testament Example of Biblical Interpretation* (SNTSMS, 36; Cambridge: Cambridge University Press, 1979), pp. 77 and 179, n. 89.

Hebrews 5.7ff. appears to reflect knowledge of the Gethsemane story (Mk 14.32–42 par.) and Hebrews 13.12 of Jesus' death outside Jerusalem. While a number of formative influences have been mooted for Hebrews, among them Platonism, Philo, the Dead Sea Scrolls and Gnosticism,[133] the Epistle is essentially a work of theology which has been generated by a rich religious imagination operating principally on the Old Testament (especially on Ps. 110 and Gen. 14).

As before, I shall comment on this theology with regard to the specific areas which have guided our comparison with the Gospel thus far, namely ecclesiology, Christology, soteriology and eschatology. Not only the background of thought, but also the nature of the community addressed in the Epistle have constituted a problem. Scholars are divided as to whether the Epistle was written to Jewish Christians, to Gentile Christians, or simply to Christians *per se*.[134] The Epistle's arguments in support of the superiority of Christian institutions over Jewish ones (of the Son over angels, of Jesus over Moses, of the heavenly high priest over the Levitical one, of the new covenant over the old) is buttressed at the same time by a detailed and comprehensive knowledge of, and dependence upon the Old Testament, and especially the sacrificial system. Its audience, for this reason, can reasonably be seen as Jewish Christians, who, in danger of apostasy (Heb. 6.4–6; 10.23, 26) or merely of conservatism (Heb. 5.12–14; 6.1–3), are either 'on the brink of lapsing into their original Jewish beliefs',[135] or 'of remaining as Christians under the covert of the Jewish religion'.[136] On the other hand, the terms 'Jew' or 'Gentile' do not appear, and, as with 1 Peter, there is no evidence of the Jew–Gentile dispute evident in Mark and Paul, nor indeed of any hostility between them. Where the addressees of Hebrews are concerned, they are 'the people of God' who are to enter into the 'sabbath rest'

---

[133] See Bruce, 'Hebrews' in *IDB(S)*, pp. 394–5; L. D. Hurst, *The Epistle to the Hebrews. Its Background of Thought* (SNTSMS, 65; Cambridge: Cambridge University Press, 1990); Wilson, *Hebrews*, p. 27.

[134] See Kümmel, *Introduction*, pp. 398–401.

[135] Williamson, 'Hebrews' in *DBI*, p. 273.   [136] Manson, *Hebrews*, p. 24.

denied to the Israel of old, the wilderness generation (Heb. 3.7–4.13, especially 4.9).

With regard to Jewish institutions, the writer of the Epistle to the Hebrews, like Mark, has an 'interior' view of purity and the laws governing it (Heb. 9.9–10; 13.9 and Mk 7.1–23) as well as a spiritual view of sacrifice (Heb. 10.1–10; 13.15–16 and Mk 12.32–4). For both writers, the Temple is man-made (Heb. 9.11, 24 and Mk 14.58). In what are admittedly very different contexts, each nevertheless is concerned with the sabbath and its implications for the follower of Jesus (Heb. 3.7–4.13 and Mk 2.23–3.6), both employing the 'hardening' motif of unbelieving Israel or the Jewish authorities in connection with it (Heb. 3.7ff. and Mk 3.5). In offering a rebuke to its target audience for its lack of courage in making spiritual progress, of advancing beyond the fundamentals, Hebrews offers a picture similar to that painted of the original disciples of Jesus in Mark. Likewise, in presenting Jesus himself as 'the apostle ... of our confession' (Heb. 3.1), as the one who 'goes ahead' of his disciples on the road to salvation (Heb. 2.10; 4.14; 6.20; 12.2 and Mk 10.32; 10.52; 14.28; 16.7), the two writers strike certain common notes.

It is in the area of Christology and soteriology, indeed, that these resemblances are to be seen. Unlike the evangelist, the writer of Hebrews shows little interest in, or knowledge of, the Jesus tradition, as the paucity of references to that tradition indicate. Nevertheless, '[n]o New Testament book', it is claimed, 'emphasizes the humanity of Jesus more emphatically than does Hebrews' (see, for example, Heb. 2.17; 5.7; 12.3),[137] and in this it can be compared with Mark. On the other hand, both writers are clearly of the view that their subject is 'more than human', is indeed divine, and, in the case of Hebrews, as with 1 Peter (though not Mark), even sinless (Heb. 4.15; 7.26; 1 Pet. 2.22; contrast Mk 1.4, 9; 10.18). In the case of Hebrews, as with 1 Peter, other 'lower' estimates of Jesus – Jesus as teacher, prophet, exorcist – have clearly been left far behind, with no apparent necessity to engage them. Miracles now attest 'the message declared by angels' and by the one addressed as 'the

---

[137] Ladd, *Theology*, p. 574. See also Graham, 'Mark and Hebrews' in Cross (ed.), *Studia Evangelica 4,1*, p. 415; Scott, *Hebrews*, p. 61.

Lord' (Heb. 2.2, 3; cf. 12.14; 13.20). Like Mark, but unlike Matthew, the writer has little truck with Jesus as an earthly Messiah or royal Son of David. The second evangelist provided no family tree for the Jesus of his Gospel, and the Christ of Hebrews, like Melchizedek, is similarly 'without father or mother or genealogy' (Heb. 7.3). Where Mark used the Messianic Psalm 110 to argue for the concept of 'Christ' as 'Lord' rather than 'Son of David' (Mk 12.35–7 and Ps. 110.1), the author of Hebrews employs the same Psalm to argue for the concept of 'Christ' as 'priest after the order of Melchizedek' (Heb. 7 and Ps. 110.4). As Mark used but qualified the notion of Jesus as the apocalyptic Son of Man ('The Son of Man *must* suffer', Mk 8.31), so too the focus of the Epistle's Christological presentation is on 'the heavenly man' who, nevertheless, achieves his salvific purpose through suffering. As 'son of man' made 'for a little while lower than the angels', he is 'crowned with glory and honour because of the suffering of death' (Heb. 2.5–9). Hence it is 'fitting that he, for whom and by whom all things exist, in bringing many sons to glory, should make the *pioneer* of their salvation perfect through suffering' (Heb. 2.10).

The word translated here (and in 12.2) as 'pioneer' (*archēgos*; see also Heb. 4.14; 6. 20) is one encountered elsewhere, as we have noted, only in Acts 3.15 and 5.31. In Mark, however, Jesus too, as we have observed, 'precedes' his disciples on his lonely way to the cross (Mk 10.32, 52), and thence to 'Galilee' (of the Gentiles) where henceforth his living presence is to be discovered (Mk 14.28; 16.7). Likewise, in Hebrews, as pathfinder, he 'passes through the heavens' (Heb. 4.14), 'entering', as 'forerunner', 'into the inner shrine behind the curtain' (Heb. 6.19–20). It is tempting, therefore, to see the Epistle's bold theological claim that Christ entered the heavenly sanctuary, opening a 'living way ... through the curtain' (Heb. 10.20), represented in narrative form in the Gospel's statement that at the death of Jesus, 'the curtain of the temple was torn in two, from top to bottom' (Mk 15.38).[138] While Hebrews also shares with Mark some other Christological images (e.g. the 'shepherd'

---

[138] Graham, 'Mark and Hebrews' in Cross (ed.), *Studia Evangelica 4,1*, p. 415. Cf. Bacon, *Mark*, p. 332.

motif, cf. Heb. 13.20 and Mk 14.27),[139] the supreme point of contact lies in their mutual 'Son of God' Christology. For Mark, as we saw, this is the supreme title. For the writer of the Epistle, too, it is a favourite one (Heb. 1.2, 5; 4.14; 5.5; 6.6; 7.3; 10.29).[140] Where the pre-existence of the Son is germinal in the Gospel rather than a more developed element of doctrine, the Christology of the author of Hebrews has clearly begun to develop along this line (e.g. Heb. 1.1–4).[141] Where the Son's status is subject to secrecy in the Gospel, in the Epistle he is 'now risen, ascended, and seated at God's right hand, waiting for the subjection to him of all his enemies'.[142]

If 'Son of God' is one of the poles around which the author's thought about Christ revolves, the other is represented by the title 'high priest' (e.g. Heb. 2.17; 3.1; 4.14; 5.10; 6.20).[143] The central theme, indeed, of the Christology of Hebrews is the high priesthood of Christ.[144] This Christology, on the other hand, is not shared by Mark, nor by the Gospel tradition as a whole, despite attempts to detect it.[145] In the expressive words of J. Héring, by '[s]eizing upon the figure of Melchizedek who appears only in Genesis 14 and later in Psalm 110, the author with remarkable wisdom has found the Archimedean point which enables him to lift from its hinges the entire Jewish cult going back by tradition to Moses and Aaron'.[146] In terms reminiscent of the prologue of John's Gospel (Jn 1.1ff.; see also Col. 1.15ff.), the writer of Hebrews in addition presents Jesus as the sustainer of creation, as God's word or even his wisdom (Heb. 1.1–3), and in this, of course, he also departs from Mark. His Christology is explicitly a high one. Where Mark had to present his epiphany Christology as a secret for the initiated, the author presupposes it. Where Mark had to engage a Jesus tradition that entertained lower estimates of his subject, the author of Hebrews, apparently restrained by only its barest elements, and obviously inspired by the Old Testament, could

---

[139] See A. Nairne, *The Epistle of Priesthood* (Edinburgh: T. & T. Clark, 1913), p. 185.
[140] See Ladd, *Theology*, p. 577.   [141] See Lindars, *Hebrews*, p. 42.
[142] Williamson, 'Hebrews' in *DBI*, p. 273.
[143] See Ellingworth, *Hebrews*, p. 67.   [144] See Ladd, *Theology*, p. 578.
[145] See, for example, Lk. 12.8 par.; 22.32; Jn 17 and Bruce, *Hebrews*, p. liii.
[146] Héring, *Hebrews*, p. xi.

soar to greater heights (see especially Heb. 1.8; see also 2 Pet. 1.1 variant reading).

If 'Son of God' describes for Hebrews Jesus' Christological status, 'high priest' defines his soteriological function. Since that function is not only to act as the perfect high priest (Heb. 4.14–5.10; 7), but also to present the perfect sacrifice (Heb. 9.11–10.18), then the Epistle's emphasis on the sacrificial death of Christ brings it yet again into relation with Mark (as well as Paul). Each writer entertains a *theologia crucis*, and in the case of Hebrews a theology of the cross *par excellence*. The one expresses it in a deceptively simple and straightforward narrative, with an interpretative saying (Mk 10.45), an account of the Last Supper (Mk 14.22–5) and a passion story (Mk 14–15), the other in an obviously comprehensive and loftier theological discourse. Each presents Jesus as 'the mediator of a new covenant' (Heb. 9.15; 12.24 and Mk 14.24), the writer of Hebrews developing, or even, some would say, making explicit what is only implicit in the Last Supper accounts.[147] Both use the Old Testament to express their passion theology, the evangelist to describe (and subtly interpret) Jesus' death with intertextual allusion (see the use of Psalm 22 or Isa. 53 in the passion narrative),[148] the writer of Hebrews to promote it with a series of proof-texts. Each too uses the language of faith (e.g. Mk 4.40; 5.34; 9.23–4; 11.22 and Heb. 11) albeit in different ways.[149]

If parallels can be seen in Christology and soteriology, then what about eschatology? As with Mark (see Mk 13 especially 13.30ff.), a future consummation is awaited. Judgment has yet to come (Heb. 6.2; 9.27; 10.27, 30–1; 12.23, 29; 13.4) and the parousia is still expected (Heb. 9.28; 10.13, 25).[150] Prominent in Mark, the Kingdom of God rarely appears in Hebrews (Heb. 1.8; 12.28), although certain related images are used in scattered

---

[147] See S. Lehne, *The New Covenant in Hebrews* (JSNTSS, 44; Sheffield: JSOT Press, 1990), pp. 83, 86, 88, 90, 119. See also Bacon, *Mark*, p. 331.

[148] See W. R. Telford, *Mark* (New Testament Guides; Sheffield: Sheffield Academic Press, 1995), p. 107.

[149] 'Faith is discovered to be less than the personal, saving relationship with Jesus which it had been in Paul and even in the Synoptic writers; it has assumed a much more academic, noetic quality', Hughes, *Hebrews and Hermeneutics*, p. 137.

[150] See J. M. Scholer, *Proleptic Priests. Priesthood in the Epistle to the Hebrews* (JSNTSS, 49; Sheffield: JSOT Press, 1991), p. 202.

passages throughout (e.g. Heb. 2.5 ('the world to come'); 3.7–4.13 ('God's sabbath rest'); 6.5 ('the age to come'); 9.15 ('the promised eternal inheritance'); 10.25 ('the Day drawing near'); 11.16 ('the heavenly country')). Jesus' resurrection is only mentioned once (Heb. 13.20). A Platonic scheme focusing on the earthly world below and the heavenly world above eclipses temporal notions of 'this age' and 'the age to come', and this spatial dualism leads some scholars to claim that the Epistle's futurist eschatology is therefore residual rather than fundamental to its thought.[151] What is clear is that the major thrust of the Epistle's eschatological presentation is a 'realized' one, and in line, therefore, with the redactional direction of the Gospel.[152] Emphasis is placed on the 'heavenly session' of Christ, on his present role on behalf of believers at the right hand of God. Where Mark was concerned to present the earthly life of Jesus as that of the divine 'Son of God', the death of Jesus as the suffering 'Son of Man', and the return of Jesus as his ultimate vindication, 'Heb', according to R. H. Fuller, 'makes the chief NT contribution to that part of Christology which concerns the heavenly work of Christ between his exaltation and the parousia, namely, as a priestly work in which his once-for-all sacrifice is the ground of his continued intercession and appearance before God for the faithful on earth (7:25; 9:24)'.[153]

MARK AND REVELATION

If Hebrews contributes to a 'realized' eschatological trend which is already in evidence in Mark, then the final book in the New Testament canon, the Apocalypse or Revelation to John, in common with its latest writing, 2 Peter, vigorously reasserts the traditional expectation (e.g. Rev. 3.11, 'I am coming soon'). Mark too, of course, has a parousia expectation, but it is qualified by his Christology and soteriology. Though dominated

---

[151] For an opposing view, see Ladd, *Theology*, p. 572; Scott, *Hebrews*, p. 61.

[152] 'The eschatological focal point in Hebrews is clearly in the past, at the death and exaltation of Christ', Attridge, *Hebrews*, p. 28. See also Scholer, *Priests*, p. 206.

[153] Fuller, *Introduction*, p. 150.

by eschatology, Revelation, like the Gospel, has a rich theology which only at times, however, transcends its major concern. Again the differences resulting from genre, as well as presentation, need to be noted. While Mark incorporates within its narrative matrix an 'eschatological discourse', sometimes referred to as the 'little apocalypse' (Mk 13), Revelation presents a series of visions (Rev. 4.1–22.5) in a major apocalypse, set within an epistolary framework (Rev. 1–3, esp. 1.4–8 and 22.6–21). Where the Markan Jesus addresses the community through his sayings and parables (e.g. Mk 4.1–34), the heavenly figure of Revelation communicates through letters addressed to the seven churches (Rev. 2–3). Whereas the Markan evangelist offers his theology in story form, the seer of the Apocalypse uses powerful imagery and symbolism.

Although Revelation shares with Mark, 1 Peter and Hebrews a preoccupation with suffering, persecution and martyrdom, it nevertheless presents a very different reaction to these experiences.[154] Instead of counselling patient forbearance or an *imitatio Christi*, it treats its tormentors with vituperation (e.g. Rev. 2.20–3), calls for vengeance upon them (Rev. 6.9–11) and conjures up vindictive images of their punishment (e.g. Rev. 14.9–11). In contrast to the respectful, or at least quietist attitude adopted by other New Testament writings (e.g. Mk 12.13–17; Rom. 13.1–7; 1 Pet. 2.13–17), the Apocalypse evinces an implacable hatred towards the Roman state which it pictures as a beast (Rev. 13) and denounces as 'Babylon the great, mother of harlots' (e.g. Rev. 17–18). Judging by the seven letters, the bad,

---

[154] For general background on Revelation, see the standard introductions, commentaries and dictionary articles: e.g. G. R. Beasley-Murray, *The Book of Revelation* (New Century Bible; London: Marshall, Morgan & Scott, 1974); G. B. Caird, *The Revelation of St John the Divine* (Black's New Testament Commentaries; London: A. & C. Black, 1984); J. M. Court, *Revelation* (New Testament Guides; Sheffield: Sheffield Academic Press, 1994); J. M. Court, 'Revelation of John' in *DBI*, pp. 593–5; Duling and Perrin, *New Testament*, pp. 447–69; E. S. Fiorenza, 'Revelation, Book of' in *IDB(S)*, pp. 744–6; Fuller, *Introduction*, pp. 184–90; Kümmel, *Introduction*, pp. 452–74; R. H. Mounce, *The Book of Revelation* (The New International Commentary on the New Testament; Grand Rapids, MI: Eerdmans, 1977); J. Sweet, *Revelation* (SCM Pelican Commentaries; London: SCM Press, 1979). For theological treatments, see e.g. R. Bauckham, *The Theology of the Book of Revelation* (New Testament Theology; Cambridge: Cambridge University Press, 1993); Bultmann, *Theology*, Vol. II, pp. 173–5; Ladd, *Theology*, pp. 619–32.

highly Semitized Greek, and his familiarity with the OT (in its Hebrew/Aramaic form) as well as the Jewish prophetic and apocalyptic literature, the author would appear to have been a Jewish-Christian prophet or visionary who wielded considerable charismatic influence over communities of fellow-believers in Asia Minor (Rev. 1.4, 9; 2–3). Curiously, the suggestion has been made that the writer may himself have been John Mark, the author of the Gospel, but such a view has been just as quickly dismissed.[155] Though perhaps incorporating earlier visionary material, the Revelation was probably composed in the closing years of Domitian's reign (81–96 CE), a date which coheres with the promotion of the Emperor-cult, the state-sanctioned persecution envisaged (e.g. Rev. 2.10, 13; 3.10; 6.9; 13.4, 12ff.; 14.9, 11; 16.2; 19.20; 20.4) and the external evidence.[156]

Where source or tradition-relations are concerned, there are few signs of direct literary dependence on the letters of Paul or the Gospel of John, the Revelation emanating, it appears, from prophetic-apocalyptic circles in Asia Minor independent of, though not necessarily uninfluenced by Paulinism or Johannine Christianity.[157] The book is the product of a Jewish apocalyptic Christianity which resisted (and to a limited extent survived) the Hellenization (and Gnosticization) of Christianity (especially under the influence of Paul), of a tradition which had roots going back, it seems, to Jesus, the eschatological prophet, and of a community which continued to proclaim both his eschatological message and his imminent return as Messiah. One intriguing link with Acts lies in the author's derogatory reference to the Nicolaitans (Rev. 2.6, 15), a group, according to Eusebius, claiming allegiance to Nicolaus, one of the seven Hellenist leaders of the primitive church (see Acts 6.1–6 and Eusebius, *Eccl. Hist.* III.29.1ff.). As with Hebrews, allusions to

---

[155] See Mounce, *Revelation*, p. 25; A. S. Peake, *The Revelation of John* (London: Joseph Johnson, 1919), p. 46.

[156] See J. Stevenson, *A New Eusebius: Documents illustrative of the History of the Church to A.D. 337* (London: SPCK, 1968), pp. 8–10.

[157] See E. S. Fiorenza, *The Book of Revelation. Justice and Judgment* (Philadelphia, PA: Fortress Press, 1985), p. 5; Sweet, *Revelation*, p. 41. Cf., however, Fuller, 'Rev knows the earlier NT writings: Mt and Lk, the Pauline epistles (except Past)', *Introduction*, p. 187.

the Synoptic tradition are relatively slight. While reference is made to the crucifixion (Rev. 11.8; see also 5.6) and the ascension (Rev. 12.5), there is little mention of the life of the historical Jesus. Jesus' name is infrequent, and, where it occurs, is often used simply in connection with his 'testimony' (namely his proclamation of the coming Kingdom of God), whose faith in such the community is called upon to share (Rev. 1.1, 2, 5, 9; 12.17; 14.12; 17.6; 19.10; 20.4; 22.16).

The one prominent exception lies in the striking correspondences to be found between the content and structure of Revelation itself (especially Rev. 6.1–7.1; 8.1) and the 'little apocalypse' of Mk 13 par. The eschatological discourse presents its readers with a series of signs both presaging and attending the end-time: the appearance of (false) eschatological agents (Mk 13.6, 21–2); a period of tribulation and calamity (13.7–8, 14–20, 24–5); the persecution of the righteous (13.9, 11–13); an act of sacrilege ('the abomination of desolation') perhaps associated with the anti-Christ (13.14); the foreshortening of the (predetermined) days (13.20); cosmic disturbances (affecting sun, moon and stars) following on from terrestrial disasters and human calamities (13.24); the appearance of the redeemer figure, God's own eschatological agent (13.26); the eschatological role of angels and the gathering and preservation of the elect (13.27). Although these are conventional elements of Jewish apocalyptic eschatology, the fact that these elements coincide so obviously in the Apocalypse of John has led some scholars (e.g. R. H. Charles) to argue that Revelation was dependent on a documentary source underlying the Synoptic Gospels.[158] The sequence occurring in Mark 13 has indeed been seen as 'decisive for the thematic development' of the Revelation.[159] Whether this is so or not, the 'seven seals' section (6.1–7.1; 8.1) at least appears to represent, according to J. M. Court, 'a development of the apocalyptic tradition in continuity with the Synoptic

---

[158] See J. M. Court, *Myth and History in the Book of Revelation* (London: SPCK, 1979), pp. 43–81, esp. 49. See also G. R. Beasley-Murray, *Jesus and the Last Days. The Interpretation of the Olivet Discourse.* (Peabody, MA: Hendrickson, 1993); Sweet, *Revelation*, pp. 19–21.

[159] Fiorenza, *Revelation*, p. 62, citing the view of A. Farrer, *The Revelation of St John the Divine* (Oxford: Clarendon Press, 1964), p. 20.

Gospels'.[160] '[T]he seals', he concludes, 'represent a reapplication of the tradition to the new circumstances of the church in the years following the fall of Jerusalem'.[161]

But what of Revelation's theology, and the relation of that theology to the community and its understanding of itself, the person and role of Jesus, and the imminent consummation? The Jewish-Christian features of the community are abundantly apparent. Worship of God is defended in a very Jewish way (see the uncompromising monotheism of Rev. 15.3–4; 19.9–10; 22.8–9), and that worship (as reflected in the heavenly liturgy) shows parallels with the Jewish synagogue.[162] The cosmology and eschatology are also particularly Jewish (see, for example, Rev. 19–22 with its emphasis on the Messianic millennium, the final judgment, the new heavens and the new earth, the descent of the new Jerusalem).[163] In sharp contrast with the openness displayed by the Markan community, especially over the food laws (Mk 7.1–23), that of the Apocalypse insists on little compromise with Gentiles or pagan society, railing mercilessly against those accommodating themselves too easily with it (compare, for example, Rev. 2.14, 20–1, 24 with Acts 15.28–9, 1 Cor. 8 and Rom. 14.13–23). While the Lamb's death seems to secure universal admission ('from every tribe and tongue and people and nation') to the true Israel, and 'hast made them a kingdom and priests to our God' (Rev. 5.9–10; cf. 1.6), yet it is clear that Jewishness itself is of continuing value (Rev. 2.9; 3.9). The 'church' of the Apocalypse is a community which emphasizes strict obedience to God's commandments, loyalty to which is underscored by repeated judgment 'on the basis of works' (Rev. 2.2, 5, 19; 3.1, 8, 15; 9.20–1; 12.17; 14.12; 20.12–13; 22.12). Where the evangelist's regard for the Jerusalem temple is at best dubious (Mk 11.17; 13.1–2; 14.58; 15.38), the apocalyptist's knowledge of, and reverence for the Jerusalem temple is apparent throughout. A similar reverence extends to the

---

[160] Court, *Myth and History*, p. 54.   [161] *Ibid.*, p. 70.
[162] See P. Prigent, *Apocalypse et Liturgie* (Neuchâtel: Delachaux et Niestlé, 1964), pp. 46–76; Sweet, *Revelation*, pp. 41–2.
[163] See N. Perrin, *The Kingdom of God in the Teaching of Jesus* (The New Testament Library; London: SCM Press; Philadelphia, PA: Westminster Press, 1963), pp. 68–73.

original twelve, whose names are inscribed on the foundations of the new Jerusalem (Rev. 21.14).

'The Christianity of Revelation', then, 'has to be termed a weakly Christianized Judaism',[164] or rather, as I would prefer, a weakly Paulinized Jewish Christianity. What makes it Christian is the central place it gives to Jesus in its Christology, soteriology and eschatology. Nevertheless, his role, it can be argued, is fundamentally different from that in the Gospel (or in Paul). 'John's Christology, and therefore his theology', it has been claimed, 'is firmly anchored in the Jesus of history',[165] yet the lack of reference to the Jesus traditions found in the Gospel makes this claim a debatable one. Though considered by some scholars as 'advanced', the Christology of the Apocalypse of John is essentially that of a martyred but vindicated eschatological prophet now deemed returning Messiah, and need be understood as no more developed than that.[166] The whole panoply of Jewish Messianic titles and images are applied to him: e.g. 'one like a son of man' (Rev. 1.13; 14.14?); 'the lion of the tribe of Judah' (5.5); 'his (i.e. God's) Christ' (11.15; cf. 20.6); 'the Lamb' (5.6ff.; 6.1ff. *et passim*);[167] the 'Lord of Lords and King of Kings' (17.14; 19.16); the returning warrior-king (19.11ff.); 'the root (and the offspring) of David' (5.5; 22.16); 'the morning star' (22.16). Only on one occasion is he called the 'Son of God' (Rev. 2.18) but comparison with Rev. 21.7 indicates that this title may be meant in a Jewish rather than Hellenistic sense, denoting therefore an ethical rather than a metaphysical relationship. It is true that he is 'Alpha and Omega', as God is (Rev. 1.17; 2.8; cf. 1.8; 21.6), and 'his head and his hair' recall the description of the Ancient of Days in Dan. 7.9 (1.14), that he possesses the seven spirits of God (3.1; 4.5; 5.6; cf. Isa. 11.2), that he is 'the beginning of God's creation' (3.14) as well as 'the Word of God' (19.13) and that, as 'the Lamb', he is frequently linked with God (7.10; 14.4; 21.22; 22.1, 3), receiving adulation

---

[164] Bultmann, *Theology*, Vol. II, p. 175.   [165] Caird, *Revelation*, p. 290.

[166] *Pace* T. Holtz, *Die Christologie der Apokalypse des Johannes* (Berlin: Akademie Verlag, 1971); G. R. Beasley-Murray, *The Book of Revelation* (New Century Bible; London: Marshall, Morgan & Scott, 1974), pp. 24–5.

[167] Mentioned some 29 times, the Lamb is never, however, explicitly identified with Jesus.

from the heavenly court (5.8–14). Yet the name of God is *never* given to Jesus, and the apocalyptist goes out of his way to state that God *alone* is to be worshipped (Rev. 19.9–10; 22.8–10). Jesus is 'the faithful witness, the firstborn of the dead (namely the first of the resurrected sons of the new age) and the ruler of the kings on earth' (Rev. 1.5; see also 3.14).

While the soteriology of the Apocalypse also centres on Jesus, his saving work appears to be limited, in the main, to two main tasks. As 'the (Messianic) Lamb', his role (as martyred but vindicated eschatological prophet) is to open the seals (Rev. 5.5ff.) and (as the resurrected one, the 'firstborn of the dead') to return as conquering warrior-king dispensing judgment upon the nations (14.1ff.). As 'one like a son of man' (an angelic being? see Rev. 1.1, 13; 14.14ff.), he (Jesus?) 'reaps the earth' with his sickle, and as 'the Word of God', he will 'smite the nations' with the sword of his mouth and 'rule them with a rod of iron' (19.11ff.). With such powerful images of military conquest, it is difficult to see how this picture coheres with the portrait of Jesus painted in Mark, and in particular with its theology of the cross. Although no detailed doctrine of redemption is outlined in Revelation,[168] one major route out of the theological difficulty has been to point out certain repeated references to the death of Christ (e.g. Rev. 1.5; 5.6, 9; 7.14; 11.8; 12.11; 13.8) and even to that death as a 'ransom' (Rev. 5.9). In referring to 'the blood of the Lamb', the author of Revelation has engaged in what A. Farrer has described as 'a rebirth of images'.[169] In the words of G. B. Caird, '[t]he Old Testament leads John to expect a Messiah who will be the Lion of Judah, but the facts of the gospel present him with a Lamb bearing the marks of slaughter (vv. 5–6). The Old Testament predicts the smashing of the nations with an iron bar, but the only weapon the lamb wields is his own Cross and the martyrdom of his followers (ii. 27; xii. 5; xix. 15).'[170] This then, it is claimed, is the master-image in light

---

[168] See Peake, *Revelation*, p. 202.

[169] A. Farrer, *A Rebirth of Images* (Westminster: Dacre Press, 1949), esp. pp. 17–18.

[170] Caird, *Revelation*, pp. 292–3. Cf. also Beasley-Murray, *Revelation*, p. 24; Kümmel, *Introduction*, pp. 461–2.

of which the whole of the Apocalypse should be read. The Lamb's sword is the power of the gospel (Rev. 1.16; 2.12, 16; 19.15) and what the slain Lamb signifies is not military power but 'the power of redemptive love'.[171]

If Revelation is to be read in this way, as an implicit *theologia crucis* expressed in the language of apocalyptic, then it could be said to resemble Mark whose theology of the cross was expressed in the form of a narrative. But is this how it should be read? There are insuperable difficulties in 'domesticating' the violent images of Revelation in this way (e.g. Rev. 14.10–11, 19–20; 19.11–21), and we are in serious danger of reading a Pauline (or Markan) theology into Revelation rather than letting it speak for itself. The 'Lamb' also appears as an apocalyptic symbol for a warlike Messianic figure in 1 Enoch 90, 'a sword issuing from his mouth' or 'slaying the wicked with the breath of his lips' being conventional descriptive motifs for his saving activity – but hardly with peaceful persuasion in view! (Compare 4 Ezra 13; Isa. 11.4 as well as Rev. 19.11, 12, 15, 21.)[172] The Lamb, as D. H. Lawrence recognized, is a 'lion in sheep's clothing ... [W]e never see it slain, we only see it slaying mankind by the million'.[173] The titles of God in the Apocalypse, and of his Christ, are always ones of power, never of love, and its world-view dominated by a thirst for vengeance (Rev. 6.9–10) and the hope of reigning in glory (Rev. 2.26–7; 3.21; contrast Mk 10.41–5). This view is reinforced when we consider the Apocalypse's eschatology.

Where the Markan redactor reveals ambiguity about apocalyptic and has already begun to have doubts about the proximity of the parousia (Mk 13.32ff.),[174] the apocalyptist reiterates in clear tones its imminence (Rev. 1.1, 3, 7; 3.11; 22.6, 7, 10, 12, 20). Revelation offers us the boldest example in the New

---

[171] See Sweet, *Revelation*, p. 50.

[172] See C. K. Barrett, *The New Testament Background. Selected Documents* (London: SPCK, 1987), pp. 325–6. Cf. also C. H. Dodd, *The Interpretation of the Fourth Gospel* (Cambridge: Cambridge University Press, 1953), p. 232.

[173] D. H. Lawrence, *Apocalypse and the Writings on Revelation* (Cambridge Edition of the Letters and Works of Lawrence; Cambridge: Cambridge University Press, 1980), pp. 99, 100.

[174] See Telford, *Mark*, pp. 135–7; Telford, 'History of Developments' in Telford (ed.), *Interpretation*, pp. 21–2.

Testament of a futurist eschatology. It presents the most power-ful and extensive statement of the conventional apocalyptic hope. In line with the historical Jesus, and with the Gospel of Mark, its supreme preoccupation is with the coming Kingdom of God, and its main theological symbol, as E. S. Fiorenza points out, is therefore the throne.[175] 'The question, God or Satan,' however, 'is now posed as the question of the kingship of God and Christ or the dominion of the Roman Caesar and the goddess Roma. This cosmic-mythological and political alter-native is reflected in the lives of the Christians who represent the kingdom of God on earth (1:6; 5:10), but are still in danger of losing their right to participate in the eschatological kingdom by becoming followers of the beast.'[176] Entertaining a different perspective on power (contrast especially Mk 10.35–45), the writer of the Apocalypse envisages that kingship as resulting in rewards for the righteous, and destruction for the wicked, the Messianic kingdom being established upon the corpses of God's enemies (Rev. 19.11–21). It is difficult therefore to agree with those who claim that Revelation shares with the rest of the New Testament a 'realized' (and therefore a non-apocalyptic or spiritual) understanding of salvation as well as a futurist one,[177] and easier to concur with D. H. Lawrence that it is the Judas of the New Testament.[178] Were it not for Mark's eschatological discourse, it would be tempting even to conclude that in Revelation we see the Jewish-Christian Christology that the evangelist himself was tilting against. Where our earliest Gospel sought to present a *theologia crucis*, the final book in the Christian canon appears to end, in all its resounding triumphalism, with a *theologia gloriae*.

[175] Fiorenza, 'Revelation' in *IDB(S)*, p. 745.   [176] *Ibid.*
[177] See, for example, Caird, *Revelation*, pp. 296, 300.
[178] 'And just as inevitably as Jesus had to have a Judas Iscariot among his disciples, so did there have to be a Revelation in the New Testament', Lawrence, *Apocalypse*, p. 67.

CHAPTER 4

Mark in the church and in the world

Having discussed the place of Mark's theology in the New Testament, it now remains for me to make some concluding remarks not only on the place of Mark in history but also on its relevance for the contemporary world. Although it is clear to us today that Mark's contribution to the theological history of Christianity has been a not inconsiderable one, the value attached to the Gospel both by the church and by the academy over the centuries may be described as ambiguous.[1] On the one hand, its use as a source (albeit with modifications) by Matthew and Luke in the first century, as well as by Tatian (in the composition of his *Diatessaron*, *c.* 170 CE) in the second, its traditional connection with the apostle Peter in the early second century, and its designation as one of the four pillars of the church by Irenaeus later that century,[2] are all factors which attest its significance for the early church. On the other hand, quotations from the Gospel of Mark are relatively uncommon among second-century writers, and commentaries on or expositions of the Second Gospel even more so. It was not until the fifth century indeed that the first of these (by Victor of Antioch)

---

[1] For discussion, see S. P. Kealy, *Mark's Gospel. A History of its Interpretation from the Beginning until 1979* (Ramsey, NJ: Paulist Press, 1982); R. P. Martin, *Mark – Evangelist and Theologian* (Exeter: Paternoster, 1979), pp. 29–50; V. Taylor, *The Gospel According to St Mark* (London: Macmillan; New York: St Martin's Press, 1996), pp. 1–25; W. R. Telford, 'Mark, Gospel of' in *DBI*, pp. 424–8; W. R. Telford, 'The Interpretation of Mark: a History of Developments and Issues' in Telford (ed.), *The Interpretation of Mark* (Edinburgh: T. & T. Clark, 1995), pp. 1–13; W. R. Telford, *Mark* (New Testament Guides; Sheffield: Sheffield Academic Press, 1995), pp. 26–34.

[2] See *Adversus Haereses*, III, xi, 8.

214

appeared.[3] Apart from that of Bede in the eighth century, and certain medieval and post-Reformation expositions, there were few treatments of the Second Gospel in subsequent centuries to rival those devoted to the other Gospels. Mark's position in canonical lists is also indicative of its position in the eyes of the early church. It is almost never placed first among the Gospels, and in some cases even last.[4] The use of the term 'the Second Gospel' itself reflects the early church's view of the sequence in which the canonical Gospels were written (Matthew, Mark, Luke, John). This traditional order owes much to Augustine's theory that Mark (despite the contradictory claims of Papias and Irenaeus regarding Markan dependence on Peter) was no more than an abbreviation of the Gospel of Matthew, this 'First Gospel' being the product, it was believed, of an apostle and an eye-witness, and a work therefore of superior literary and theological value. It was only in the latter half of the eighteenth century, when the Augustinian view was challenged, that centuries of relative neglect for the Gospel of Mark were brought to an end.

The factors which brought about this change in the Gospel's fortunes, particularly in the academy, and which have propelled it into prominence in the nineteenth and twentieth centuries, are associated, of course, with the advent of the modern critical approaches to the biblical text which were discussed in chapter one. The first of these was the application of source criticism which, through the critical endeavours of scholars such as K. Lachmann, C. H. Weisse and H. J. Holtzmann, led to the establishment of the priority of Mark and the development of the so-called 'Markan hypothesis'. Deemed the earliest Gospel, and as such the repository of data on the historical Jesus in its most primitive form, Mark was the bedrock text for the so-

[3] 'No commentary on this Gospel was written before that of Victor of Antioch (in the 5th century) who complained that he could not find any treatment of this gospel comparable with expositions of Matthew and John', Martin, *Mark*, p. 30. According to M. Cahill, 'The Identification of the First Markan Commentary', *Revue biblique*, 101 (1994), pp. 256–68, the first formal full-length commentary on Mark was the seventh-century *Commentarius in Evangelium secundum Marcum*. Transmitted in connection with the writings of Jerome, this was enormously influential, Cahill claims, in the history of Markan exegesis.

[4] Martin, *Mark*, p. 30.

called Liberal Lives of Jesus which flourished in the nineteenth and early twentieth centuries. The second of these was the application of form criticism to the Gospel which, in its classic phase between the Wars, exposed the degree to which the Gospel was the product of fragmentary community tradition. In the hands of scholars such as K. L. Schmidt, M. Dibelius and R. Bultmann, 'Formgeschichte' threw light on the influence of the early church's theology on the pre-Markan tradition while simultaneously undermining the Gospel's trustworthiness as a connected biographical account. Building upon form criticism's findings, but shifting its emphasis, redaction criticism, after the Second World War, produced a further refinement on the Gospel by concentrating on its editorial elements. Pursuing insights first suggested by W. Wrede at the start of the century, or R. H. Lightfoot some time later, redaction critics such as W. Marxsen and N. Perrin used the new method to open a window into the evangelist's mind, and to establish more scientifically the degree to which his own theology had shaped the traditions to which he had become an heir. A further consequence of redaction criticism, however, has been the high-lighting of not only the theological but also the literary achievement of the evangelist. While the three historical-critical methods have continued to be applied fruitfully to the Gospel, a particular feature of the last quarter of the twentieth century has been the application to Mark of the methods and approaches of the newer literary criticism.

In sum, the last two to three centuries have seen the restoration of the Gospel of Mark to its rightful place as one of the major products of nascent Christianity. While the traditional view of Mark is still held, to a lesser extent in the academy, and to a greater extent in the church, three major shifts in emphasis, within this period, have been discernible within mainstream scholarship. In the nineteenth and early twentieth centuries, the historical emphasis has been uppermost. Mark, in other words, has been seen as a *historian*, albeit of an untutored kind. Historical optimism has in turn given way to a greater appreciation of the theological nature of his work, with the evangelist being appreciated much more as a *theologian*. A further, more recent, shift in emphasis has been the literary one, the notion of Mark as (to some degree) an *author* being no longer ruled out of court even by scholars influenced by the traditional historical-critical methods. It is arguable indeed that these literary approaches have hence secured for the Gospel a further lease of life.

THE CONTEMPORARY SIGNIFICANCE OF MARK

Mark and discipleship: some theological issues and observations

But what of the contemporary significance of Mark? What is its worth in today's world? What does it have to say to our generation? Given that it is our earliest written record of first-century Jesus traditions, it is clear that it will retain its value as a historical document (for scholar and believer alike), despite the formidable problems that its interpretation as such presents. Given too that this record has reached us in the form of a connected narrative, a Jesus 'story', and that this 'story' has generated a succession of further literary formations, the en-during value of Mark as a literary composition cannot also be underestimated. It was this text after all which first established a literary 'image' of Jesus in the popular mind and, as a con-sequence, it has exercised a profound influence upon western culture. The current and escalating interest in the influence of the Gospel in literature, especially in fiction and film, is a testament to this.[5] But does the Gospel have anything to say to a world fast approaching a new millennium? Does it impinge in any way on the theological, ethical, political, gender or ethnic issues which form or inform the agenda(s) of our own age?

At first sight, it is not clear that it does, given the contingent nature of the text, particularly with regard to its socio-historical situation as well as its ideological perspective. The Gospel of Mark was composed in a very different world from our own. It

[5] See W. R. Telford, 'The New Testament in Fiction and Film: A Biblical Scholar's Perspective' in J. G. Davies, G. Harvey and W. Watson (eds.), *Words Remembered, Texts Renewed. Essays in Honour of J. F. A. Sawyer* (Sheffield: Sheffield Academic Press, 1995), pp. 360–94.

was written to address the issues and concerns of a first century Mediterranean community struggling to find its identity and mission not only within the political and cultural context of the Graeco-Roman Empire but also within the religious context of the Jewish-Christian tradition to which it was a reluctant heir. The religious ideas which it presents do not rest easily with the post-modern ethos of present society. Rationalism since the enlightenment has undermined any literal acceptance of the Markan miracles. The ministering presence of angels (1.13) or the evil influence of demons (5.1–13) are not the stuff of our everyday experience. Despite our current prophets of doom, the end of the world is no more imminent for us than it was in reality for Mark, despite his predictions to the contrary (Mk 13, especially 13.30). In the eyes of our generation too, 'the concept of Jesus as bearing the judgement of God,' to quote Ernest Best, 'seems immoral to some; why should men not bear their own judgement?'[6] The Christological titles with which the evangelist expressed the significance of Jesus in his day are likewise culturally bound, and therefore less acceptable, even where they are comprehensible, as vehicles for modern estimates of Jesus. Mark's harsh portrait of the Jews, which appears to be an inevitable concomitant of his Christology and soteriology, is also a feature of his Gospel which many today would disavow.

Against this, nevertheless, is the fact that, in the eyes of the church, the Gospel of Mark remains a sacred text, a religious icon, an 'inspired' word from God whose major contribution to the life of faith is the vivid picture it presents of Christian discipleship and of the one whom Mark believed to be the believer's supreme role model. Its value as a theological document lies therefore in these twin motifs of Christology and discipleship.[7] Powerfully portrayed are the misunderstanding, lack of spiritual perception, cowardice, faint-heartedness and

---

[6] E. Best, *Mark. The Gospel as Story* (Studies of the New Testament and its World; Edinburgh: T. & T. Clark, 1983), p. 146.

[7] For some recent discussion on Mark's understanding of discipleship, see, for example, E. Best, *Disciples and Discipleship. Studies in the Gospel According to Mark* (Edinburgh: T. & T. Clark, 1986); T. J. Geddert, *Watchwords. Mark 13 in Markan Eschatology* (JSNTSS 26; Sheffield: JSOT Press, 1989); G. Twelftree, 'Discipleship in Mark's Gospel', *St Mark's Review [Canberra]*, 141 (1990), pp. 5–11.

fear that are the constant enemies of the disciple. Repeatedly emphasized is the need for faith (1.15; 4.20; 4.40; 5.34; 6.5, 6; 9.20–4; 10.52; 11.22–3),[8] and prayer (1.35; 9.29; 11.24–5; 14.32–42).[9] Of major importance is the central section of the Gospel (8.27–10.45) where a combination of various stories and sayings on the subject of discipleship are set within the context of Jesus' journey or pilgrimage to Jerusalem, his instructions to his disciples taking place 'on the way' or 'on the road' (8.27; 9.33, 34; 10.17, 32, 46, 52) to his appointment with death ('the way of the cross').[10] A recurring theme is not only the nature but the cost of discipleship, especially in terms of suffering and persecution. The Markan Jesus summons the disciple to 'take up his cross and follow me', and a number of passages in this central section explore the implications of this call (8.27–35; 9.30–7; 9.38–50; 10.2–16; 10.17–30).[11] Two contrasting ways of life are offered to the disciple (and hence to the reader): saving one's life out of fear, or losing one's life for others (8.35).[12] Even some of the minor characters in the Markan story can be seen as paradigmatic disciples, Bartimaeus, for example (10.46–52),[13] or 'the naked young man' (14. 51–2).[14] Stripped of their particularity, these 'discipleship' motifs represent, then, a timeless challenge to all believing Christians, in this generation as well as in Mark's.

---

[8] For the distinction between 'kerymatic' faith in Mark, i.e. Christological faith associated with commitment and discipleship, and 'petitionary' faith, i.e. trust in the miracle-worker to effect specific requests, see C. D. Marshall, *Faith as a Theme in Mark's Narrative* (SNTSMS, 64; Cambridge: Cambridge University Press, 1989). For a different analysis of this Markan motif, see M. R. Thompson, *The Role of Disbelief in Mark. A New Approach to the Second Gospel* (New York and Mahwah, NJ: Paulist Press, 1989).

[9] See S. E. Dowd, *Prayer, Power and the Problem of Suffering: Mark 11:22–25 in the Context of Markan Theology* (SBLDS, 105; Atlanta, GA: Scholars Press, 1988).

[10] See Telford, *Mark*, pp. 140–1.

[11] See D. H. Juel, 'The Way of the Cross: Markan Texts for Late Pentecost', *Word and World*, 14 (1994), pp. 352–59. See also J. B. Green, *The Way of the Cross. Following Jesus in the Gospel of Mark* (Nashville, TN: Discipleship Resources, 1991).

[12] See D. Rhoads, 'Losing Life for Others in the Face of Death. Mark's Standards of Judgment', *Int*, 47 (1993), pp. 358–69.

[13] See J. N. Suggitt, 'Bartimaeus and Christian Discipleship (Mark 10:46–52)', *JTSouthAfr*, 74 (1991), pp. 57–63.

[14] See S. R. Johnson, 'The Identity and Significance of the Neaniskos in Mark', *Forum*, 8 (1992), pp. 123–39.

Mark and the law: some ethical issues and observations

So much for the church but what about the world? So much for theology but what about ethics?[15] How does the Gospel's particular understanding of religion and religious practice relate to the realities as well as the concerns of modern society, and what has it to contribute to the issues that dominate secular discussion? What has its particular perspective on ritual purity (7.1–23), for example, to say to a world which has experienced the impact of HIV/AIDS?[16] What relevance has its debates on what is permissible on the sabbath (2.23–3.5) for a society which is increasingly abandoning a statutory day of rest encompassed by religious taboos? Can its seemingly radical attitude to wealth and status (10.17–31) really be entertained in a world that has seen the triumph of capitalism, the virtues of competition and the mass benefits (notwithstanding the disadvantages) of the consumer society? What has its rigorist attitude towards divorce and remarriage (10.2–12) to say to a society which has fought to free itself from marital restraints? While everyone in today's world can admire the Markan Jesus' concern for children (9.33–7; 10.13–16), and not a few side with his penalty for the child-abuser (9.42), some might be appalled by his insensitivity to the rights of animals (5.11–13) or even of trees (11.12–14, 20)! In an age that has learned to be suspicious of esoteric cults and new religious movements, how can a text which purports to support family values (10.2–16) at the same time sanction the relativization of family ties (3.31–5) or even the disruption of families in the name of religious commitment (10.29–30; 13.12–13)? 'Render to Caesar the things that are Caesar's, and

---

[15] For general discussion on ethics in Mark's Gospel, see, for example, J. L. Houlden, *Ethics and the New Testament* (Penguin Books; London and Oxford: Penguin/Mowbray, 1973), pp. 41–6; H. C. Kee, *Community of the New Age. Studies in Mark's Gospel* (Philadelphia, PA: Westminster Press, 1977), pp. 151–61; J. T. Sanders, *Ethics in the New Testament. Change and Development* (Philadelphia, PA: Fortress Press, 1975), pp. 31–40; W. Schrage, *The Ethics of the New Testament* (Philadelphia, PA: Fortress Press, 1988), pp. 138–43; D. O. Via Jr., *The Ethics of Mark's Gospel – In the Middle of Time* (Philadelphia, PA: Fortress Press, 1985).

[16] For a dialogue between the two, see A. H. Cadwaller, 'The Hermeneutics of Purity in Mark's Gospel: A Consideration for the AIDS Debate', *Pacifica*, 5 (1992), pp. 145–69.

to God the things that are God's' (12.17) is a memorable injunction, but how in the end does it enable us to quantify the individual's duties to the state or determine the legitimate limits of individual freedom or state intervention?

Contradictions in the text apart, one obvious response to the above is that it is unfair to demand precise ethical answers to specific modern questions from an admittedly ancient text, especially when the author's concerns are so very different from our own. Close study of the Gospel, moreover, has led a number of scholars to comment on the relative paucity of ethical rules actually to be found in Mark.[17] While the evangelist does offer his readers the famous and still relevant 'love command' (12.28–34), or catalogues the vices that they are presumably to avoid (7.21–2), he presents only relatively few passages (10.1–12, 13–17; 12.13–17) which give some guidance on the duties of Christians either to each other, or to society at large. Several reasons have been proffered for such. J. L. Houlden, for example, has taken the lack of ethical material in Mark as evidence of gnostic tendencies on the part of the evangelist,[18] as well as of the eschatological perspective that permeated his thought.[19] J. T. Sanders, likewise, is of a similar opinion in respect of the second of these factors.[20] An additional consideration to be borne in mind is that the primary thrust of the Gospel is Christological, as I have argued, and not ethical.

Where Mark's contribution to ethical debate is concerned, however, this is not the end of the matter, and some further comments are in order. It is also possible to discern in Mark an underlying concern for 'spirituality', 'interiority', 'the inward

---

[17] See, for example, E. Best, *Following Jesus. Discipleship in the Gospel of Mark* (JSNTSS, 4; Sheffield: JSOT Press, 1981), p. 14; Houlden, *Ethics*, pp. 41–2.

[18] Houlden, *Ethics*, pp. 41–2.

[19] 'For this writer then, as for John, it appears that facing and settling moral problems, in the everyday sense, was not a primary concern ... For Mark, the End, though not immediately to appear (xiii, 7), was not far away', *ibid.*, p. 45.

[20] 'One will have to say, then, that Mark has very little interest in the welfare of the world or its inhabitants other than to persuade as many of them as possible to repent and follow. His imminent eschatology is so much the basis of his outlook that he cannot even pass on Jesus' command to love in its original meaning; instead, he appeals for what one today would have to call retreat from the world and its problems, Sanders, *Ethics*, p. 33. For a dissenting opinion, however, see Schrage, *Ethics*, p. 139.

disposition of the heart' or 'core values' which transcends his culture's concern for ritual or cultic purity, or for the 'external' morality that is expressed in rules or regulations. 'Food taboos are abandoned', according to Houlden, 'not by a mere alteration of the rules, but because of a wholly different conception of what constitutes uncleanness in the sight of God (vii, 1–23).'[21] In sharp contrast to the Qumran sectarians, where ritual purity was a major preoccupation,[22] the Markan approach to defilement has this 'internal' or 'moral' quality ('the things which come out of a man are what defile him', 7.15) and the solution for such defilement, one observes, is a Christocentric one ('the Son of Man has authority on earth to forgive sins', 2.10).[23]

The situation is similar with regard to the question of sabbath observance. While there is uncertainty over whether the historical Jesus actually broke the sabbath commandment or merely engaged in legitimate debate over what was permissible,[24] it is clear in Mark that it is a concern for human life as well as for the original intention of the sabbath that makes Jesus challenge the imputed casuistry of the Pharisees, and which leads to the evangelist's Christological conclusion. 'Thus, the sabbath law must give way, not before a set of amended regulations but before a God who has only one choice when it comes to saving life or destroying it (iii, 4), and before the Son of Man who is the sabbath's lord (ii, 28)'.[25] In a context where the rigour of the Pharisees was only matched by that of the Essenes,[26] it is easier

[21] Houlden, *Ethics*, p. 43.

[22] See Kee, *Community*, p. 98; F. G. Martinez and J. T. Barrera, *The People of the Dead Sea Scrolls. Their Writings, Beliefs and Practices* (Leiden, New York and Cologne: E. J. Brill, 1993), pp. 156–7.

[23] For recent discussion of the notion of 'purity' in Mark, see R. P. Booth, *Jesus and the Laws of Purity. Tradition History and Legal History in Mark 7* (JSNTSS, 13; Sheffield: JSOT Press, 1986); J. H. Neyrey, 'The Idea of Purity in Mark's Gospel', *Semeia*, 35 (1986), pp. 91–128; J. Neyrey, 'A Symbolic Approach to Mark 7', *Foundation and Facets Forum*, 4 (1988), pp. 63–91.

[24] See, for example, S. Bacchiocchi, *From Sabbath to Sunday. A Historical Investigation of the Rise of Sunday Observance in Early Christianity* (Rome: Pontificia Universitas Gregoriana, 1977); H. Weiss, 'The Sabbath in the Synoptic Gospels', *JSNT*, 38 (1990), pp. 13–27.

[25] Houlden, *Ethics*, p. 43.

[26] See M. Black (ed.), *The Scrolls and Christianity* (Theological Collections, 11; London: SPCK, 1969), p. 100.

in our day to sympathize with a figure who appears to champion freedom over regulation, or human well-being over religious scruples.

This emphasis on the value of life itself over against worldly success (8.36, 37), as well as the absolute claim that Jesus himself makes on the disciple (8.35) also informs the evangelist's attitude to wealth and status, and can be interpreted as qualifying what appears otherwise to be an impossibly radical, even unpalatable position. A stake in society through family and property are not necessarily evil of themselves, nor repudiated for their own sake, or else the Markan Jesus would not have promised them as concrete rewards to his disciples in exchange for their overriding commitment (10.28–30). As H. C. Kee points out:

Peter's challenge as reported in Mark 10.28 ... suggests that in the Markan community the break with family, home, personal and economic security, and even the seeming irresponsibility towards one's own offspring, would be compensated for in the new pattern of relationships and identity that would develop in the Christian community, culminating in the full achievement of blessedness in the age to come (10.31).[27]

Allegiance, then, to the new community, born of discipleship, with its faith in Jesus and its commitment to 'the way of the cross' is the prism through which the evangelist's ethical concerns are refracted, and it is his religious allegiance which relativizes (rather than destroys) the claims of worldly institutions.

Something similar can be seen in the Markan attitude to marriage and the family.[28] Where the evangelist is concerned, marriage will not exist in the new age (12.25). As an institution, it too must take second place, if need be, to Jesus and the

---

[27] Kee, *Community*, p. 153. See also Schrage's comment on this passage: 'These verses emphasize ... that renunciation and sacrifice are not undertaken for ascetic reasons or in hope of eschatological reward. They will be repaid in this age with concrete material and personal reward within the community as the family of God (*familia dei*)', *Ethics*, p. 142.

[28] For a discussion of discipleship and family ties in Mark, see S. C. Barton, *Discipleship and Family Ties in Mark and Matthew* (SNTSMS, 80; Cambridge: Cambridge University Press, 1994), pp. 57–124. For a more general perspective, both biblical and contemporary, see S. C. Barton (ed.), *The Family in Theological Perspective* (Edinburgh: T. & T. Clark, 1996).

demands of the gospel (10.28–30). On the other hand, marriage in this age is to be regarded as an indissoluble union (10.2–12). Here, as in the case of the sabbath, the Markan Jesus appeals to the institution's original divine intention. In contrast to his approach to the sabbath, however, his rigid attitude to the marriage law outmatches that of the Pharisaic school (even the stricter Shammaites), and is paralleled only among the Qumran sectarians.[29] Here, too, given the discrepancies between the Synoptic and Pauline divorce pericopae, there is uncertainty over the nuances of the historical Jesus' attitude to the marriage law,[30] but it is nonetheless clear that, for Mark, lifelong monogamy was the norm for both partners. Although this is still the ideal for many Christians, the difficulties of applying the Markan Jesus' teaching to the complex problems of divorce in the modern world are clearly formidable.[31] Some scholars have commented on what seems to be an unusually legalistic position for Jesus, and have attempted to interpret this teaching in light of his alleged concern for the rights of women as well as of children. If such is the underlying intention of the Markan Jesus' teaching, then it obviously impinges on contemporary concerns.[32] Whether the passage should be so interpreted is a moot point, but the ideal of lifelong monogamy presented by the Gospel, its regard for 'family values' (even when displaced by the new community of faith) and its repeated emphasis on Jesus' identification with the child make it at least a worthy partner in any modern discussion on these issues. Where ethics are concerned, then, the Gospel has a continuing capacity to remind the reader that he or she must go 'back to basics'. True greatness lies in service (9.33–7), true fulfilment in self-giving (8.35), true happiness in 'receiving the kingdom of God like a

---

[29] See the advocacy of lifelong monogamy in 11Q Temple Scroll[a] (11Q19) LVII.17–18 as well as Cairo Damascus Document[a] IV.20–21 = 4Q Damascus Document[f] 3 1–2 where there is a similar, though not identical, appeal to Gen. 1.27.

[30] See, for example, E. P. Sanders and M. Davies, *Studying the Synoptic Gospels* (London: SCM Press; Philadelphia, PA: Trinity Press International, 1989), pp. 324–8; B. Vawter, 'Divorce and the New Testament', *CBQ*, 39 (1977), pp. 528–42.

[31] For a succinct and measured statement on the subject, see Taylor, *Mark*, p. 421.

[32] Kee, for example, has seen in this Markan passage on divorce 'a conception of something close to full equality and mutual responsibility between members of both sexes', *Community*, p. 155.

child' (10.15). In these general respects, if not in its particularities, the Markan Gospel has still much to offer to contemporary ethical debate.

Mark and the cross: some political issues and observations

If the 'spirituality' reflected in Mark's Gospel still has relevance
for our own day, then what can be said for its 'take' on politics,
a subject that has come to dominate the contemporary world.
The enigmatic saying of the Markan Jesus, previously referred
to ('Render to Caesar the things that are Caesar's, and to God
the things that are God's', 12.17) has long been used by
Christianity to justify a separation between the spiritual and the
material, between the sacred and the secular, between politics
and religion, between the community of faith and the political
order.[33] Usually interpreted, along with Romans 13.1–7, as
articulating a theory of the relation between church and state,
the passage has often bolstered in particular a quietist position
in this regard.[34] That an ambiguous utterance of this kind
should be allowed to bear the weight of any such developed
doctrine is questionable, but does this mean that the evangelist
has nothing otherwise to contribute to political discussion? The
contrary is surely the case, for when one considers the Gospel as
a whole, then it is obvious that its major motifs (strength versus
weakness, power versus love, conflict and its resolution, the
nature of authority, the necessity of suffering, etc.) have a
bearing upon the subject. Indeed there is a sense in which, the
particularities aside, the Gospel may be said to be ultimately
concerned with the ideology of power,[35] and that, in a deeper
sense, its major aim is to expound the true nature of power, and
to connect it with the notion of redemptive suffering.

[33] For a discussion of different interpretations of this passage, see M. A. Corner and
C. R. Rowland, *Liberating Exegesis* (Biblical Foundations in Theology; London: SCM
Press, 1990), pp. 106–7.

[34] For an opposing view, see Herzog, 'Dissembling', *PerspRelSt*, 21 (1994), pp. 339–60.
Questioning this standard assumption, Herzog regards both passages as examples of
the coded 'double-speak' of the weak when forced to reveal their political hand in
public.

[35] See W. C. Placher, 'Narratives of a Vulnerable God', *Princeton Seminary Bulletin*, 14
(1993), pp. 134–51.

Throughout this study of the Gospel, I have commented on the notion that there are opposing Christologies at work in the Markan text. In promoting Jesus as the Messianic 'Son of David', or as the apocalyptic 'Son of Man' (or even, some would say, as the Hellenistic 'divine man'), these Christologies distinguish themselves by their triumphalist estimate of his person and role, and hence by their understanding of the nature of *power*. In seeing him as Messiah *despite*, and not *because of*, his death, and by looking to his second return or parousia to effect humankind's salvation, neither of these perspectives accords a significant place to the cross in its soteriological scheme. In assessing the significance of the Markan redaction on these traditions, furthermore, we have observed Mark's repeated emphasis on the suffering, death and resurrection of Jesus (8.31; 9.31; 10.33–4; 10.45; 14.24). As with Paul, but by means of narrative rather than theological discourse (compare, for example, 1 Cor. 1.18–25 with Mk 15.31–32), Mark communicates to his readers the claim that Jesus discloses his true identity (as Son of God) and achieves his essential victory (as Son of Man) through his redemptive suffering on the cross. By emphasizing 'the way of the cross' as 'the way of love and service',[36] the evangelist has succeeded in transforming Jesus' own self-giving into a timeless icon with the capacity to shatter all the pretensions that surround worldly notions of power (see especially Mk 10.42–5). By opposing a 'theology of glory' (*theologia gloriae*), and its concomitant understanding of earthly power, with a 'theology of the cross' (*theologia crucis*), wherein God's 'power is perfected in weakness' (2 Cor. 12.9), the evangelist may be credited with producing a critique of illegitimate authority or abusive power which is still capable of challenging the power structures of today's world, whether personal or institutional.

[36] 'The main purpose of his [the Markan Jesus'] teaching is to bring his followers to an understanding of his own Cross, not only as redemptive, but also as a way of life for themselves; they must take up their crosses as he did and serve as he served. Thus it is not that he only enlightens their minds but that he calls for them to go on the way of discipleship, which is the way of love and service', E. Best, *The Temptation and the Passion: the Markan Soteriology* (SNTSMS, 2; Cambridge: Cambridge University Press, 1965), p. 190.

The relevance of the Gospel in such general terms to contemporary power relationships or to modern political realities is clear, but there is at least one body of opinion that would claim that Mark has a much more definite political edge than the somewhat abstract account above would suggest. A variety of socio-political, and even Marxist readings of the Gospel have been undertaken in recent years, all springing from the desire to situate Mark realistically (and not just theologically) within the socio-historical currents of his day (and ours). For liberation theologians, the Gospel of Mark is 'poor man's literature'[37] in that it sides with the oppressed against the oppressor. A truly subversive text (10.31), it seeks to overturn not only those religious ideas that it deems false but the underlying institutional and oppressive power structures which are assumed to give rise to these ideas in the first place.

One such contemporary reading is that of F. Belo, a Christian lately turned Marxist, whose somewhat difficult book attempts to apply materialist theory and insights to the Gospel.[38] With an egalitarian ethic derived from Deuteronomy and the prophets, the Jesus of Mark represented a threat, it is claimed, to conventional understandings of family, wealth, and status, and to contemporary Jewish leadership as mediated by the priests through the Temple.

So what we find in Mark's Gospel is an account of conflict: between on the one hand the reign of God and the action of the eschatological salvation outside the Temple and on the other hand the firm view of the opponents that the prevailing culture, concerned as it is with the support of a society which divides, marginalizes, justifies wealth and makes economic gain out of theological virtue, is inimical to the radically new.[39]

Jesus' death resulted from his ideological challenge to the Temple, then the foremost economic and political (as well as

---

[37] See J. Cárdenas Pallares, *A Poor Man Called Jesus. Reflections on the Gospel of Mark* (Maryknoll, NY: Orbis, 1982).

[38] F. Belo, *A Materialist Reading of the Gospel of Mark* (Maryknoll, NY: Orbis, 1981). For an admirably clear account of Belo's views, see Corner and Rowland, *Liberating Exegesis*, pp. 93–114. For comment, see J. Volckaert, 'Mark, A Subversive Reading', *Vidyajyoti*, 46 (1982), pp. 246–52.

[39] Corner and Rowland, *Liberating Exegesis*, p. 114.

religious) institution of his day. Although he was crucified for essentially practical reasons, his death was subsequently transformed by theological doctrine to such an extent that the sting was drawn from its original revolutionary (socio-political) implications. 'The cross', in the words of Corner and Rowland, 'becomes an ideological device which justifies the socio-economic realities and warns against naive idealism.'[40]

A further contemporary 'political' reading of Mark's story of Jesus is that represented by C. Myers.[41] The periphery, Mark's story tells us, and not the centre, is where God is at work, the cross representing the beginning of the new world order. With a socio-political strategy that may be described as 'non-aligned radicalism' or 'revolutionary non-violence', the evangelist's aim, according to Myers, is to subvert, on behalf of the common people, the dominant ideology of his culture (and ours). 'Mark', Myers claims, 'looks for the end of the old world and the inauguration of the new, but it is discipleship – which he equates with a specific social practice and costly political engagement – that will inaugurate this transformation.'[42] Writing in response to the crisis created by the Jewish War, the evangelist spoke to and for a community of revolutionary activists whose pursuit of this radical discipleship involved them in non-violent resistance to Rome, opposition to the Jewish ruling class, and friction with those who sought to suborn them into the War. 'The profile of Mark's community', he therefore concludes, 'does not fit in the strictures designed by sect-sociology, nor does it fit the caricatures of millennial groups. It must be taken seriously on its own terms, as a distinct socio-political strategy in a determinate formation, and indeed as an ideology of practice that begs to be heard in our own time.'[43]

One of the most recent attempts to address current political concerns through the lens of Mark's Gospel is that by R. R.

---

[40] *Ibid.*, p. 101.
[41] C. Myers, *Binding the Strong Man. A Political Reading of Mark's Story of Jesus* (Maryknoll, NY: Orbis, 1988). See also C. Myers, *Who Will Roll Away the Stone? Discipleship Queries for First World Christians* (Maryknoll, NY: Orbis, 1994).
[42] Myers, *Strong Man*, p. 416.   [43] *Ibid.*, p. 444.

Beck.[44] Beck's theme is the ideology or myth of violence in modern society, and in particular the contemporary assumption that violence has had, and still has, a constructive part to play in bringing about civilization. After examining how certain narratives (the western stories of Louis L'Amour are taken as an exemplar) both legitimate and perpetuate myths of redemptive violence, he turns to the Gospel of Mark in order to gauge how it contributes to our understanding of conflict, and in particular to its stance regarding non-violent as opposed to violent means of conflict resolution. Applying narrative criticism to the Gospel, and focusing upon the literary patterns of conflict to be found there, Beck exposes the underlying ideological message conveyed by the Markan narrative. While entering into conflict, indeed refusing to avoid it, the Markan Jesus at the same time confounds the expectations of 'constructive violence', Beck claims, by demonstrating his unwillingness to engage in such violence himself. With its underlying ideology of non-violent resistance to evil, then, and in its presentation of Jesus as the true model for such, the Gospel, by thus engaging the myth of violence, offers a clear message for contemporary society.

'Political' readings of Mark, such as these, clearly highlight the contemporary significance of Mark, although many would wish to distance themselves from the left-wing agenda or perspective that is frequently associated with liberation theology. The tendency of such treatments is to treat the religious ideas of the text as a secondary manifestation of underlying economic or political realities, or the theology as a form of false consciousness. As a result, they may be doing violence themselves to the author's theological integrity. At times the ambiguities of the Markan text can frustrate even the liberation theologian's efforts to suborn it into his or her world-view, as, for example, when the Markan Jesus is made to defend an act of extravagance which could have garnered resources for the poor, and to speak (almost flippantly) of the permanent availability of the poor for charitable dispensation (14.3–9)![45]

---

[44] R. R. Beck, *Nonviolent Story. Narrative Conflict Resolution in the Gospel of Mark* (Maryknoll, NY: Orbis, 1996).

[45] This passage has often been used to defend theology over politics, or to promote an

Mark and women: some gender issues and observations

If the subject of violence is one of the preoccupations of the present day, then the subject of gender is another. A great deal of attention has been directed to issues of masculinity and femininity in our post-modern society, and a great deal of interest taken in 'images' of male and female in the modern media. This interest focuses not only on the nature of these images, and how they are conveyed, especially by literature and film, but also on how in turn they influence cultural under-standings of gender, for better or for worse. Feminism has done much to encourage this interest, with its exposure of the patterns of dominance and submission which have traditionally governed relations between the sexes, and with its critique of the oppressive structures of patriarchy. One focal point for feminist theology has been the place of women in the early Christian movement,[46] and the role and status of women in the New Testament, especially the Gospels.[47] Special interest has been taken in figures such as Mary Magdalene,[48] and it is now a common claim that she and other women played a significant role within the early Jesus movement.[49] It is no surprise, then, that issues of gender have been discussed in connection with the Gospel of Mark. Feminist interpretation has interpreted Markan soteriology in terms of liberation from patriarchy,[50] and questions regarding the understanding of gender in the ancient world, as well as our own, have been raised in connec-

---

evangelical gospel over a social one. For a liberation theologian's interpretation of the passage, see R. S. Sugirtharajah, ' "For you always have the poor with you": an Example of Hermeneutics of Suspicion', *Asia Journal of Theology*, 4 (1990), pp. 102–7.

[46] See, for example, M. Fander, *Die Stellung der Frau im Markusevangelium. Unter besonderer Berücksichtigung kultur- und religionsgeschichtlicher Hintergründe* (Münsteraner Theologische Abhandlungen, 8; Altenberge: Telos, 1989).

[47] See, for example, M. Evans, *Women in the Bible* (Exeter: Paternoster, 1983), pp. 44–60.

[48] See, for example, R. Atwood, *Mary Magdalene in the New Testament Gospels and Early Tradition* (European University Studies, Series 23: Theology 457; Bern, Berlin and Frankfurt: Lang, 1993).

[49] See, for example, C. Ricci, *Mary Magdalene and Many Others. Women who Followed Jesus* (Minneapolis, MN: Fortress Press, 1994).

[50] See M. S. Medley, 'Emancipatory Solidarity: the Redemptive Significance of Jesus in Mark', *PerspRelSt*, 21 (1994), pp. 5–22.

tion with such passages as Mark 6.17–29.[51] By far the majority of recent studies, however, have occupied themselves with the role and status of women in Mark.[52]

Women figure in the Gospel in a handful of passages: Mark 1.29–31 (Peter's mother-in-law); 3.31–5 (Jesus' mother); 5.21–4, 35–43 (Jairus' daughter); 5.24–34 (the haemorrhaging woman); 6.17–29 (Herodias and her daughter); 7.24–30 (the Syrophoenician woman and her daughter); 12.41–4 (the poor widow); 14.3–9 (the anointing woman); 15.40–1, 47 (the ministering women – Mary Magdalene, Mary and Salome – and others); 16.1–8 (the women at the empty tomb – Mary Magdalene, Mary and Salome). They appear in the context of healing stories (1.29–31; 5.21–43; 7.24–30), in other isolated stories and incidents (3.31–5; 6.17–29; 12.41–4) and in the narrative of the passion and resurrection (14.3–9; 15.40–1, 47; 16.1–8). In total, the women are thirteen in number (if the daughter of the Syrophoenician woman is counted, although she does not make an appearance, and the 'many other women' of Mk 15.41 are not). Some of them are specifically named (Herodias, Mary Magdalene, Mary, Salome), or by reference to associated men (Peter's mother-in-law, Jesus' mother, Jairus' daughter), others are unnamed (the haemorrhaging woman, the poor widow, the anointing woman).[53] Encountered usually by Jesus as isolated individuals in private, women only become prominent as his followers (where the Markan reader is concerned), or as belonging to his circle, from Mark 15.40 onwards, that is, in the

---

[51] See J. A. Glancy, 'Unveiling Masculinity. The Construction of Gender in Mark 6:17–29', *Biblical Interpretation*, 2 (1994), pp. 34–50.

[52] See Telford, 'History of Developments' in Telford (ed.), *Interpretation*, p. 12; Telford, *Mark*, p. 111; Fander, *Stellung*. For a Japanese feminist perspective, see H. Kinukawa, *Women and Jesus in Mark. A Japanese Feminist Perspective* (Bible & Liberation; Maryknoll, NY: Orbis, 1994).

[53] For individual studies of some of these nameless women, see, for example, S. C. Barton, 'Mark as Narrative. The Story of the Anointing Woman (Mk 14:3–9)', *ExpT*, 102 (1990–1), pp. 230–4; M. Fander, 'Frauen in der Nachfolge Jesu. Die Rolle der Frau im Markusevangelium', *EvTh*, 52 (1992), pp. 413–32; M. Minor, 'The Women of the Gospel of Mark and Contemporary Women's Spirituality', *Spirituality Today*, 43 (1991), pp. 134–41; D. Rhoads, 'Jesus and the Syrophoenician Woman in Mark. A Narrative-Critical Study', *Journal of the American Academy of Religion*, 62 (1994), pp. 343–75.

crucifixion and resurrection narrative.[54] Although 'words-and-deeds *chreiai*' about women are rare in the ancient world,[55] Mark's women are essentially minor characters who do little in the context of the Gospel to propel the plot forward.

A key issue, then, is whether we should regard the evangelist's portrayal of women as positive or negative. The vast majority of commentators have opted for the former view, claiming that women emerge in Mark as 'hidden heroes', following Jesus on his way to the cross, demonstrating courage, showing faith, offering service, in short, exemplifying the marks of true discipleship.[56] The anointing woman, for example, has been taken as the model disciple, expressing 'in a nutshell' the overall message of the Gospel itself.[57] Mark's exemplary treatment of women as minor characters in his Gospel has been taken as a function of his 'reversal theme' ('many that are first will be last, and the last first', 10.31),[58] their role in the narrative acting as a counterpoint to that of the male disciples, whose discipleship (and leadership), by contrast, are found wanting.[59] It is the women who in the final analysis act as witnesses to both his death and his resurrection, and therein, notwithstanding their silence, lies their ultimate significance.[60]

If this assessment of the role of women in the Markan Gospel

---

[54] See W. Munro, 'Women Disciples in Mark?', *CBQ*, 44 (1982), pp. 225–41.

[55] See M. A. Beavis, 'Women as Models of Faith in Mark', *BTB*, 18 (1988), pp. 3–9.

[56] *Ibid.*; Fander, 'Frauen', *Evth*, 52 (1992), pp. 413–32; E. S. Fiorenza, *In Memory of Her* (New York: Crossroad, 1983), pp. 316–23; J. A. Grassi, 'The Secret Heroine of Mark's Drama', *BTB*, 18 (1988), pp. 10–15; J. A. Grassi, *The Hidden Heroes of the Gospels. Female Counterparts of Jesus* (Collegeville, MN: Liturgical Press, 1989); W. J. Harrington, 'Mark as Story', *Priests & People*, 8 (1994), pp. 243–7; J. Kopas, 'Jesus and Women in Mark's Gospel', *Review for Religious*, 44 (1985), pp. 912–20; Minor, 'Women', *Spirituality Today*, 43 (1991), pp. 134–41.

[57] See Barton, 'Mark as Narrative', *ExpT*, 102 (1990–1), pp. 230–4.

[58] See Fiorenza, *Memory*, p. 318; A. Gill, 'Women Ministers in the Gospel of Mark', *Australian Biblical Review*, 35 (1987), pp. 14–21; E. S. Malbon, 'Fallible Followers. Women and Men in the Gospel of Mark', *Semeia*, 28 (1983), pp. 29–48.

[59] See A. B. Lane, 'The Significance of the Thirteen Women in the Gospel of Mark', *Unitarian Universalist Christian*, 38 (1983), pp. 18–27; J. J. Schmitt, 'Women in Mark's Gospel', *Bible Today*, 19 (1981), pp. 228–33; M. J. Selvidge [Schierling], 'Women as Leaders in the Marcan Communities', *Listening*, 15 (1980), pp. 250–6. The thirteen women in Mark are taken by Lane to correspond to the thirteen male disciples in the Gospel (the twelve plus Levi).

[60] See Fiorenza, *Memory*, pp. 321–2; P. J. Hartin, 'The Role of the Women Disciples in Mark's Narrative', *Theologia Evangelica*, 26 (1993), pp. 91–102; L. Schottroff, 'Die

is correct, then it raises the question of the evangelist's motivation(s) in portraying them so positively, especially when the male disciples are treated so harshly. Some have suggested that the evangelist's exemplary treatment of the women reflects the true state of affairs in the Markan community, where women, it is claimed, were treated as equals, and occupied positions of influence or even leadership,[61] others that it reflects the situation of the early church where more women than men were martyred for their faith.[62] On the other hand, it could simply represent the obverse side of his attack on the male disciples, the women (along with other minor characters) being elevated, in literary terms, in order to highlight *per contrarium* his criticism of the Jerusalem leaders.

Before accepting, however, the basic premise of a Markan intention to elevate women, for whatever reason, a number of factors can be mentioned which suggest a different picture. In the first place, it should be noted that Mark's portrayal of women is neither extensive nor uniformly positive (see, for example, the depiction of Herodias and her daughter, 6.17–29). Apart from individual cameos, their narrative role is largely confined, as has already been observed, to the passion narrative. Overall the evangelist appears to have only taken a moderate interest in women and their roles, if we are to judge by the fact that there are relatively few female characters, and little teaching with regard to them.[63] Male characters, as I have remarked, propel the plot throughout, with the female characters playing only a very passive role. The Markan text indeed appears to be coloured by an androcentric mindset, the virtues displayed by the women (humility, submissiveness, service, etc.) embodying those of the ancient world, and not the modern.[64] They are not

mütigen Frauen aus Galiläa und der Auferstehungsglaube', *Diakonia*, 20 (1989), pp. 221–6.

[61] Cf. Fiorenza, *Memory*, pp. 321–2; Lane, 'Thirteen Women', pp. 18–27; Munro, 'Women Disciples', pp. 225–41; Selvidge, 'Women as Leaders', pp. 250–6.

[62] Cf. Fander, *Stellung*.

[63] See B. Witherington, *Women in the Earliest Churches* (Cambridge: Cambridge University Press, 1988), pp. 158–66; B. Witherington, *Women and the Genesis of Christianity* (Cambridge: Cambridge University Press, 1990), pp. 225–8.

[64] See M. E. Cotes, *Images of Women in the Gospel of Mark* (unpublished dissertation, Manchester University, 1993).

actually given the title 'disciple' (*mathētēs*), moreover,[65] and it is by no means clear that they functioned as leaders in the Markan community. In the crucial role as witnesses to the resurrection ('Go tell his disciples . . .', 16.7), they failed, as we observed in chapter two, saying 'nothing to any one, for they were afraid' (16.8). In this respect, then, they are no better than their male counterparts, for whom, indeed, in narrative terms, they act as 'stand-ins.' Their late presence in the Gospel, in a definite narrative role, need be accounted for by no more than the necessity on the part of the evangelist to carry the story forward in view of the absence of the male disciples (14.50). By likewise displaying the fear, stupidity and disobedience predicated of the male disciples elsewhere by the evangelist, the womenfolk of the Jerusalem community can be seen, in the end, to come under the same harsh judgment as their menfolk. Mark's treatment of the women is therefore not as simple as it may seem, and the case for a positive or negative treatment should at least be given an open verdict.

Mark and the Jews: some ethnic issues and observations

If Mark's portrayal of women represents a modern concern, then his treatment of the Jews reflects an even greater one. The 'image' of the Jews in the Gospel of Mark touches upon one of the burning issues of our day, namely the question of anti-Semitism and its relation to the New Testament, particularly the Gospels.[66] The question is an important one for Christians and Jews alike and has given rise to a vigorous debate in recent times.[67] The answers offered and the claims made have significant implications for relations between Christianity and

---

[65] For a dissenting view, see J. Dines, 'Not to be Served, but to Serve: Women as Disciples in Mark's Gospel', *Month*, 26 (1993), pp. 438–42.

[66] While a growing body of opinion argues that the anachronistic term 'anti-Semitism' should be replaced, where the New Testament is concerned, by the more appropriate terms 'anti-Jewishness' or 'anti-Judaism', the term remains in vogue as a cogent reminder of the disastrous effects that anti-Jewish sentiments within the New Testament have had in the more recent history of Jewish–Christian relations.

[67] See, for example, J. D. G. Dunn, 'The Question of Anti-semitism in the New Testament Writings of the Period' in J. D. G. Dunn (ed.), *Jews and Christians: The Parting of the Ways A.D. 70 to 135. The Second Durham–Tübingen Research Symposium on*

Judaism, · and especially for the current Jewish–Christian dialogue. On the one hand, there are those, following R. R. Ruether, who would claim that anti-Semitic attitudes are built into the very structure of the Christian myth and that '[t]he foundations of anti-Judaic thought were laid in the New Testament'.[68] This view is shared by J. Hellig,[69] for example, who holds that the very roots of the negative image of the Jew, and of the demonization of Jews are to be found in these writings. On the other hand, there are those who argue that the New Testament is not *necessarily* anti-Semitic, although it can provide, and indeed has provided, a basis for anti-Semitic consequences or effects.[70] Anti-Jewish comments in the New Testament oppose Judaism theologically but are not directed against Jews, *qua* Jews. Anti-Jewish passages are in a minority and are not used with any frequency until the Crusades and modern times.[71] The New Testament is no more anti-Jewish, it is claimed, than the Old Testament or Hebrew Bible, the prophetic tradition being prominent in pointing out Israel's spiritual ills, the prophets vehemently railing against their erring compatriots.[72] By the measure of Hellenistic conventions and contemporary Jewish polemic, moreover, the New Testament's slander against fellow Jews is remarkably mild.[73]

A key trend in recent years, among New Testament scholars, has been the assertion that anti-Semitic statements or attitudes in the New Testament are the product of contingent situational

Earliest Christianity and Judaism (Durham: Mohr–Siebeck, 1989), pp. 177–211 for an excellent summary of the debate.

[68] See R. Ruether, *Faith and Fratricide: The Theological Roots of Anti-Semitism* (New York: Seabury Press, 1974), p. 226.

[69] J. Hellig, 'The negative image of the Jew and its New Testament roots', *JTSouthAfr*, 64 (1988), pp. 39–48.

[70] See G. Baumbach, 'Das Neue Testament – ein Judenfeindliches Buch? Zur Frage nach der Entstehung und Verbreitung antijüdischer Tendenzen im frühen Christentum', *Die Zeichen der Zeit*, 40 (1986), pp. 138–142.

[71] See L. H. Feldman, 'Is the New Testament Anti-Semitic?', *Humanities*, 21 (1987), pp. 1–14; L. Feldman, 'Is the New Testament Anti-Semitic?', *Moment [Washington, DC]*, 15 (1990), pp. 32–5, 50–2.

[72] See C. Goldstein, 'Is the New Testament Anti-Semitic?', *Liberty [Silver Springs, MD]*, 87 (1992), pp. 11–15; J. D. Levenson, 'Is there a counterpart in the Hebrew Bible to New Testament Antisemitism?', *Journal of Ecumenical Studies*, 22 (1985), pp. 242–60.

[73] See L. T. Johnson, 'The New Testament's Anti-Jewish Slander and the Conventions of Ancient Polemic', *JBL*, 108 (1989), pp. 419–41.

factors.[74] Different portrayals of Jews in the New Testament reflect the differing situations of the writers and their communities, especially with regard to the particular stage reached in what has now been termed 'the parting of the ways' between the two religions.[75] Anti-Judaism decreases as we regress towards Christian origins, while later writers intensified the anti-Judaism of their sources in light of their search for religious identity, their developing Christology, their response to socio-political factors (the desire to appease Roman opinion, the concern to distance themselves from Jewish nationalism, etc.) and so on.[76] The less hope that a Christian writer had for a successful mission to fellow Jews, it is observed, the more animosity is shown.[77]

A particular feature of scholarly debate in the last ten years or so has been the contention that disputes between early Christians and Jews in the New Testament were for the most part intra-Jewish disputes and had the character of 'sibling rivalry'.[78] Anti-Jewish statements in the New Testament are seen as childlike polemics against the emergent Christian sect's older and more firmly established 'mother religion'.[79] The general thrust of the argument, therefore, is to support the view

[74] See, for example, J. C. Beker, 'The New Testament View of Judaism' in J. H. Charlesworth (ed.), *Jesus and Christians: Exploring the Past, Present and Future* (New York: Crossroad, 1990), pp. 60–75.

[75] See E. Trocmé, 'Les Juifs d'après le Nouveau Testament', *Foi et Vie*, 90 (1991), pp. 3–22.

[76] See M. J. Cook, 'Confronting New Testament attitudes on Jews and Christians: four Jewish perspectives', *Chicago Theological Seminary Register*, 78 (1988), pp. 3–30; J. Neusner and E. S. Frerichs (eds.), *'To See Ourselves as Others See Us': Christians, Jews, 'Others' in Late Antiquity* (Scholars Press Studies in the Humanities; Chico, CA: Scholars Press, 1985); G. N. Stanton, 'Aspects of early Christian–Jewish polemic and apologetic', *NTS*, 31 (1985), pp. 377–92.

[77] See E. E. Johnson, 'Jews and Christians in the New Testament. John, Matthew and Paul', *Reformed Review*, 42 (1988), pp. 113–28.

[78] See Dunn, 'Anti-Semitism' in Dunn (ed.), *Jews and Christians*, pp. 177–211; C. A. Evans and D. Hagner (eds.), *Anti-Semitism and Early Christianity: Issues of Polemic and Faith* (Minneapolis, MN: Fortress Press, 1993); D. Sänger, 'Neue Testament und Antijudaismus: Versuch einer exegetischen und hermeneutischen Vergewisserung im innerchristlichen Gespräch', *Kerygma und Dogma*, 34 (1988), pp. 210–31.

[79] See N. A. Beck, *Mature Christianity. The Recognition and Repudiation of the Anti-Jewish Polemic of the New Testament* (Selinsgrove, PA: Susquehanna University, 1985); R. A. Everett, 'The Christian Responsibility in Anti-Semitism', *Judaism*, 36 (1987), pp. 377–81.

that 'anti-Jewish trends in Christianity' are 'peripheral and accidental, and not grounded in the New Testament itself'.[80] According to R. W. Klein, indeed, the New Testament offers more resources than obstacles to Jewish–Christian dialogue today.[81]

Be this as it may, the fact remains that in the Gospels, and particularly in the earliest of the Gospels, the reader is confronted with a portrait of the Jews which has been used by subsequent generations of Christians to justify persecution. A particular charge levelled against Jews by their persecutors was that of being the spiritually blind executioners of Jesus of Nazareth, their Christ, and, insofar as that figure is seen as an incarnation of God, as the perpetrators of deicide, as God-slayers. Given that this portrait owes much to Mark's presentation, it is therefore fair to ask whether religious anti-Semitism has any basis in the attitudes expressed by the evangelist, whether he himself can be considered 'anti-Semitic' or 'anti-Jewish', and, if so, to what degree, and with what significance?

The question was raised in chapter two, one recalls, in connection with the discussion of Mark's treatment of the Jewish leaders in relation to that of Jesus, but has been postponed until now. There I concluded that for Mark, as for Paul, Jesus is more than the Jewish Messiah confessed as such by his original Jewish followers in the person of Peter; he is the divine *Son of God*, a status recognized only by the supernatural world (the demons) and by a Gentile centurion at his crucifixion. The Markan Jesus, the Son of God *incognito*, is depicted as being misunderstood or rejected by various representative Jewish leadership groups and in turn as repudiating their authority and their doctrine. This Markan Jesus is a commanding figure who is shown constantly in a favourable light vis-à-vis these Jewish leaders ('he taught with authority, and not as the scribes,' 1.22). He is depicted as condoning the breaking of the sabbath (2.23ff.; 3.1–6). In chapter 12, he is placed in the contrived but

---

[80] See G. Baum, *Is the New Testament Anti-Semitic?* (Glen Rock, NJ: Paulist Press, 1965) and Dunn, 'Anti-Semitism' in Dunn (ed.), *Jews and Christians*, p. 177.

[81] See R. W. Klein, 'Anti-Semitism as Christian Legacy: the Origin and Nature of our Estrangement from the Jews', *Currents in Theology and Mission*, 11 (1984), pp. 285–301.

dramatically appropriate setting of the Jewish Temple and shown being confronted by and besting in argument each of the leadership groups of the nation in turn: the chief priests, elders and scribes, the Pharisees, the Herodians and the Sadducees.

If any New Testament writing deserved to be described as anti-Semitic, therefore, Mark would be a good candidate. The treatment of Judaism and the Jewish leaders amounts almost to 'a pronounced campaign of denigration', in the words of one of the scholars cited (S. G. F. Brandon). Jewish lustration practice is disparaged, as are other Jewish practices (7.1–23). Judaism is implied to be obsolescent (2.21–22 – new wine is not be placed in old wineskins). The Jewish leaders are depicted as hard of heart (2.1ff.; 3.5), as hypocrites (7.6–7), as guilty of the unforgivable sin in questioning the source of Jesus' power (3.28–30), and as wicked murderers for rejecting Jesus (the beloved Son of the vineyard owner) and the prophets before him (12.1ff.). All the Jewish leadership groups are shown implausibly as plotting his death, with Jesus anticipating their culpability in the passion predictions (8.31; 9.31; 10.33–4). They act with stealth and deviousness (14.1–2), are accused of acting out of envy (15.10), and are depicted as cruelly mocking Jesus on the cross (15.31–2).

Not only these Jewish leadership groups but Jesus' own family and friends are represented as rejecting him (3.31–5). 'Who are my mother, brothers, sisters?' Jesus asks, and answers, 'Those who do the will of my Father.' Thus, blood relationship is repudiated and a spiritual relationship with Jesus is emphasized. This failure to recognize and confess Jesus as 'Son of God' extends even to the original Jewish disciples, who are shown as remarkably obtuse, even fearful, stupid, cowardly and treacherous. In the Gospel, furthermore, we see the attempt on the part of Judaism (and also of Jewish Christianity) to come to terms theologically with the rejection of the claims of Gentile Christianity for Jesus. In one of the most remarkable passages in the New Testament, the Old Testament, we observed, is pressed into the service of theological explanation. In Mark 4.12, Isaiah 6.9–10 is employed to argue that Jesus' original parabolic teaching had as its very purpose the hardening of Jewish hearts. That had been the historical outcome; this must, therefore, have been the intended effect. It is this theological datum – not merely the motif of 'spiritual blindness' but the predestined rejection by the Jews of the Son of God – that carries with it the germ of further religious anti-Semitism (1 Pet. 2.7–8).

Is Mark anti-Semitic, then, or anti-Jewish? Various views have been expressed in regard to this. On the one hand, it has been argued that the evangelist's hostility is confined to the Jewish authorities and not to the nation as a whole. In his controversies with these leaders, his Jesus remains within the limits of intra-Jewish dispute (e.g. in sabbath observance or divorce), and does not overstep the bounds of acceptable Jewish behaviour (e.g. by repudiating his people).[82] As the feeding stories may indicate, Mark sees in the Christian community a place for Jew and Gentile alike. This tendency on the evangelist's part may be strengthened by the observation that the treatment of the Jewish leaders is not uniformly negative. One anonymous scribe is treated sympathetically (12.28–34), as are two named members of the Jewish establishment, Jairus, a ruler of the synagogue (5.22–4, 35–43), and Joseph of Arimathea, a respected member of the council (15.42–7). In light of this, E. S. Malbon concludes:

Being a foe of the Marcan Jesus is a matter of how one chooses to relate to him not a matter of one's social or religious status and role. And the same is true of being a friend of Jesus. Furthermore, the Jewish religious establishment (although subdivided) is but one major category of foes of the Marcan Jesus. Other categories are the Roman political establishment (Herod, Pilate, soldiers) and nonhuman foes (unclean spirits, demons, Satan) ... Thus Mark challenges both the absolutism of 'good' and 'bad' (no one is a perfect disciple) and the absolutism of types determined by status and role (no one is ruled out as a disciple). By suggesting that even presumed foes can be followers, Mark opens up the category of disciples; by indicating that even known followers can sometimes fail, Mark deepens the meaning of discipleship.[83]

---

[82] See H. Baarlink, 'Zur Frage nach dem Antijudaismus im Markusevangelium', *ZNW*, 70 (1979), pp. 166–93.

[83] E. S. Malbon, 'The Jewish Leaders in the Gospel of Mark: a Literary Study of Marcan Characterization', *JBL*, 108 (1989), pp. 276, 277, 280. For a dissenting view, see J. D. Kingsbury, 'The Religious Authorities in the Gospel of Mark', *NTS*, 36 (1990), pp. 47–50.

On the other hand, it cannot be denied that the various Jewish leadership groups (Pharisees, Herodians, Sadducees, chief priests, elders, scribes) are *for the most part* united as a single body or character in opposition to Jesus, and that there are also hints that the evangelist's horizons extend to *all* Jews (7.3–4 'the Pharisees *and all the Jews*', as well as 7.6).[84] Even accounting for their leaders' machinations, it is the Jewish crowd who in the end call for Jesus' crucifixion (15.13). For killing his heir, God will destroy the tenants and give the vineyard to others (12.9). The evangelist also links Jesus' family with his opponents (3.21, 22), as we have seen, and has Jesus repudiate in effect his blood ties with the former (3.31–5). The matter of the Mark's attitude to the Jews is hard, therefore, to resolve.

Modern enlightened Christian opinion would of course repudiate all expressions of religious anti-Semitism. Gone are the days when 'a pair of female statues [*Ecclēsia* and *Synagōga*] was erected in Gothic cathedrals in Europe to symbolize the Church triumphant and the Synagogue rejected and fallen. The Church is represented as a proud but modest maiden crowned and holding the *Ecclēsia* in one hand, and sometimes a staff in the other. The Synagogue is depicted as a blindfold wanton, and her characteristic appurtenances are a broken staff (2 Corinthians 3:14), broken tablets of the Law and a fallen crown.'[85] Christian reaction against anti-Semitism found significant expression in the decree of the Vatican Council (in 1965–6) exonerating Jews from the guilt of crucifying Jesus, although there was some opposition to this. A modern Christian would claim that all humankind shares responsibility corporately and spiritually for the death of Jesus.

A dilemma still faces the Christian, however, whose faith is born of and is reflected in New Testament writings such as the Gospel of Mark. If it is a matter of divine revelation that Jesus of Nazareth is to be considered more than a Jewish prophet, teacher and exorcist, as Mark maintained, and that he is to be

---

[84] See W. A. Johnson, 'The Jews in Saint Mark's Gospel', *Religion and Intellectual Life*, 6 (1989), pp. 182–92.

[85] J. Heinemann, J. Gutmann, C. Roth and others, 'Anti-Semitism' in *Encyclopaedia Judaica* (Jerusalem: Keter Publishing House, 1972), pp. 91–2.

worshipped as the 'Son of God', and therefore as no less than the incarnation of God, then all who reject this view – and Jews would be in this category – must be considered in Christian theology as 'spiritually blind'. Yet the position of the church, based on that self-same theology, claims that all men are brothers, and that they are to be treated with love, justice and respect. As a corollary they are not to be regarded, because of their different traditions, views or perspectives, as 'spiritually inferior'. In uttering his (in)famous theory of the parables (4.11–12), the Markan Jesus appears to consign his Jewish hearers to such a position, and the question that remains therefore is whether a Christianity based on such a declaration can really shed its anti-Jewishness and yet stay true to its revelatory claims.

Select bibliography

BIBLIOGRAPHICAL RESOURCES

For a comprehensive and classified coverage of bibliographical resources on the Gospel of Mark, the following are helpful. Neirynck is the most up to date. For publications after 1992, the student should consult *NTA* which gives periodical abstracts on Mark, as well as book notices (see Gospels–Acts).

Humphrey, H. M., *A Bibliography for the Gospel of Mark 1954–1980* (Studies in the Bible and Early Christianity, 1; New York and Toronto: Edwin Mellen Press, 1981).

Neirynck, F. *et al.* (eds.), *The Gospel of Mark. A Cumulative Bibliography 1950–1990* (BETL, CII; Leuven: Leuven University Press/Peeters, 1992).

New Testament Abstracts.

COMMENTARIES

Among the standard commentaries, the following should be noted:

Anderson, H., *The Gospel of Mark* (New Century Bible Commentary; Grand Rapids, MI: Eerdmans, 1981). A very good popular commentary based on the Revised Standard Version, which is well-informed (up to its date of publication) by modern scholarship. It has in particular an excellent sixty-page introduction to the Gospel. Published in paperback in 1981.

Cranfield, C. E. B., *The Gospel according to St Mark: an Introduction and Commentary* (Cambridge Greek Testament Commentary; Cambridge: Cambridge University Press, 1959). Reprinted frequently with revised additional supplementary notes, but essentially predating contemporary approaches and understandings of the Gospel.

Guelich, R. A., *Mark 1–8:26* (Word Biblical Commentary, 34A; Dallas,

TX: Word, 1989). The most recent large commentary. Careful, cautious, conservative scholarship with a well-balanced discussion of the problems. Guelich's untimely death has unfortunately deprived us of a second volume from his own hand.

Gundry, R. H., *Mark. A Commentary on His Apology for the Cross* (Grand Rapids, MI: Eerdmans, 1992). A hefty commentary! Offers an exposition of each pericope which engages scholarly views and pays special attention to Mark's grammar and style.

Hooker, M. D., *The Gospel According to St Mark* (Black's New Testament Commentaries; London: A. & C. Black, 1991). Though taking account of modern scholarship on the Gospel, this excellent 'middle of the road' commentary, in running style, does not, in the tradition of the series, 'overburden the reader with names and theories'.

Lane, W. L., *The Gospel According to Mark. The English Text with Introduction, Exposition and Notes* (The New International Commentary on the New Testament, 2; Grand Rapids, MI: Eerdmans; The New London Commentary on the New Testament; London: Marshall, Morgan & Scott, 1974). Detailed, conservative scholarship based on the American Standard Version of 1901.

Mann, C. S., *Mark. A New Translation with Introduction and Commentary* (Anchor Bible, 27; Garden City, NY: Doubleday, 1986). A substantial seven hundred-page commentary in a series aimed at the general reader with no special formal training in Biblical Studies. The only major modern commentary to be based on 'the Griesbach hypothesis', namely that Mark is a simple conflation of Matthew and Luke. Mann's 'Mark' for that reason is at odds with the more sophisticated author revealed by modern literary-critical study of the Gospel.

Nineham, D. E., *The Gospel of St Mark* (Pelican Commentary; London and New York: A. & C. Black, 1968). The classic commentary on the English text and still worth buying. Though first published in 1963, its scholarly insights and forward-looking approach have anticipated later developments.

Schweizer, E., *The Good News According to Mark* (London: SPCK, 1971). Translated from the German, this commentary is by a major scholar on Mark's Gospel who has contributed much to our understanding of the evangelist's theological achievement.

Taylor, V., *The Gospel According to St Mark* (London: Macmillan; New York: St Martin's Press, 1966). The classic commentary on the Greek text. Preserves much of value but its emphasis on the historicity of the Gospel has been long overtaken by modern preoccupation with the Gospel's literary and theological aspects.

Helpful condensed treatments are to be found in the following one-volume commentaries or dictionaries:

Cranfield, C. E. B., 'Mark, Gospel of' in G. A. Buttrick (ed.), *The Interpreter's Dictionary of the Bible* (New York and Nashville, TN: Abingdon Press, 1962), Vol. III, pp. 267–77. A conservative interpretation of the Gospel, now decidedly dated. Should be read in conjunction with N. Perrin's article in the later supplementary volume.

Perrin, N., 'Mark, Gospel of' in K. Crim (ed.), *The Interpreter's Dictionary of the Bible, Supplementary Volume* (Nashville: Abingdon Press, 1976), pp. 571–3. A succinct discussion of more recent approaches and issues by an American scholar who dominated Markan studies in the seventies.

Mally, E. J., 'The Gospel according to Mark' in R. E. Brown, J. A. Fitzmyer and R. E. Murphy (eds.), *The Jerome Biblical Commentary* (London: G. Chapman, 1968), pp. 21–61. A scholarly treatment in a Catholic commentary recognised for its erudition. Now eclipsed by *The New Jerome Biblical Commentary* (1989).

Harrington, D. J., 'The Gospel according to Mark' in R. E. Brown, J. A. Fitzmyer and R. E. Murphy (eds.), *The New Jerome Biblical Commentary* (London: G. Chapman, 1989), pp. 596–629. Introduction rather brief but the most recent condensed commentary there is.

Telford, W. R., 'Mark, Gospel of' in R. J. Coggins and J. L. Houlden (eds.), *A Dictionary of Biblical Interpretation* (London: SCM Press; Philadelphia, PA: Trinity Press International, 1990), pp. 424–8. Reviews the history of interpretation of Mark and the variety of critical approaches to it.

Wilson, R. McL., 'Mark' in M. Black and H. H. Rowley (eds.), *Peake's Commentary on the Bible* (London: Thomas Nelson, 1962), pp. 799–819. Now decidedly dated (as the bibliography indicates) but useful for its concentrated exposition of the text.

The major foreign-language commentaries include:

Ernst, J., *Das Evangelium nach Markus. Übersetzt und Erklärt* (Regensburger Neues Testament; Regensburg: F. Pustet, 1981). Draws on recent Markan research to accent literary and theological questions.

Gnilka, J., *Das Evangelium nach Markus* (Evangelisch-Katholischer Kommentar zum Neuen Testament, II 1/2; Zurich, Einsiedeln and Cologne: Benziger, 1978; Neukirchen and Vluyn: Neukirchener Verlag, 1979). A major work of German scholarship which in its moderate assessment of the Gospel perhaps comes closest to representing the consensus (if such exists) on matters which divide the scholars. Includes discussion on the history of interpretation.

Lührmann, D., *Das Markusevangelium* (Handbuch zum Neuen Testament, 3; Tübingen: Mohr–Siebeck, 1987). One of the most recent major German commentaries and one which, while still in the German mainstream, comes closest to incorporating insights from the newer literary studies.

Pesch, R., *Das Markusevangelium* (Herders Theologischer Kommentar zum Neuen Testament, II, 1/2; Freiburg, Basle and Vienna: Herder, 1976/1977). A magisterial commentary of meticulous conservative scholarship which views Mark as a relatively unoriginal collection of historically reliable traditions which determined, along with his own minimal editing, the structure of his Gospel. Further editions published I [4]1984; II [3]1983.

Schmithals, W., *Das Evangelium nach Markus* (Ökumenischer Faschenbuchkommentar zum Neuen Testament, 2/1 & 2/2; Gütersloh: Mohn, 1979). Represents two extremes of interpretation by seeing Mark as the ultra-conservative editor of an extensive underlying source written by someone with great theological originality.

SPECIAL STUDIES

The following offer useful treatments of Mark by way of general background:

Best, E., *Mark. The Gospel as Story* (Studies of the New Testament and its World; Edinburgh: T. & T. Clark, 1983). Based on a series of lectures, this book, by a prominent British scholar, offers observations on and reactions to a number of Markan issues and problems (e.g. Mark's purpose and continuing significance, the passion, Christology, etc.).

Hengel, M., *Studies in the Gospel of Mark* (Philadelphia, PA: Fortress Press, 1985). Three essays by a prominent German scholar on the Gospel's origin and situation, literary, theological and historical problems, and the titles of the Gospels and Mark.

Hooker, M. D., *The Message of Mark* (London: Epworth Press, 1983). Eight lectures on Mark's message by another prominent British scholar.

Kee, H. C., *Community of the New Age. Studies in Mark's Gospel*

(Philadelphia, PA: Westminster Press, 1977). One of the most important works on Mark in the last twenty years.

Martin, R. P., *Mark – Evangelist and Theologian* (Exeter: Paternoster, 1979). A classic guide to the Gospel, and notable for its account of and engagement with scholarship up until the end of the seventies.

Pesch, R., *Das Markus-Evangelium* (Wege der Forschung, 411; Darmstadt: Wissenschaftliche Buchgesellschaft, 1979). A collection of classic essays in German by various scholars.

Telford, W. R., *Mark* (New Testament Guides; Sheffield: Sheffield Academic Press, 1995). A more recent study guide to the Gospel approached from the point of view of history, literature and theology.

Telford, W. R. (ed.), *The Interpretation of Mark* (Studies in New Testament Interpretation; Edinburgh: T. & T. Clark, 1995). After a 61–page introduction to Markan studies, this volume presents thirteen articles in English by prominent Markan scholars. A twenty-page select bibliography is also included.

THE THEOLOGY OF MARK

In addition to the works above, the following offer reflections on Mark's theology, either as a whole or with respect to specific aspects or passages:

Baarlink, H., *Anfängliches Evangelium* (Kampen: Kok, 1977).

Boring, M. E., 'The Christology of Mark: Hermeneutical Issues for Systematic Theology', *Semeia*, 30 (1984), pp. 125–53.

Bultmann, R., *Theology of the New Testament* (London: SCM Press, 1952/1955), *passim*.

Burkill, T. A., 'St Mark's Philosophy of History', *New Testament Studies*, 3 (1957), pp. 142–8.

Conzelmann, H., *An Outline of the Theology of the New Testament* (The New Testament Library; London: SCM Press; Evanston, IL: Harper & Row, 1969), pp. 140–4.

Conzelmann, H., 'History and Theology in the Passion Narratives of the Synoptic Gospels', *Interpretation*, 24 (1970), pp. 178–97.

Dewey, J., *Markan Public Debate. Literary Technique, Concentric Structure, and Theology in Mark 2:1–3:6* (Society of Biblical Literature Dissertation Series, 48; Chico, CA: Scholars Press, 1980).

Donahue, J. R., *The Theology and Setting of Discipleship in the Gospel of Mark* (Milwaukee, WI: Marquette University Press, 1983).

Dowd, S. E., *Prayer, Power and the Problem of Suffering: Mark 11:22–25 in* the Context of Markan Theology (Society of Biblical Literature Dissertation Series, 105; Atlanta, GA: Scholars Press, 1988).

Evans, C. F., *The Beginning of the Gospel. Four Lectures on St Mark's Gospel* (London: SPCK, 1968).

Evans, C. F., *Explorations in Theology* (London: SCM Press, 1977).

Geddert, T. J., *Watchwords. Mark 13 in Markan Eschatology* (Journal for the Study of the New Testament Supplement Series, 26; Sheffield: JSOT Press, 1989).

Goppelt, L., *Theology of the New Testament. Volume One: The Ministry of Jesus in its Theological Significance* (Grand Rapids, MI: Eerdmans, 1981), *passim.*

Grässer, E., 'Jesus in Nazareth (Mark VI.1–6a). Notes on the Redaction and Theology of St Mark', *New Testament Studies*, 16 (1969–70), pp. 1–23.

Jeremias, J., *New Testament Theology. Part One: The Proclamation of Jesus* (The New Testament Library; London: SCM Press, 1971), *passim.*

Kertelge, K., 'The Epiphany of Jesus in the Gospel (Mark)' in W. R. Telford (ed.), *The Interpretation of Mark* (Edinburgh: T. & T. Clark, 1995), pp. 105–23.

Kingsbury, J. D., *The Christology of Mark's Gospel* (Philadelphia, PA: Fortress Press, 1983).

Kümmel, W. G., *The Theology of the New Testament according to is Major Witnesses Jesus – Paul – John* (Nashville, TN and New York: Abingdon Press, 1973), *passim.*

Ladd, G. E., *A Theology of the New Testament* (Grand Rapids, MI: Eerdmans, 1974), *passim.*

Lindemann, A., 'Erwägungen zum Problem einer "Theologie der synoptischen Evangelien" ', *Zeitschrift für die neutestamentliche Wissenschaft und die Kunde der älteren Kirche*, 77 (1986), pp. 1–33.

Marshall, C. D., *Faith as a Theme in Mark's Narrative* (Society for New Testament Studies Monograph Series, 64; Cambridge: Cambridge University Press, 1989).

Martin, R. P., 'The Theology of Mark's Gospel', *South Western Journal of Theology*, 21 (1978), pp. 23–36.

Matera, F. J., *The Kingship of Jesus. Composition and Theology in Mark 15* (Society of Biblical Literature Dissertation Series, 66; Chico, CA: Scholars Press, 1982).

Robbins, V. K., 'The Healing of Blind Bartimaeus (10:46–52) in the Marcan Theology', *Journal of Biblical Literature*, 92 (1973), pp. 224–43.

Schreiber, J., *Theologie des Vertrauens. Eine Redaktionsgeschichtliche Untersuchung des Markusevangeliums* (Hamburg: Furche, 1967).

Schulz, S., 'Mark's Significance for the Theology of Early Christianity' in W. R. Telford (ed.), *The Interpretation of Mark* (Edinburgh: T. & T. Clark, 1995), pp. 197–206.

Schweizer, E., *Theologische Einleitung in das Neue Testament* (Grundrisse zum Neuen Testament 2; Göttingen: Vandenhoeck & Ruprecht, 1989), pp. 115–21.

Schweizer, E., 'Mark's Theological Achievement' in W. R. Telford (ed.), *The Interpretation of Mark* (Edinburgh: T. & T. Clark, 1995), pp. 63–87.

Thompson, M. R., *The Role of Disbelief in Mark. A New Approach to the Second Gospel* (New York and Mahwah, NJ: Paulist Press, 1989).

Index of references

Church Fathers

NT Apocrypha and Pseudepigrapha

Other Ancient Writers

Index of names

Index of subjects